D1566238

BREAD
and
RESPECT

$\mathcal{B}$READ
and
RESPECT
The Italians of Louisiana

A. V. Margavio and Jerome J. Salomone

PELICAN PUBLISHING COMPANY
Gretna 2002

*The word "Pelican" and the depiction of a pelican are trademarks
of Pelican Publishing Company, Inc., and are registered
in the U.S. Patent and Trademark Office.*

Library of Congress Cataloging-in-Publication Data

Margavio, Anthony V., 1938-
  Bread and respect : the Italians of Louisiana / A. V. Margavio and
Jerome J. Salomone.
     p. cm.
Includes bibliographical references and index.
  ISBN 1-58980-023-0 (hardcover : alk. paper)
  1. Italian Americans—Louisiana—History. 2. Italian Americans—
Louisiana—Social conditions. 3. Immigrants—Louisiana—History.
4. Louisiana—History. 5. Louisiana—Social conditions. 6.
Louisiana—Ethnic relations. I. Salomone, Jerome J., 1934- II. Title.
  F380.I8 M37 2002

                                                    2002001457

*Excerpts from WORLD OF OUR FATHERS, copyright © 1976 by Irving
Howe, reprinted by permission of Harcourt, Inc.*

Jacket illustration courtesy Southern Louisiana University

Printed in the United States of America

Published by Pelican Publishing Company, Inc.
1000 Burmaster Street, Gretna, Louisiana 70053

To Mary, the mother of Jesus, in the same spirit in which the drummer boy drummed for the Christ child. This tired world—we include ourselves—with its penchant for shallow dreams and broken promises would do well to imitate your constancy. Draw us closer to your Son. Viva Maria!

Contents

Acknowledgments

In the 1980s we announced to a number of our friends that we would write a book on the Italians of Louisiana. After writing it, we realized it wasn't worth reading. We are more than a bit red-faced over this broken promise. Without the persistence of our friends, we would have gone to our graves with promises to keep. We hope this version of the story of the Italians in Louisiana satisfies the expectations of our readers and our long-suffering friends.

To our wives, Sandy and Ruscilla, who bore our children and suffered our inattention for more years than they should have, we offer our undying gratitude.

Joseph Maselli assisted us in numerous ways. He has tirelessly promoted the Italian heritage locally and nationally. Founder and editor of the *Italian-American Digest,* Joseph worked with others to establish the American-Italian Museum and Library in New Orleans. He continues to labor energetically on behalf of Italian causes. We salute him and all the other fine men and women who have worked to promote the Italian legacy in the United States of America.

Prof. Carlo Di Maio, our Roman friend, colleague, and expert Italian linguist, has been generous with his time and advice. He carefully read the manuscript and corrected our misuse of the Italian language. No amount of thanks can express our gratitude for this assistance. Genie Hawkins was a conscientious, competent, and cheerful editor who rearranged sentences and cleaned up grammar to make this a more readable document. Scott Rabalais found enough time from his job covering LSU football for the *Morning Advocate* to read and comment on our work. Southeastern Louisiana University librarians Paul Haschak, Lori Smith, and Donna K. Hughes-Oldenburg helped us, and Laura Zammit, Nancy Tatman, Gayle Campbell, Pattie Steib, Gary Russell, and Carlos Lopez of the Center for Faculty Excellence rendered key technical support. Laura was the technical project director and Nancy assisted her in formatting the manuscript for publication. Their professionalism was indispensable. Dr. William Bankston and a graduate student obtained important demographic material we were unable to locate for ourselves. We also wish to thank Victoria Mocsary, who prepared the photographs, Nga Bui, who arranged the bibliography, professors Merrill Lee Johnson and Andre Skupin of the Geography Department of the University of New Orleans, for their technical assistance on our maps, and Daniel Margavio, for carrying the map project to completion. Special thanks go to Pelican Publishing Company's editor in chief and our editor, Nina Kooij (who better not cut this sentence!), for her patient efforts.

Southeastern Louisiana University provided funds for our research through its Research and Grants Committee and through the Department of Sociology and Criminal Justice.

BREAD
and
RESPECT

CHAPTER ONE

Yearnings

More people of Italian ancestry live outside of Italy than in it. Since the time of Julius Caesar over two thousand years ago, Italy has sent its citizens from its peninsula and two main islands, Sardinia and Sicily, to the four corners of the earth. Sometimes they went as powerful conquerors, sometimes as powerless peasants, but always as carriers of the culture that was theirs in their native land. Today, millions upon millions of sons and daughters of Italy make their homes in nations around the world, including the United States of America, where, between 1820 and 2000, more than 5,400,000 Italian immigrants settled. Estimates of their contemporary descendants in North America run as high as 26,000,000. More than 70,000 Italian immigrants made Louisiana their home. Their descendants currently number in the hundreds of thousands. We want to tell their story.

When sympathetically reporting the activities of your own ethnic group, it is ever so easy to engage in what Mario Puzo calls "retrospective falsification"—remembering the good but not the bad, therefore erroneously manufacturing or embellishing the "successes" of the past.[1] Many descriptions of the Italian immigrant in Louisiana and elsewhere have far exceeded the bounds of truth and modesty. Bruno Roselli's description of the

New Orleans community is a good example of this kind of ethnic boast.[2] Analyzing inscriptions on tombstones and relying
on his linguistic talents, Roselli painted a picture of the early
Italian community that raised embellishing the truth to a
grand art. While the creative use of tombstone inscriptions can
be applauded (indeed, some excellent studies have been conducted on ancient cities, notably Rome, using this technique),
the one-sided argument pursued in this twenty-eight-page
book is transparent. It resembles an overly praiseworthy eulogy
at a funeral where everyone in the church knows the deceased
to have been a scoundrel. Aware of this problem, we wish only
to pursue and to relate the story that documented facts can
support. If we have inadvertently fallen into the same trap here
and there, we beg the reader's indulgence.

The reader who desires to know immediately the major thesis of this work need not search long. We intend to show how
Italian culture shaped the lives of the immigrants to Louisiana
and, in turn, how experiences in Louisiana modified the Old
World values and culture the Italians brought with them. In
order to do this, we extend to the reader an invitation to travel
back to the Italy of 100 years ago—to the Italy the immigrants
left behind, an Italy of order and confusion, of beauty and ugliness, of tranquility and unrest. There are no compass settings,
no maps, no astronomical charts, and no mariner's crafts that
can help us arrive at our desired destination. For the place we
wish to take the reader is not the Italy of earth, and air, and sea;
it is the Italy of the mind—of the images, nurtured in the soils
of Italy and especially Sicily, that the immigrants carried with
them to their new home in Louisiana. What was it about the
Old Country and *la via vecchia* (the old way) that shaped their
values, attitudes, and sentiments? What were the tastes, sights,
and smells of their previous life? What were their trials and
tribulations, their yearnings for tomorrow, their desperate
needs for bread and respect? As the Italians of that time and
place understood it, what were their lives and homeland like

before the turn of the twentieth century? To answer these questions is to begin to understand what the immigrants brought with them to the New World, and to discover the legacy they bequeathed to their children in Louisiana and the United States of America.

We hope to achieve our purpose by exploring the dominant cultural values which embody and animate Italian life using the national character approach as a guide. This approach, also known as the culture-personality school, was first developed by Ruth Benedict and Margaret Mead.[3] The national character approach assumes that each society has a unique configuration of cultural traits and these, taken as a whole, provide the society's members with shared understandings and values. It is precisely a society's value configuration that gives rise to its basic personality type, or national character.[4] This is so because personality traits not consistent with the dominant values are discouraged, while character traits and behaviors consistent with the major cultural values are reinforced. Therefore, a typical or modal personality for each society is a natural response to that society's cultural values. To oversimplify, Japanese are industrious people because Japanese culture places a premium on effort and achievement; opposite tendencies are discouraged. Americans seek independence and individualism because of the enormous collective emphasis placed on these highly praised "cultural virtues." By the same argument, Italian artistic spirit exists in the context of a society that reveres art.

How do we recognize dominant values when we see them? Three indicators, reflected in three basic questions, seem to point to them. First, how extensive are the values? Are they held to be important by large numbers of inhabitants, rich and poor, powerful and impotent, respected and disfavored, or are they held to be essential by certain special interests whose desires run counter to those of other interest groups? Second, how long have those who embrace the values subscribed to them? Are they fads, or are they enduring properties of the people?

And finally, how strongly are the values felt by those who possess them? Are they something people can take or leave without batting an eye, or are they near and dear to the hearts of the people, something for which they willingly make great sacrifices? Naturally, when values are widely held and strongly felt over a long period of time they make their imprint on the psyche. In other words, the dominant values encourage the formation of a type of personality or national character in that society. *Encourage* is a well-chosen word because no culture ever imprints itself so completely on the personalities of those enveloped by it that they become psychological clones of one another.

The Italian immigrants who came to Louisiana brought with them a set of strongly held values that comprised what amounts to a philosophy of life—an all-embracing way to view themselves, others, and all else in the universe. That philosophy of life rested squarely on the foundation of eight highly prized values that we call yearnings. When our yearnings for the things we cherish remain unsatisfied, we feel an emptiness and hunger for their fulfillment. For that reason the immigrants' yearnings are metaphorically depicted as hungers. They are the enduring hungers for *bread, respect, fortune, security, drama, justice,* and *beauty.* To this list, a hunger not found on Italian soil is added. The hunger of *memory* is an outgrowth of transplantation to Louisiana soil. Not unique to Louisiana's Italians, the hunger of memory is found whenever a people remove themselves, or are forcibly removed by others, from the land of their ancestors. It is a concern for their roots that is occasioned by adaptation to a new country. In America, it is a yearning expressed most characteristically by the third- and fourth-generation European immigrant. This kind of nostalgia affects those who possess it with a sense of loss, a perception of historical discontinuity. It manifests itself chiefly in a desire to return, if only spiritually, to the land of their ancestors. Taken one at a time, these attributes are not unique to Italians, for all humans desire these same things. When these hungers are taken together, however, the Italians' quest for their fulfillment reveals a historical and sociological story different from any other.

Strictly speaking, the narrative we have written is neither a history nor a sociology of the Italians. To be sure, it contains historical facts and sociological observations—the particular and the general. History records distinct, often very personal, facts of times, places, and persons. Sociology, like all the social sciences, searches for general implications hidden in specific facts. At its best, sociology illustrates how personal facts and experiences are related to the general social and cultural conditions within which they occur. At its worst, sociology, with its dispassionate analysis, disembodies history and, in the process, loses the drama of human emotions. We wish to avoid that kind of sterility by including biographical sketches, personal stories, and fact-based fictional vignettes to enliven the facts as we see them. To be sure, we want to engage not only the head but the heart as we relate the legacy of Louisiana's Italian immigrants. There is good reason to emphasize feeling alongside reason because to describe Louisiana's Italians without capturing their dramatic emotional persona is not to describe them at all.

While, in a general way, our guide is the anthropological tradition on national character, our specific inspiration comes from the Italian journalist Luigi Barzini, who has admirably captured the unity of Italian culture and national character in his widely acclaimed study, *The Italians*. To his ideas we have added dramaturgical elaboration, a literary style that embraces imagery the immigrants themselves might have used to express their ideas and feelings.[5]

The major cultural values that are the building blocks of Italian culture are not independent of each other but rather are interrelated at different levels. To understand them one must know how they spring from the overarching Italian cultural theme about life and nature. As much as the Romans admired the Greeks, one might think Aristotle's admonition to be moderate in all things would be appealing to the Italians.

Nothing could be farther from the truth. For them, moderation is a fault. In both their praise and condemnation, Italians aim for the superlative. The singular idea in Italian culture that unifies the whole fabric of Italian life is that life and nature need embellishment. Ordinary things must be dramatized, clothed in radiant garments, garnished until the tasteless, boring, and drab are at first hidden and then subsequently transformed into objects larger and grander than life. This symphonic theme can be heard in a thousand melodies, each of which echoes a variant of itself. Through art, science, religion, folklore, and in countless other ways, embellishment transforms the ordinary, the humdrum, into something special, exciting, and larger than life. Adornment of persons, places, things, and events dramatizes mundane affairs, thereby creating the theatrical production that, depending on the individuals involved, more often than not, results in high drama or spectacle. In so doing, elaboration does not merely conceal that which it finds distasteful but rather transforms it by making it extraordinary. In the process, the imagination is propelled toward the extremes and away from the average. The Italian mentality is not so intolerant of ugliness and banality as it is of middling ugliness and banality. By embellishing the everyday fabric of life, human emotions are stretched to the extremes, thus creating a tapestry of drama in which the level planes of emotion and expression have no place. Embellishment cultivates vice with the same passion that it cultivates virtue, giving expression to a world that produces the greatest saints as well as the greatest sinners. Need we be reminded, Francis of Assisi, Catherine of Siena, and Anthony of Padua (who really was Portuguese) are saintly exemplars, while Caesare and Lucrezia Borgia and Machiavelli are known to history as virtue's antithesis. Italian culture, in this fashion, "creates" people whose base minds are downright devilish, while their enlightened ones keep company with the angels. Italians' woes are the greatest sorrows, while their joys are celestial. In such a world, there is little room for emotions like tranquil plains, but only those that resemble mountain peaks and valleys.

Perhaps an example will help clarify our meaning. It is not very Italian to experience mere marital difficulty. For the Italian with marital trouble, life is a veritable Golgotha, a crucifixion. By the same token, what the Italian experiences as celestial joy in marriage, others would prosaically call marital happiness. The end result is that social reality is expanded by exaggeration and elaboration.

Hyperbole is common. Consider a conventional expression of farewell. An American is likely to say something like, "I wish you well," "Have a nice day," or some other bland formula. An Italian might say, *"Santo e Ricco."* In doing so, he is expressing a profound contradiction. He is, in effect, saying, "I desire that you possess the sanctity of St. Francis and the wealth of Rockefeller!" Everyday conversation is full of this kind of overstatement, not only in what is said but also the manner in which it is said. The Italian is expected to use voice, hands, facial muscles, and, indeed, the whole body to communicate and animate thoughts, feelings, and actions. This kind of extravagance is encountered not just in interpersonal greetings and relationships but is found throughout the institutional life of Italy, in the pageantry of its festivals, as well as in the arts, especially music, painting, and sculpture.

Nothing in Italian life escapes this process of elaboration, certainly not the style of cooking. Italians raise this activity to a high art. Even with simple dishes, the process of expansion and dramatization is in evidence. Consider how the lowly tomato is transformed into an elegant sauce. It is indicative of the Italian character to embellish food further by attaching dramatic labels to the products of the kitchen. The name of a Sicilian dessert admirably reflects this tendency. The most opulent and decadent treat ever devised by human hands is appropriately called "The Triumph of Gluttony"!

But how have these cultural values, character traits, and

dramatizations survived the ocean crossing? Have they with-stood the corrosive power of time unchanged, been modified, or been altogether abandoned? To explore these matters we must first return to Italy.

CHAPTER TWO

Bread

THE OLD COUNTRY

"The Song of the Immigrants"

Wolves have warmed themselves on our fleece and eaten our
flesh.
We are the generation of sheep.
Wolves have sheared us to the bone while we protested only to
God.
In time of peace we sickened in hospitals or jails.
In time of war we were cannon fodder.
We harvested bales of grass, one blade for us, the rest for the
wolves.
One day a rumor spread—there was a vast and distant land
where we could live *meno male.*
Some sheep went and returned, transformed, no longer sheep
but wolves and they associated with our wolves.
"We want to go to that vast and distant country," we sheep said.
"We want to go."
"There is an ocean to cross," the wolves said.
"We will cross it."
"And if you are shipwrecked and drowned?"
"It's better to die quickly than suffer a lifetime."
"There are diseases."

"No disease can be more horrible than hunger from father to
son."
And the wolves said, "Sheep, there will be deceivers. . . . "
"You've been deceiving us for centuries."
"Would you abandon the land of your fathers, your brothers?"
"You who fleece us are not our brothers. The land of our
fathers is a slaughterhouse."
In tatters, in great herds we in pain beyond belief journeyed to
the vast and distant land.
Some of us did drown.
Some of us did die of privation.
But for every ten that perished a thousand survived and endured.
Better to choke in the ocean than be strangled by misery.
Better to deceive ourselves than be deceived by the wolves.
Better to die in our way than to be lower than the beasts.

This poem, printed in the book *La Storia*,[1] was first published by an anonymous author in 1880 in a German newspaper and reproduced by Ferdinando Fontana in 1881. It speaks
poignantly to the desperate plight of the Italian peasant in
southern Italy at that time and for many preceding centuries.
Yet despite their incessant struggle, relief from hunger, pain,
and injustice escaped them. While every word in this song
drips with emotion, one line screams for further attention: "No
disease can be more horrible than hunger from father to son."
Not every Italian who left Mother Italy did so because of the
enduring *hunger* to escape hunger, but the search for bread,
the yearning for a chance to earn a decent livelihood, and the
absence of hope that they would ever be able to do so at home
was undoubtedly the single most important reason for their
emigration to America.

The decision to leave or not to leave was, to say the least, not
an easy one. Even for those who meant to return, and many
did, there was an enormous uncertainty about such a long and
improbable journey, especially for someone who previously
had never gone beyond his own village. For the great majority

of those who chose to come to America, the decision meant to leave permanently and completely—permanently, because they would never come back to family and homeland in their lifetimes, and completely, because for the poverty-stricken, illiterate peasants there would be little or no likelihood of correspondence between families split apart by the Atlantic. For most of them, leaving meant total separation from their former lives. All they brought with them to the dock when they boarded the ship, in many instances, were a few scraps of clothing, a few crumbs of food, and their remembrances of the lives they were leaving behind. Yet they left by the millions, nearly 5.5 million of them in the thirty years after the unification of Italy in 1870.[2] Millions more would leave southern Italy for North and South America and other parts of the world in the years to follow.[3] It is one of the great ironies of history that immediately upon Italy's attainment of nationhood, millions of Italians would abandon their newly established country. To explain this unexpected turn of events we must return to the Italy of that time.

The peninsula of Italy extends from the Alps some 700 miles southeast into the Mediterranean. The "toe" of the familiar boot shape of Italy is a mere 2 miles from the island of Sicily across the Strait of Messina. The whole country covers a little over 116,000 square miles. Sicily is a little less than 10,000 square miles. The other large Italian island, Sardinia, is a little over 9,000 square miles.

The country can be divided into a northern and southern half.[4] The southern half, or *Mezzogiorno,* includes insular Italy. A line from Naples on the Mediterranean Sea to Pescara on the Adriatic Sea has been taken as the unofficial boundary between the two Italies. Northern Italy is more urban and industrial and contains the best agricultural lands. Southern and insular Italy are predominately areas of agricultural villages. The rivers of the north carry large volumes of water. The rivers of the south carry less. Rain in the north is adequate and falls when agricultural lands need it. Rain in the south is inadequate and generally arrives too late for agricultural purposes. In modern times, the southern provinces of Italy have been less progressive and more provincial than the northern provinces. It was in the north that industry first came. It was the north that most benefited from the unification of Italy in the nineteenth century.

Southern Italy has always been like a stepchild in the family of the Italian national state. The powerlessness of the south, especially Sicily, after unification merely continued the political and social troubles of the region, which have deep roots, extending back into the centuries. The chief problem has always been political insecurity. Rulers have come and gone with new rulers taking their places, yet the peasants' lot has never been their concern. Exploitation, heavy taxation, and callous treatment have been the peasants' daily bread.

This bleak picture contrasts markedly with the Sicily of ancient times. When most of Europe was still inhabited by barbaric tribesmen and Roman legions in garrisons guarded the empire's outposts, Sicily had already experienced the benefits and the misfortunes of previous civilizations. The Pearl of the Mediterranean had been colonized previously by both Greece and Carthage. From her strategic position in North Africa, Carthage colonized the western half of Sicily. The island's minerals and grains contributed to the wealth of the Phoenician merchants at Carthage.

Somewhat later, Greeks established colonies on the island, challenging the Carthaginians. In 480 B.C., Greek forces decisively defeated the Carthaginians at Himera, Sicily. But by 420 B.C., Carthage had once again expanded her influence, eventually covering most of the island.

By the third century B.C., Rome competed with Carthage for dominance in the Mediterranean. After a near defeat in the Second Punic War at the hands of Hannibal, Rome decisively settled the issue in her favor in the third and final war against the Carthaginians. By the third century B.C., Sicily had become the first province of Rome and the breadbasket for the emerging empire. Cities, aqueducts, libraries, arts, and Doric temples were all hers long before most of Europe was transformed by Roman culture.

With the collapse of Rome's Western Empire in 496, Vandals and Ostrogoths conquered Sicily. In 535, the Byzantine Empire controlled Sicily, and Greek became the official language. Subsequently, Byzantine rulers were replaced by the expanding Islamic World.

During the 200 years of Arab rule, Sicily experienced the benefits of Moslem science, art, and literature. Irrigation and the introduction of new crops, including lemons and oranges, improved agriculture. However, the Arabs also brought goats to the island. Unlike cattle, which do not eat the pasture to its roots, goats chew grass down to the soil, thereby damaging root systems and hastening soil erosion over the ensuing years.

With the expansion of trade in Europe and a reduced threat from Islam, Europe began to influence former Moslem lands along the Mediterranean. By the eleventh century, Normans conquered the island and joined it with southern Italy to create the Kingdom of the Two Sicilys. Under the Normans, the island gradually came into the orbit of Western Europe. By the thirteenth century, a brief German rule was followed by French control of the island. The Sicilians ended French rule in a violent uprising in 1282 but not before Sicily had become the cultural center of Italy. For the next several hundred years, Spain, Savoy, and Austria, in that order, ruled Sicily. The invasion of Sicily by Garibaldi and the subsequent revolt of the people ended Bourbon rule, which had begun in the early eighteenth century. In 1860, Sicily became part of the Kingdom of Italy.

The colonizers took far, far more than they gave. The once rich island of earlier times became one of the most backward areas of Europe by the modern era. Deforestation, poor agricultural practices, excessive water withdrawal, and salt and sulphur mining had their detrimental effects on the land.[5] Sicily yielded her harvests and her resources with great human toil and, ultimately, with devastating consequences.

The historical accounts that describe the fall of Sicily and southern Italy from a once proud position in the ancient world are long and tortuous. We have only sketched here what others have recorded in volumes.

Foreign invaders drastically altered the area. To be sure, they brought with them the benefits of civilization. Doric temples, Roman aqueducts, and Saracen art and science created a unique cultural ensemble. In addition, the earlier rulers and colonizers left their mark in the many place names and linguistic survivals. There are areas of Sicily and southern Italy that have Greek place names and where the Greek language survives in the local dialects. This influence is most marked on the eastern side of Sicily. In continental Italy, it is quite noticeable in the area of the "heel" of the boot or Salentino peninsula, an area sometimes referred to as the "Grichia."

Racially, southern Italians and Sicilians are different from the alpine stock found in northern Italy, but one occasionally finds red hair, fair skin, and light-colored eyes in the otherwise Mediterranean-racial-type area. These traits are reminders of the many foreign rulers Sicily and southern Italy have had in their long history as a toy of foreign powers. Yet through it all, the lot of the peasant seems never to have changed. Even under local rule after unification the fate of the peasants (*contadini*) remained unchanged. Current conditions are still the worst in all of Western Europe. One comparatively recent study of a south Italian village (Calimera) reported that fifteen families owned almost all the land in this village of 5,700 people.[6] The unemployment situation reflected the poverty of the village. Nearly half of the population was not gainfully employed. The great majority of the workers were landless peasants or non-agricultural wage workers (day laborers) willing to accept any job.

It was from the landless peasantry that the overwhelming majority of Louisiana's Italian population originated. The peasants' destiny has been universally tied to their relationship to the land. Therefore, it is essential to examine the state of agriculture and the land tenure system in the *Mezzogiorno* if we are to understand the root causes of the abject poverty and powerlessness of the peasants, and their reluctance to leave the land they loved.

Historically, the great majority of the peasants did not own the land they worked; they were tenants instead. For the most part, the agricultural lands (*latifondi*) were in the hands of barons who were absentee owners. They generally cared little for those who worked the land and had little or no contact with their tenants.[7] Overseers (*gabellotti*) managed the estates for the barons, who preferred to live in the cities. The *gabellotti* were at times ruthless in extracting the rents. Some three-quarters of what a peasant produced generally went to a *gabellotto*.

The few peasants who owned property held small, scattered parcels, hardly suitable for more than the meager survival of their families. They did escape the suffocating rents of the *gabellotti* but not the heavy taxes of an increasingly oppressive government. The unification of Italy, it was hoped, would offer the peasant of the *Mezzogiorno* some relief, but instead, nationhood exacerbated the misery in the south. Enactment of the Grist Tax on grain placed such a heavy burden on the *contadini* it was not uncommon for the tax collector to be met with gunfire! They had to mortgage their property to pay their taxes. They then lost the land when they were unable to repay their loans. Many of the *contadini*, in this fashion, were reduced to agricultural wage workers, thereby effectively transforming them into a rural proletariat.

When the modern nation of Italy was coming into existence in the 1860s, 80 percent of the population depended upon agriculture for their livelihood. What industry there was, was nearly exclusively in the north. The farther north one traveled up the boot of Italy, the more industrial the landscape. Milan and Turin, located in the northern provinces of Lombardy and Piedmont respectively, had already shown signs of becoming mighty industrial cities. To encourage the further industrial development of the north, the newly installed Italian government instituted tariffs on goods manufactured in the south, placing products made there at a competitive disadvantage. As a consequence sales dropped, profits dried up, and the few factories in the south were forced to close, dumping those former factory workers into an ever growing pool of agricultural laborers in the *Mezzogiorno*.

To add to their suffering, in the 1870s, Italy's vineyards were struck by phylloxera (plant lice particularly destructive to grapes), which came across the Alps from France. Many vineyards had to be destroyed. Those that survived produced greatly diminished crops that were poor in quality. Added to southern Italy's other problems, this was another step toward an economic catastrophe. In 1880, France initiated a tariff on Italian wines, further hindering exports to that country.

Unification had other deleterious effects on the poverty-stricken peasants in the south. Military conscription was soon begun, a turn of events not favored by the southern Italian peasants. They saw military service as a device to protect the government, the landed rich, and industrial entrepreneurs in the north. Southern peasants viewed all these perceived governmental objectives with great suspicion if not with an outright animosity. If their centuries of experience meant anything, there was good reason to distrust, even hate, their new governors. After all, all their other governors were eminently worthy of their contempt.

One of the early initiatives of the new government was to assert itself as an instrument of order. To ensure the security of the people, officials began an aggressive program of law enforcement to sweep the streets clean of Italy's criminal element. This led to large-scale imprisonment. Since the south had a long history of criminal activity, especially theft and banditry, it naturally provided most of the prisoners.

Among the landless peasants, the *tenant system* did not encourage efficient use of the land. The absentee owners generally were interested in a short tenancy because it was the easiest way of protecting themselves against inflation.[8] This practice reduced incentives for improving the land and favored quick-cash crops like wheat, while discouraging crops such as grapes and olives that require several years before production can be realized. Any improvements to the land were forfeited at the expiration of the contract. Furthermore, tenancy was uncertain. The landlord could turn the tenant out any time he wished.

Elsewhere in Europe, the absentee-landlord tenancy produced conditions similar to the conditions found among the *contadini* of Sicily. In Ireland during the nineteenth century the same system prevailed and produced the same results.[9] Both in Ireland and Italy, nature seemed to conspire against the peasant. In nineteenth-century Ireland, the potato rot caused widespread starvation. In southern Italy and Sicily the climate had become more arid. Over the period of several centuries less and less rain fell. At times, even drinking water was in short supply. A common village scene included the barrel men with their horse-drawn carts crying in the streets their familiar call, *"Cori allegru! Cori vivu! Veni e assaggia la me acqua!"* (Heart's cheer! Heart's cheer! Come and taste my water!)

Deforestation, drought, land erosion, heavy taxation, unscrupulous rulers, corrupt police, and organized banditry were the peasants' constant companions, especially in the late nineteenth century. Not surprisingly, many peasants sought relief through immigration. The intensity of their discontent is aptly reflected in the great number who left their homeland to seek a better life in the Americas and elsewhere.[10] Of those arriving in the United States, the great majority settled in the northern cities where industrial jobs were available.[11]

And yet there was another side to peasant life. Life in the village with its festivals and religious holidays gave some brief,
intermittent respite from the yoke. Unlike in America, where
the farms are isolated, in Sicily and southern Italy the farmers
live in the village and generally work in the outlying fields.
Most villages of 100 years ago contained from 1,000 to 5,000
people, but some were much larger. The piazza, with its church
and municipal building, was the center of town. The better
houses were located close to the village square. Farther out
were the one- and two-room houses of the peasants, who neither had—nor gave much thought to—privacy. They spent
their leisure socializing in the village square. Recent studies of
southern Italian village life suggest that little has changed in
this regard.

The village of the nineteenth century was the whole world
for the peasant. This *campanilismo,* as it is called, was not
merely the parochialism that is found in small towns. It is a
total world view that constricts the peasants' perspective to the
peal of the village church bells. With the peasants confined in
such a small universe, not only are the larger world's concerns
excluded from their purview, but even the concerns of the
neighboring villages are too distant for their attention.

Outsiders were met with suspicion. Peasants could not
understand why anyone would be interested in their village.
The lack of restaurants in many villages today is evidence that
strangers still have no place in their world. Visiting with villagers from other communities was infrequent. When it
occurred, locals believed the visitors should bring their own
provisions with them or be fed and sheltered by relatives. This
suspicion of outsiders was not confined to the occasional
stranger; it included all those in authority as well, from local
politicians to the national government. Locals characteristically distrusted the law and the police. These attitudes, no
doubt, have their roots in the mistreatment of Sicilians by foreign rulers. Each new wave of foreign conquerors added new

layers of distrust and suffering to their collective memories. With each foreign ruler, peasants found new reasons to trust only familiar village faces. Even then there was the risk of betrayal adding to *la miseria*. After all, men could be enticed with money or offers of power. The circle of trust in time grew smaller and smaller to include primarily kinsmen and selected members of the village who were not instruments of the police, the barons, or the *Mafiosi*.

The *contadini*'s distrust of outsiders was manifested wherever they immigrated. In the new country, typically, the peasants identified more closely with fellow villagers than with other Italians and more closely with Italians than with non-Italians. Companionship was sought out first among *paesani*, those who came from the same village and quite likely were bound by ties of marriage or godparenthood.

If the social and economic conditions in southern Italy and Sicily were the "push" factors motivating the peasants to leave their homeland, then the lure of easy money and opportunity in America and elsewhere were the pull factors. But their reasons for leaving are not easily distilled into simple concepts. Many, if not most, immigrants wanted only to sojourn abroad. Their dream initially was to get a job, save their money, get rich, and return to Italy. The statistics bear out that many realized this dream, at least partially, for many did return.[12] How many is not known with much accuracy. What can be said confidently, however, is that proportionately more Italians returned to Italy than was true of any other European ethnic group.

It is easy to understand how peasants in Italy and Sicily might hear of America and New York, but how did they come to learn about places in Louisiana as provincial as rural Terrebonne and Lafourche parishes? What was the attraction of Louisiana? The answer is to be found in the aftermath of the American Civil War and subsequently in the combined activities of sugar planters, parish police juries, the state of Louisiana, and steamship agents.

NEW ORLEANS AND PALERMO:
THE CITRUS CONNECTION

Before the development of the citrus industries of
California, Texas, Florida, and Louisiana, Mediterranean growers supplied the United States. In the early nineteenth century,
New Orleans, the second-largest port in the country, was
receiving a significant portion of these imports. A thriving
trade existed between New Orleans and Palermo, Sicily. In
1880, the *Daily Picayune* recorded the arrival of a British
steamship that had left Palermo on November 3, met with
rough water, sustained some damage, but arrived safely on
December 16 at the Calliope Street Wharf. On board were 210
Sicilians from Palermo and vicinity and cargo consisting of
lemons, preserved tomatoes, figs, olives, and oil.[13] Other ships
outbound from Sicily carried similar stores of lemons, limes,
olives, oil, dried figs, and other products to New Orleans,
where a sizeable portion of those goods was sold in the New
Orleans retail market; the remainder was loaded on steam-
boats and carried to ports upriver like Natchez, Memphis, St.
Louis, and Cairo, Illinois. On the return trip, vessels from New
Orleans carried cotton and grain, especially rice and wheat, as
cargo to various European ports before returning to Palermo
to be reloaded for another trip to New Orleans. By the middle
of the nineteenth century, a small but significant colony of
Italians was thriving in the Crescent City as a direct result of
this uninterrupted commercial activity. With the expansion of
the U.S. citrus industry in the late 1800s, the amount of fruit
imported from Mediterranean ports dwindled, but by that
time immigrants from Sicily had become the main "cargo" regularly arriving at the Port of New Orleans.

Perhaps, at this point, we should recall the significance of the
Port of New Orleans in the history of the United States. Almost
from the moment of its founding by Frenchman Jean Baptiste
Le Moyne, Sieur de Bienville, in 1718, the city prospered despite

setbacks resulting from early serious hurricanes, disease, and Indian wars. By 1721, New Orleans already had 300 inhabitants and was the commercial center of the region. By 1728, its population exceeded 1,000 optimistic citizens, whose hopefulness led them to believe that the day was not far off when New Orleans would be "an opulent city and the metropolis of a great and rich colony."[14] Their hopefulness was not in vain, though it would be nearly one hundred years before New Orleans could legitimately claim to be the Queen City of the South. John Kemp calls the fifty years preceding the Civil War New Orleans' magnificent half-century; he is correct. Consider these facts: Between 1801 and 1817, the number of ship arrivals in New Orleans increased from 181 vessels per year to 542. In 1840, New Orleans was the fourth-largest city in the United States, challenging New York as the leading port in the nation. By 1860, New Orleans was, indeed, both opulent and great. So much prosperity had been generated by and channeled through its port that the 1860 census revealed Louisiana residents—not including slaves, of course—had one of the highest per-capita incomes in the nation.[15]

The Crescent City served as the port of embarkation and debarkation for people, natural resources, and manufactured products for the entire Mississippi Valley. It should be recalled, the big cities of the northeastern seaboard were not very well connected to the emerging cities along the Mississippi River prior to the Civil War.[16] The Mississippi River served as the maritime highway for the interior of this burgeoning nation of ours. Because of its strategic location, New Orleans was either the starting point or the ending point for all waterborne traffic through the Gulf of Mexico. Though the Civil War did not diminish the long-term significance of the Mississippi River to the country or the importance of New Orleans to the Mississippi Valley, it did profoundly affect everything else in Louisiana.

When Gen. Robert E. Lee surrendered the Army of Virginia to Gen. Ulysses S. Grant at Appomattox on April 9, 1865, the

American Civil War, for all practical purposes, was over. Only then could the Emancipation Proclamation, issued two years earlier by President Lincoln to free the slaves, be fully and permanently implemented. Over four million blacks throughout the former slave states were no longer bound to their owners or the land. Though delayed by unfulfilled hopes of receiving "forty acres and a mule," eventually, over one and one-half million ex-slaves and free blacks left the South for other regions of the country. The withdrawal of federal troops in 1877 marked the end of Reconstruction in Louisiana. From then until the end of the century there was a large, steady out-migration of blacks from the state, especially from the agricultural areas. Even before this exodus, Louisiana was short of agricultural laborers. Thus, from the point of view of plantation owners, the departure of black field hands only worsened an already bad situation.

Louisiana's two main plantation crops following the Civil War were sugar and cotton. Of the two, sugar production was the most labor intensive, especially during the harvesting season. As a result, *la zuccherata*, the sugarcane grinding season, required an influx of large numbers of migrant laborers. To a lesser but significant extent, additional migrant laborers were needed during the harvesting of the cotton crop. As it happens, cane harvesting takes place between late October and January. It is important to harvest the crop before any hard, late-winter freezes reduce the sugar content or, far worse, cause it to sour in the stalks. Cotton, on the other hand, matures in summer. Sugar is grown in South Louisiana while cotton is mainly grown in the central and northern portions of the state. As we shall see later, many Italian immigrants were itinerant workers finding odd jobs in the city, then moving to the sugar plantations in the fall and early winter, perhaps returning to the city in late winter and spring, traveling upstate to work the cotton plantations, then repeating the cycle.

One special case of black out-migration is noteworthy. So

many blacks left Louisiana for Kansas after Reconstruction that their departure came to be known as the Kansas Fever. The Kansas Pacific Railroad line between New Orleans and Kansas City was in full swing, making transportation widely available and reasonably affordable. Also, blacks had favorable impressions of Kansas owing to the successful campaign by abolitionists there, prior to the Civil War, to bring Kansas into the Union as a free state. Other reasons for the black exodus from Louisiana to Kansas and elsewhere included the precarious status of the tenant in the farm-tenancy system, intimidation of black voters, the periodic outbreak of yellow fever, and active recruitment by labor agents in Kansas and agents for the railroad. No accurate figures are available indicating how many people left the state during this Kansas Fever "epidemic," but estimates for Louisiana and Mississippi in just two years, 1878 and 1879, place the figure between 5,000 to 10,000.[17] The blacks who remained in Louisiana agriculture following the Civil War were viewed with a growing suspicion by the planters and their overseers because of Negro unrest on the plantations. There were slowdowns and strikes, prompting the growers to consider free blacks unreliable agricultural workers. Newspapers across the state began to run articles questioning the wisdom of continued dependence of agriculture on black workers. Actually, while this skepticism gained widespread attention in the news, most planters knew the future of large-scale agriculture in the state was linked to the continuing use of Negro plantation field hands.

The need to replace the blacks who left Louisiana, the growers' dissatisfaction with free blacks, and the expansion of agricultural lands following the Civil War resulted in the absolute necessity to recruit plantation workers from outside the area.

In response to these circumstances, the Louisiana Association of Sugar Planters, a private lobby, was instrumental in getting the Louisiana legislature to create the Louisiana Bureau of

Immigration in 1866, a state agency that immediately began to publish and distribute pamphlets in the United States and Europe praising the opportunities associated with plantation labor in the state. Soon thereafter, immigration committees were founded and funded by parish police juries in the sugar parishes. Agents representing these organizations were joined by steamship agents in attempting to entice American farmers from the Midwest to relocate in Louisiana. When that failed, interest turned to Chinese laborers, who were considered good but unreliable workers. Their interests tended to be in the cities and in becoming fishermen. The planters then turned their attention to white immigrants from Europe and eventually focused on southern Italy, particularly Sicily. Before the contract labor laws were passed that prohibited entry of immigrants with work contracts, agents representing planters worked a number of European cities. However, Sicilians were the only group to respond in significant numbers to their attempts at recruitment. There is no way to tell accurately how many immigrants responded to the efforts to attract workers to the sugar plantations. Estimates range from a low of 16,000 to an improbable high of 80,000.[18] It was, however, the impetus of the sugar industry that opened the "immigration gates" to Louisiana from Italy. Before those gates were largely closed by the Immigration Act of 1924, over 100,000 Italians had come through the Port of New Orleans as immigrants to the United States of America.

Almost immediately the sugar planters hailed the Sicilian immigrants as excellent workers. Usually their virtues were contrasted with the real or presumed vices of the black workers they only partially replaced. The praise was well deserved,[19] although the Italians were not content to remain on the plantations very long as landless field hands. They wanted more, as evidenced by their relentless drive to achieve economic independence.

As table 1 indicates, approximately 70,000 Italian immigrants arrived at the Port of New Orleans from 1898 to 1929. Additionally, on average, about 2,000 arrived annually from the period 1880 to 1898, or about 36,000, which brings the total to 106,000. Although an Italian community existed in New Orleans as early as the Civil War, attracted by the growing business opportunities centered on the port, it was a small community. By 1930 the depression and the Quota Laws enacted during the 1920s drastically reduced the immigration not only of Italians but others as well and especially those from southern and eastern Europe.

HOW MANY CAME AND WHERE DID THEY GO?

Table 1

Italian Immigrants Arriving at the Port of New Orleans, 1898-1929

Period	Number of Immigrants
1898-1901	8,453
1902-5	18,450
1906-9	13,153
1910-13	6,326
1914-17	8,140
1918-21	8,208
1922-25	3,698
1926-29	3,509
Total	**69,937**

Sources: *Annual Report of the Commissioner-General of Immigration to the Secretary of Labor* (fiscal year ended June 30, 1920 and 1930). *Annual Report of the Commissioner-General of Immigration to the Secretary of Commerce and Labor* (fiscal year ended June 30, 1905). *Annual Report of the Commissioner-General of Immigration Treasury Dept. Document No. 2148* (fiscal year ended June 30, 1899).

Apparently, Italian immigrants who wished to come to Louisiana chose New Orleans as their port of entry. The record shows that very few Italian immigrants entering from other ports identified Louisiana as their final destination. However, it is known that some did arrive from Italian colonies in other American cities. The *New Orleans Daily Picayune* reported the arrival of thirty-two Italian immigrants recruited in New York City to work on the Oakley plantation.[20] From conversations with immigrants one learns that other Italians worked as wage workers in construction or mining in the northeast before coming to New Orleans. What is not known is the number of immigrants who did so. As to those who permanently settled in Louisiana from all points of entry, one must rely on census reports.

The 1900 census reported 17,431 foreign-born Italians living in Louisiana. In 1910 the figure was 19,634. By 1920, their numbers declined to 16,634. The 1930 census reported only 13,573. Based on these census enumerations and allowing for mortality, the number of immigrants who stayed would be approximately 31,000.[21] However, this estimate could be revised upward if one assumes the census figures are under-enumerations, which is likely since the coverage rarely approaches 100 percent, particularly during the very early periods and when populations are relatively small. There may also have been a significant number of migratory cane cutters who would not be residing in the state in spring when the censuses were taken. The sugarcane harvest, of course, is in the fall. Estimating the under-enumeration to be 3 percent, a better estimate of permanent residents could be set at 32,000. Of course, this figure is a conservative guess.

Table 2

Distribution of Foreign-Born Italians in Louisiana, 1900, 1910, 1920, and 1930

Parish	1900	1910	1920	1930	Change (1900-30)
Acadia	14	25	29	16	+2

Allen	*	0	1	nr	
Ascension	1,332	578	273	196	-1,136
Assumption	770	460	181	66	-764
Avoyelles	175	178	143	79	-96
Beauregard	*	0	90	49	
Bienville	nr	nr	nr	nr	0
Bossier	9	8	47	104	+95
Caddo	20	243	337	480	+460
Calcasieu	133	494	189*	193	
Caldwell	3	20	22	5	+2
Cameron	7	3	nr	nr	-7
Catahoula	4*	0	4	nr	-4
Claiborne	1	2	9	3	+2
Concordia	12	62	12	7	-5
DeSoto	nr	1	2	2	+2
East Baton Rouge	112	384	512	576	+464
East Carroll	7	14	18	17	+10
East Feliciana	25	26	45	45	+20
Evangeline	*	nr	6	5	
Franklin	nr	5	10	8	+8
Grant	18	14	13	6	-12
Iberia	355	275	178	149	-206
Iberville	886	865	645	472	-414
Jackson	nr	71	17	nr	0
Jefferson	1,012	1,209	919	804	-208
Jefferson Davis	*	0	2	3	
Lafayette	26	66	56	60	+34
Lafourche	830	343	102	71	-759
La Salle	*	0	2	2	
Lincoln		39	2	2	+2
Livingston	2	6	5	3	+1
Madison	5	119	14	11	+6
Morehouse	1	17	11	9	+8
Natchitoches	26	42	73	36	+10
Orleans	5,866	8,065	7,833	6,821	+955
Ouachita	35	139	202	222	+187
Plaquemines	362	135	116	71	-291

Pointe Coupee	218	365	277	132	-103
Rapides	33	184	259	223	+190
Red River	1	nr	23	4	+3
Richland	nr	10	29	12	+12
Sabine	1	33	4	nr	-1
St. Bernard	123	238	190	102	-21
St. Charles	626	254	137	113	-513
St. Helena	nr	nr	10	nr	0
St. James	1,218	699	162	73	-1,145
St. John the Baptist	450	144	70	88	-362
St. Landry	157	361	300	*	
St. Martin	57	78	41	24	-33
St. Mary	1,639	1,246	593	304	-1,335
St. Tammany	32	61	16	42	+10
Tangipahoa	97	1,021	1,805	1,550	+1,453
Tensas	34	78	84	25	-9
Terrebonne	550	294	142	80	-470
Union	nr	nr	nr	nr	0
Vermilion	7	67	70	44	+37
Vernon	13	69	26	5	-8
Washington	nr	230	151	82	+82
Webster	1	3	0	1	0
West Baton Rouge	120	210	106	66	-54
West Carroll	nr	nr	nr	nr	0
West Feliciana	6	47	18	8	+2
Winn	nr	34	1	2	+2
Total	17,431	19,634	16,634	13,573	**-3,858**

Sources: Bureau of the Census, *Twelfth Census,* vol. 1, part 1 (1901), 756-58, and *Fifteenth Census,* vol. 3, part 1 (1932), 993, prepared by the Government Printing Office (Washington, D.C.).

Between 1900 and 1930 five parishes were added. La Salle was organized from part of Catahoula in 1910, Evangeline was

organized from part of St. Landry in 1911, and Allen,
Beauregard, and Jefferson Davis were organized from parts of
Calcasieu in 1913. The parishes affected by boundary changes
are marked with an *. The changes are therefore not presented.
When no immigrants are reported for a parish, *nr* (none
reported) is more honest than zero. It means probably zero,
but given the quality of the data gathering, one cannot be sure.
In computing change, nr was treated as zero.
The numbers in table 2 represent actual settlement figures
while the numbers in table 1 refer to arrivals, not settlers.

— — —

Table 2 gives the distribution of Italian immigrants. Except
for Orleans (New Orleans), the immigrants had mostly settled
in the sugarcane parishes, which can be defined as Ascension,
Assumption, Avoyelles, Iberia, Iberville, Jefferson, Lafourche,
Plaquemines, Pointe Coupee, St. Bernard, St. Charles, St.
James, St. John the Baptist, St. Martin, St. Mary, Terrebonne,
and West Baton Rouge. Notice all these parishes are in south
and south-central Louisiana. They all had sizeable Italian populations in 1900, and while they all retained some Italian presence, they steadily lost significant numbers during each of the
succeeding census years, so that by 1930 all of them were well
below their 1900 figures.

During the thirty years from 1900 to 1930, what appears to
have happened was that the immigrants moved from the sugar
plantations to the cities and their surrounding districts.
Illustrating this trend is the fact that the parishes containing
the largest cities all reported higher 1930 figures than 1900
levels even though the total number of foreign-born Italians
for the state decreased from 17,431 in 1900 to 13,573 in 1930.
Orleans reported 955 more foreign-born Italians, Caddo
(Shreveport) 460, East Baton Rouge 464, Ouachita (Monroe)

187, and Rapides (Alexandria) 190. However, not all resided within the incorporated limits of these cities. The 1930 census reported the following numbers of foreign-born Italians residing in Louisiana cities:[22]

Alexandria	161
Baton Rouge	312
New Orleans	6,821
Shreveport	294

Except for New Orleans, where the parish and city are coterminous, a significant number of the immigrants in these parishes resided in the semirural and rural areas surrounding the cities. Truck farming played a large role in this settlement pattern. This tendency was especially true for New Orleans, where large numbers of immigrants were attracted to the area east of the French Quarter roughly paralleling St. Claude Avenue. Algiers (across the river) and the old town of Carrollton were also places of settlement for immigrants engaged in truck farming and related occupations.

This settlement pattern resembles that of Sicily more than agricultural settlement in the United States generally. In Sicily the peasants lived in the village and walked or rode on a mule to work the outlying fields. The peasant was an urban villager.[23] He did not live on isolated farmlands. In the United States this pattern is by and large lacking. The closest we came to it is with truck-farming communities near large cities. We see this pattern in Louisiana, but it is also encountered in New York, New Jersey, and elsewhere.

One important exception to the general trend from the plantation parishes to the environs of cities is the unique case of Tangipahoa Parish. During the period from 1900 to 1930, the foreign-born Italian population of the parish increased by 1,453. The settlement of Tangipahoa and the immigrants' involvement in the strawberry industry of southeast Louisiana has been well documented.[24] They bought up land thought too poor for farming by native Americans and paid for it with money saved from living frugally, saving as much as half of the wages received as plantation workers.

The Italian immigrants who came to Louisiana were predominately peasants from the interior and northwestern wine and fruit growing regions of Sicily. The villages from which they came were: Contessa Entellina, Ustica, Bisacquino, Termini Imerse, Poggioreale, Corleone, Cefalu, Palazzo Adriano, Trapani, Chiusa Sclafani, Trabia, Caccamo, Gibellina, Vallelunga Pratemento, Roccamena, Sambuca, Salaparuta, and the city of Palermo.[25]

This near-total dependence on Sicily as a source of immigrants to Louisiana contrasts markedly with the national picture. Estimates vary, but probably around 25 percent of the Italian immigration to the United States was from Sicily.[26] One searches in vain for records of passengers coming in shiploads from continental Italy. There is, however, some indication that continental Italians entered the port at New Orleans aboard vessels sailing from Latin American ports.[27] These arrivals were few, however, compared to the numbers coming from Sicily. The other source of continental Italians in Louisiana was the Italian colonies in cities of the northern United States, particularly Chicago and New York.[28] They came to work the sugar plantations; some stayed. However, in proportion to the Italians from Sicily, these immigrants probably were few. A reasonable estimate is that over 90 percent of all Italian immigrants to Louisiana were Sicilians.

Besides its Sicilian character, immigration to Louisiana was unique in that it peaked earlier than elsewhere in North America. Nationally, the majority of immigrants arrived between 1901 and 1914. In Louisiana, however, over half of all Italian immigrants arrived prior to 1900. This fact is revealed in table 3.

Table 3

Year of Immigration for Louisiana and the United States (in Percent)

Location	1925-30	1920-24	1915-19	1911-14	1901-10	1900 & <	unknown
Louisiana	0.6	3.1	2.0	4.8	33.2	51.9	4.5
United States	4.6	14.8	6.2	17.2	36.4	17.8	3.0

Source: Bureau of the Census, *Fifteenth Census,* vol. 3, part 1 (1932), prepared by the Government Printing Office (Washington, D.C.).

ARRIVAL AT NEW ORLEANS

Even with the new steamships, the journey from Palermo to New Orleans could take over a month. On December 16, 1880, a British steamship arrived in New Orleans after an extraordinarily long forty-three-day journey from Palermo.[29] The vessel had met with rough weather. More typical was the experience of the *Elysia,* which left Palermo on September 28, 1890, with 1,013 immigrants and arrived at New Orleans nineteen days later.[30]

Sympathy for the immigrants was generally lacking in the reporting of their arrivals. Dispassionately, as if listing baseball scores, the *Daily Picayune* stated that two children died and one child was born during this latter passage.[31] In the same breath, the article went on to add that there were about six hundred men and three hundred women aboard. "Some brought over boxes of ill smelling cheese. . . . Some had numbers of umbrellas, each of a different violet hue." Yet, one is appreciative of the detailed descriptions of the clothing.

> The most common dress of the men were black velveteen jackets and trousers very close fitting and with huge fur caps. Those not well attired had on woolen jackets with many pockets, each

bulging, muchly patched trousers, slouch hats or red handker-
chiefs and shawls. The women, without exception, wore neither
hat nor bonnet. The hair was parted in two switches, straight
back from the faces hard and uninviting in outline. Most of
them were of a petite build, yet muscular. Their dresses were
light stuff, usually much ornamented. . . . Green, yellow, and
red predominated in the clothes which gayly covered the dark
forms of the cryless and stoical little ones.[32]

Both men and women wore earrings. The earrings of the
women reached to their shoulders.[33]

When a ship arrived it would be greeted by friends and relations of the new arrivals, crowds of curiosity seekers, and a
small army of customs officials. The immigrants did not dis-
embark immediately upon arrival, but were detained for all the
processing and medical examinations that come with entering
a foreign country. On October 21, 1900, a ship from Palermo
carrying over two thousand Sicilians anchored at Nine-Mile
Point.[34] By October 27, all but about two hundred were allowed
to land. The poor, the aged, and the infirm who would likely
be wards of the state were sent back. Their last hope to escape
poverty withered at the Press Street wharf. They would have to
resume the quest for bread in the land of their fathers.

CHAPTER THREE

Respect (*Rispetto*)

We came to America in search of bread and felt the inferiority of beggars. Everything about us was interpreted in terms of that inferiority. —Quoted in Mangione and Morreale

ANNA'S APRON

The sun had risen on the tiny village of Alia longer than anyone could remember. The whitewashed buildings, surrounding fields, and assorted animals were the only world the few thousand or so villagers had ever known. When compared to the age of the village, the oldest man around, Ernesto Paternostro, was a mere infant of ninety-five years. When the young ones asked about the origin of their village, Ernesto would once again tell the story his grandfather told him. If a significant audience of pleading children accompanied by one or two adults was gathered, he was particularly ready to perform. Staring at the distant mountains, he would assume his theatrical stance. "God created Adam and Eve and placed them in Paradise; they sinned. God was angry and drove them out. In their wanderings to find a good place to settle, they chanced upon Alia. Since the barons already owned all of the good land and the contadini were a quarrelsome lot, they continued on their way in search of a 'good place.'" Each retelling was a bit different. Details were added or subtracted as memory and wit provided.

Francesco, or "Chico," as his mother would call him except when she was angry, passed by a small audience attentively watching old man Ernesto "perform." It was a good day, for it was Sunday, a day of respite from work in the fields. Men, women, and children filled the piazza. *Chico searched the familiar figures near the fountain until his eyes found the small frame of Anna. A mere sixteen, she still bore the visage of a child. But even with her newly embroidered shawl covering her upper body, Chico could discern the delicate figure of a woman. Anna blushed and looked down momentarily. Recovering her composure, she stole a glimpse of Chico's shoulders and deep tan that nature and work in the fields had fashioned. At length, her brown eyes gazed upon his handsome face with its cleft chin that she had fancied since her childhood.*

But there were other eyes in the piazza *and many of them, especially of the married women, were watching Chico and Anna attentively. Their relatives in particular bore the duty of guarding the gates of virtue and family honor. The sentinels permitted smiles, pleasant words, and some harmless laughter but not much more. The wedding would take place when both families agreed on all the arrangements, not the least of which would be the dowry.*

Lust and abiding affection intermingled inside Chico like water and wine. At eighteen years of age, he was not expected to be capable of drawing the distinction. The wisdom of the old ones would check the recklessness of youth. Chico could only imagine the dire consequences of breaking the time-honored rules of courtship.

He stood speechless in front of Anna, gazing into her eyes. At length, realizing the awkwardness of the scene, he announced to Anna's relatives, who flanked her on both sides, that he was on his way to his uncle's house. Even so angelic a distraction as Anna could not detain Chico today. His thoughts turned to the rumors about America. He tried to imagine what his cousin would report about this faraway place. He was impatient to hear about this land that was so rich that the streets were paved with gold.

Chico nurtured a dream shared by many in the village to have a piece of good land. He did not hope for riches but enough money to buy sufficient land in his village to secure his and Anna's freedom from want. Perhaps in America he could make the money to buy his dream, he thought. Perhaps he would never have to watch the baroness wipe her soiled hands on Anna's apron again.

The truth in this bit of fiction is the common desire of the Sicilian peasant to escape from a world that offered too little bread and even less respect. It was not for want of bread alone that the *contadini* left their villages. *Rispetto* is what they also sought, but in their native land they got precious little of it. Economic hardships may be sufficient to drive men from their homes to search for survival. But the peasants of southern Italy and Sicily desired more than ample food. In their native lands they had been placed beneath the beasts of burden for longer than anyone could remember. Ignasio Silone's account of a peasant song strikingly portrays the *contadini*'s place in the social order of the Old Country.[1] According to the song, the Prince of Heaven, God Himself, is above everything. Then comes the prince of the earth, Lord Torlonia. Under him are armed guards. Under the guards are his dogs. After that, there is nothing. After nothing, there is more nothing. The peasants come next.

Bruno Arcudi has argued persuasively that the *contadini*'s hunger for respect was greater than their hunger for bread.[2] Here are peasants, the heirs of 3,000 years of civilization, who lived under the shadows of Doric temples their ancestors built. They were rightfully proud people. Their pitiful economic conditions often, however, concealed that great sense of pride and dignity. The immigrants in Louisiana who lived in shacks with inner walls papered with newspapers and cardboard boxes but who, nevertheless, took their meals only after first setting the table with the family's finest linen reflected that inner dignity. Similarly, the immigrant women who refused to be searched for contraband when they disembarked at the Port of New Orleans reflected that same sense of repute. The blindness of Americans to that dignity was sadly reflected in the *Daily Picayune*'s 1900 account of a customs official's reaction to a peasant woman who refused to be searched. The official, Mrs. Baker, "found the whole episode amusing."[3] She could not understand why the *contadina* protested being searched. After all, no contraband was found. She was not a thief or a smuggler, so why object? Because the woman had so few possessions, Mrs. Baker could not imagine she possessed dignity!

A distinction has been drawn between the honor nested in a person's status and that which is attached to the individual.[4] The honor afforded a person as an individual is called dignity and is a modern development. In 1900, the Italian conception was closer to the medieval idea that based honor on status in the community, especially family status. When the Italian immigrant demanded *rispetto*, he was thinking of his and his family's place in the community. The honor he claimed was derived from blood and name, but individuals in the family could add to, or subtract from, the family's honor. Purity of blood among the peasantry was based on the chastity of women; name was based on the behavior of men.[5] The family that was unable to preserve the chastity of its women was held in disgrace. Similarly, the family was disgraced if its menfolk lacked courage or sound judgment. Shame and honor befell persons according to their actions and befell the family that claimed them as members. But there were class differences. At that time in Sicily, aristocratic women did not need to dress quite so modestly nor be as vigilant in guarding the gates of chastity. The family name among the highborn could compensate for the laxity of individual members. In the poorer families, however, a woman's chastity was so highly regarded that it was a matter of social advertisement. Not only were nuptial sheets privately examined on the first night for the telltale signs of bridal virginity, but the sheets were hung on the balcony so that others might also see the proof! Women were required to don their aprons when leaving the house, symbolizing the momentary and obligatory nature of their errands.[6] As in all traditional societies, children were expected to give respect to adults, and wives were expected to honor their husbands.

It is important to note that honor can only be contested among equals. The *contadini* could not, of course, claim honor from noblemen. Without wealth and noble birth, the peasants aspired to be honored among their peers through their industry, moral character, and prudence. But a *contadino's* renown in his village made no impression on the aristocracy. In truth, peasants were treated badly by noblemen and their agents. And perhaps because they were, their notion of honor, although deeply rooted in the European Middle Ages, shared some kinship with the modern American conception of honor, which favors dignity of the individual. The Italian peasant who came to America had at least some sympathy for this sentiment.

In Italy, the *contadini* were hated because they were lowborn and poor. In America, while they enjoyed legal equality, they were hated because they were poor and different. Americans were oblivious to the distinctions of honor peasant families made among themselves. For the most part, immigrants to America tried vainly to keep alive their claims to honor. Those who gained respect did so by becoming materially successful, the only way capitalist America could ever bestow honor. Most immigrants worked incessantly at getting ahead. A few exceptionally lucky and industrious ones became successful. Interestingly, there is little evidence they avoided un-honorific jobs. No job was unworthy of their efforts so long as they could make a living at it. Indeed, the American characteristic of considering prestige when evaluating occupations was incomprehensible to the Italian peasant who came to this country. His work ethic, like that of the Puritans during the colonial period of American history, was indestructible; but the motivation for the Italian immigrant came from altogether different sources. The Puritan was inspired, perhaps even compelled, to work by the Protestant ethic, a collection of moral imperatives that drove them to work, invest, get rich, live an ascetic lifestyle, and await salvation. The Italian peasants' predisposition toward labor found its spiritual wellspring in medieval thought. Living for centuries under the shadow of monasticism, they saw work as a form of prayer or sacrifice, as penance for sin. Therefore, with rare exceptions for thievery and prostitution, which are sinful in themselves, all kinds of labor are considered valuable and honorable.[7] Moreover, pragmatically, they knew they either worked, or they starved to death.

Manual labor, no matter how demeaning to Americans, was eagerly sought by Italian immigrants. Their primary motivation was economic security for themselves and their families. Their occupational choices were not prompted by a concern for prestige but rather were typically conceived of in practical terms. Indeed, there is evidence to indicate that occupational choices of today's Italian-Americans continue to be based more on income than prestige considerations.

For the vast majority of Italian immigrants to America, respect escaped their grasp. The immigrant from Italy soon learned his claims to honor based on his and his family's place in the community fell on deaf ears in America. He tried to keep it alive among *paesani* and family members. The lack of respect between the immigrant and his American neighbor was mutual. The immigrant was often cool and indifferent to Americans. He found it hard to honor a people who he thought worked too little, had little loyalty to family, and whose morality he found defective. Yet, externally, the immigrants wanted to be good neighbors. They kept their distance, but when it was important to have good public relations, they knew how to ingratiate themselves. It was during settlement that the immigrant tried at first to earn and subsequently claim *rispetto*.

SETTLEMENT IN AMERICA

There has been such a striking similarity among the immigrant settlement experiences in the many urban centers of

America that there is justification for describing urban settlement in general terms. What happened in New York was, in many ways, similar to what happened in Boston, Philadelphia, Chicago, San Francisco, and other large cities. There was some small-town and rural settlement, but this involved comparatively few immigrants in America.[8] After 1880, when the frontier had already closed and homesteading had run its course, there was no free land for the taking. Without money to purchase the private land that might have been for sale, even at very inexpensive prices, the Italian peasant immigrants, most of whom arrived at this time, were left little or no option but to gravitate to the cities. Just as importantly, the jobs were in the cities—the big cities. When they came to this country, America was stretching its industrial muscles. It was in the midst of its greatest industrial expansion ever, which was taking place in the cities. That's where the work was; consequently that's where the immigrants went. When they got there, the Italians, like other ethnic European immigrants of that time, huddled together in colonies filled with their countrymen.

Most settled in the low-rent neighborhoods adjacent to the business districts in America's sprawling Northern urban centers. It was chiefly here that they made their first attempts at reconstructing their lives. In Manhattan's Lower East Side, Chicago's South Side, Boston's West End, San Francisco's North Beach, and other large American cities in the Midwest and northeastern seaboard, the rural masses of Europe tried to set down roots. Historically, America's urban slums were the inhospitable places where European immigrants tried to adapt their largely rural institutions and cultures to the urban milieu.[9] More recently, the Puerto Ricans, Taiwanese, Vietnamese, and Latin Americans have followed in the same pattern. The neighborhoods they settled into in the urban landscape go by a hundred names both generic and specific. They have been called ghettoes, racial islands, ethnic colonies, barrios, or, more exactly, Little Italy, Little Poland, Germantown, and Chinatown. The litany of names is endless. The immigrants have also been called urban villagers.[10]

These were neighborhoods in decay; living conditions were abominable. The immediate cause of the physical decay of the neighborhoods surrounding commercial centers has been attributed to a lack of municipal building codes. The absence of construction and maintenance regulations resulted in the eventual growth of urban slums on an unprecedented scale. The squalor of slums in Manhattan equaled the worst in Europe or Asia.[11]

The living conditions in these "hellholes" have been depicted in a most depressing manner.

> About 50 percent [of tenements] slept three or four in a room; and nearly 25 percent, five in a room. Toilet facilities, two to a floor at best and foul privies at worst, allowing neither the simplification of nature nor the conveniences of civilization, added to the sense of people intolerably packed together. . . . Perhaps worse was the assault of smells: the odors of human waste only intermittently carted away from backyard privies by a careless sanitation department, the stench of fish and meat starting to rot on pushcarts, the foulness of neglected sewers and gutters. Life was abrasive, clamorous.[12]

But there was another side to life in urban America's slums. The density, squalor, and health-debasing environment could be at times moderated by a strong sense of community. Particularly in the twentieth century after social reformers helped to improve living conditions, and institutional forms modeled after the "Old Country" became routine, the ethnic neighborhood could be a fortress of "Old World" life in urban America, a refuge and an island of familiar people, languages, and inviting smells surrounded by the sea of uninviting America (inhospitable Americans). Residence in these locations over time became a complex set of social arrangements, some American but mostly European, transplanted in the American landscape.

SETTLEMENT IN LOUISIANA

The experience of the immigrants in Louisiana was different from the national pattern. For one thing, there never was an

Italian slum in Louisiana. The largest and most dense concentration of Italians in Louisiana was found in the New Orleans French Quarter, one of the most desirable sections of the city and one of the most famous and unique neighborhoods in the United States of America. Through it all, the Quarter has always been affordable. Especially in 1900 when the Italian immigrants were flocking to it, there were enough inexpensive properties to accommodate even poverty-stricken newcomers. Although, because of the poverty, there was some similarity between the Quarter and ethnic slums in Northern cities, the Italian immigrants who settled there did so not because of impoverishment but because of its proximity to the farmers' market (French Market). The market attracted Italian immigrants because of the long-standing presence and influence of Italian-Americans in the operation of it. For a long time New Orleanians have maintained that the French Market was founded by the Spanish, named after the French, and controlled by the Italians! Moreover, unlike in Northern cities, there never was large-scale tenement construction either in the French Quarter or elsewhere in the city to accommodate the population growth of the city. The original buildings in the Quarter were somewhat modified to target the poor renter, but no multistoried, multifamily structures were erected to capitalize on a landlord's market as in other American cities. Indeed, even today it cannot be said that there is a tenement district within the city.

The other significant manner in which Louisiana's Italian immigrants differ from the national pattern is the large number of them who initially settled in rural communities. Only in California, where nearly half of the original immigrants went into the wine and produce industries, is there anything resembling the Italian experience in Louisiana. Consider these figures: in 1900, of 17,431 foreign-born Italians residing in Louisiana, 10,952, or 65 percent, were living in rural communities. Rural residency was 58 percent of the total in 1910, 52 percent of the total in 1920, and 45 percent of the total in

1930. As these numbers indicate, Italian immigrants gradually gravitated to the cities although very significant numbers of them remained in rural environments. Even at this writing, thousands of people of Italian ancestry can be found throughout the rural sugar parishes in South Louisiana and in Tangipahoa Parish, where their ancestors were strawberry farmers.

Settlement of Italian immigrants in Louisiana has been shaped by five factors. First, the size and pace of immigration was such that a pre-Civil War enclave of business and professional immigrants developed in the French Quarter in New Orleans. The mass immigration of the late nineteenth century represented a larger flow of peasant people who benefited from the existence of a well-established Italian colony that already had won acceptance in the city.

Second, the French Creole[13] culture of Louisiana was essentially a Mediterranean variant. The immigrant from Sicily could identify with the major social arrangements and values he found in South Louisiana. The main principle on which he and the Creole differed was the role of work in everyday life. While both enjoyed fine foods, loved games of chance, and appreciated the arts, the immigrant was much more given to a work ethic than the Creole, whose reputation for ease of living has contributed to New Orleans being called the Big Easy. This work ethic, along with frugality and an apparently inexhaustible capacity to make sacrifices to ensure a better life for their families, has been largely responsible for the Italian immigrants' economic success in Louisiana.

Third, although the geographies of Italy and South Louisiana are quite different, the temperature extremes are comparable. Subtropical Louisiana was more tolerable to the Italians, despite its high humidity, than the cold climate of Northern American cities. More importantly, the topography of South Louisiana with high and rich alluvial ridges flanking low swampy areas was inviting for a peasant who could make a successful garden even in the harsh, rocky soils of southern

Italy and Sicily. In Louisiana, the fertile alluvial soils rewarded the dedicated farmer with bountiful harvests. In New Orleans, the availability of farmland within the city limits as well as in the surrounding area was instrumental in decentralizing the Italian population by making truck farming in and around the city a profitable enterprise.

Fourth, the relatively open economic niche in the food industry was vigorously explored. Before long, the Italians became the food "kingpins" of Louisiana.

Finally, Italians in Louisiana typically immigrated and settled in family units. Married men were less prone to make the journey to Louisiana without their wives and children than to other ports of call. This circumstance naturally had a settling effect on the husbands. By contrast, Thomas Kessner described the immigration of Italians to New York as "by and large, a non-family movement of males in their productive years—without family ties to restrict them they moved freely across the city and country often joining the birds of passage in seeking the most attractive short range opportunities, ignoring business and enterprise."[14]

EARLY SETTLEMENT IN LOUISIANA

Few people realize that prior to 1870 and the start of the era of intensive immigration, New Orleans attracted thousands of Italians. The earliest Italians to set foot in Louisiana arrived as members of the De Soto expedition in the sixteenth century. During the French-Spanish regimes and in the early nineteenth century the majority of these immigrants were from the northern provinces of Piedmont, Liguria, and Lombardy. These provinces had close cultural and political ties with France. Thus it is not surprising that these Italians were attracted to Louisiana because of its French language and traditions and the business opportunities offered by the Port of New Orleans. By mid-century (1850) Louisiana had 924 Italians living within its boundaries, making it the state with the largest Italian-born population in the United States.[15]

Three Italians are known to have been in Louisiana in the 1540s with Hernando De Soto's Spanish expedition: Maestro Francisco, Cristoforo de Spinola, and Bernardo Peloso. Of the three, Francisco is the most memorable. He was an engineer who constructed bridges and boats to assist the expedition in crossing streams and rivers in their travels across the gulf coastal region of the United States. When De Soto died on the banks of the Mississippi River near Natchez in 1542, his men made their way into Arkansas before turning homeward. In 1543, Francisco was responsible for constructing a flotilla of seven vessels that would eventually take the expedition safely back to its place of origination in Mexico. On instructions from Spain, De Soto was to find gold. Of course, there was no gold to find. Finding none, Spain lost interest in the Mississippi Valley, thus opening the way for France, its political rival, to be the first European nation to establish a lasting settlement in Louisiana.[16]

The Italian mercenaries who accompanied the French explorers and settlers of the vast Louisiana Territory were, no doubt, representative of the professional soldier so frequently encountered during this period. Enrico di Tonti is the most famous of these. In 1678 he joined forces with René Robert Cavelier, Sieur de La Salle's French expedition, which explored the Mississippi Valley. Owing to financial and political delays, the expedition did not set out until early February 1682. Upon reaching the mouth of the Mississippi River later that same year the expedition claimed the whole territory drained by the river for Louis XIV, king of France. Tonti was feared and respected by the Indians, who knew him as the man with the "iron hand" because of "the hook-like claw that replaced the hand Tonti lost while fighting for the French in Sicily."[17]

After the French established New Orleans in 1718 and began to settle Louisiana, other Italians came into the area. Russell M. Magnaghi reports some of them to be undesirables who had been living in France, deserters, and tobacco smugglers.[18]

The French founded and colonized Louisiana during the

period 1718-63. In 1763, by the stroke of a pen, Louisiana was ceded to Spain as a result of the provisions of the Treaty of Paris. Spain controlled New Orleans and Louisiana for the next thirty-seven years, returning them to France in 1800. Soon thereafter, in 1803, the French sold Louisiana to the United States of America in what every American high-school student knows is the Louisiana Purchase, the greatest land deal in the history of the country. Thomas Jefferson bought Louisiana from Napoleon for $15,000,000, roughly three cents per acre. At that time, except for Texas (which belonged to Mexico), Louisiana included all the land west of the Mississippi River to the Rockies—roughly one-third of all the lands in the continental United States.

During the French and Spanish colonial periods, there was a steady trickle of Italians into Louisiana. Most of them came as members of the military, including such men as Lieutenant Maloza, Giovanni Audicio, Giuseppe Fasiny, Domingo Parsigni, Giovanni Sapia, Francesco Uberti, Pietro Rola, and Giuseppe Airoldi. The most noteworthy Italian soldier of that era was Francesco de Roggio, who commanded the Royal Genoese Grenadiers. In 1750, Captain de Roggio was sent with his command to Louisiana, where four years later he was put in charge of the marine infantry and served as commandant of the Arkansas Post. The de Roggios became a prominent family in New Orleans and Francesco's great-grandson was the famous Civil War general P. G. T. Beauregard.[19]

Not all of the Italians who came to New Orleans stayed there; some of them spread out into the countryside elsewhere in Louisiana and beyond. Giovanni Grandenigo went to Mobile initially, then removed himself to Opelousas, Louisiana, where he took up permanent residence. In 1789 he was president of the Trustees of the Catholic Church in Opelousas. Domenico Monteche settled in Natchitoches. He acquired a house, property, and black and Indian slaves. Indeed, Italian settlers introduced into New Orleans made their way up the Mississippi

River all the way to Missouri. The St. Louis militia roster of 1780 lists some Italian names though we do not know the country of their origin.

While there was a scattering of Italians beyond the environs of New Orleans, it was in, and around, the city itself where most of them lived out their lives. By the start of the nineteenth century, Italians were already beginning to make an economic, if not cultural, impact on the city. Jerome Chiapella was such an influential merchant in 1804 that his signature accompanied a petition to the United States Congress on behalf of the merchants of New Orleans protesting what they referred to as "the economic stagnation of the Port of New Orleans." Another Italian, Pietro Maspero, owned the Exchange Coffee House on Chartres Street. It was the epicenter of the city's social scene at the beginning of the nineteenth century. Gen. Andrew Jackson was received in triumph at Maspero's following the Battle of New Orleans (1815). Maspero was an entrepreneur with wide-ranging interests in business, art, optics, and auctioneering.

Two somewhat shady Italians favored the disreputable business of the pirate Jean Lafitte. They took up residence with him in Barataria Bay. With Lafitte, they were smugglers and pirates along the northern coast of the Gulf of Mexico. One of them, Louis Chighizola, was an unsavory character covered in battle scars whose distinguishing mark was his nose, or more correctly what was left of it. It had been cut off at the tip by a saber. As a consequence, he was known as Nez Coupé, "Cut Nose." Vincent Gambi was especially bellicose. He was not only in trouble with the legitimate political authorities in New Orleans but also at odds with Capt. Jean Lafitte. Contrary to Lafitte's instructions, Gambi was prone to attacking American-flag vessels. Chighizola and Gambi won pardons for their crimes as a result of their gallantry in the Battle of New Orleans in 1815, when they fought with Jean Lafitte's pirates alongside Andrew Jackson's army against the British.

Louisiana was admitted into statehood in 1812. By that time, the Italians in New Orleans were numerous enough to constitute a definable enclave. Contributing to the growth of the emerging Italian colony was the next wave of Italian immigrants, which was prompted in Italy by the political upheavals of 1820, 1821, 1830, and 1848.[20] These unsuccessful revolutions and the war of 1849 for Italian independence from Austria prompted a number of Italians to emigrate. "These early immigrants, representing an educated class of professionals, skilled craftsmen, and mercenaries from Turin, Milan, Genoa, Naples, Malta, Sardinia, and Sicily were exiled to the United States for participating in the revolutionary movement to unify Italy. Many stumbled upon New Orleans en route west."[21]

By 1840, New Orleans had a population of 102,193, including hundreds of Italians. The Italian community in Louisiana was already large enough to require the assignment of Italian Catholic missionaries to the area. An Italian opera company came to New Orleans about this time, and the physician Dr. Felix Fermento, Sr., became one of the most distinguished medical professionals in the city for his work with the sick and his research that proved the usefulness of vaccinations against smallpox.

Well before the War Between the States, New Orleans was the home of men like the painter Antonio Mondelli, sculptor Perelli, architect Pietro Gualdi, and businessmen Santo Oteri and Angelo Socola.

Magnaghi states, "By the eve of the Civil War the Italians were well established in New Orleans. They were engaged in every occupation imaginable: coffee and oyster saloon keeper, physician, merchant, poultry dealer, perfume, chocolate manufacturer, ice merchant, river trader, levee speculator, shell dealer, importer and the usual assortment of shopkeepers, craftsmen, and tradesmen."[22]

Two military units composed of Italian soldiers fought for the Confederacy in the Civil War. Organized in New Orleans soon after Louisiana withdrew from the Union, Garibaldi's Legion[23] comprised 170 men in full military arms and regalia. They fought as Company F, a component of the *Cazadores Espanoles* (Spanish Hunters). The other unit, consisting exclusively of resident aliens, was the Italian Guards Battalion. It served with the European Brigade under the command of the Louisiana Militia.

Before the great migration of southern Italians to Louisiana between 1880 and 1920, the Italian colony in New Orleans was large enough to support two Italian Catholic churches, two benevolent societies, an Italian newspaper, and even an Italian Free Masonic lodge known as Dante Lodge No. 174. Despite these developments and the Italians' substantial economic influence, they did not have a significant cultural impact on the city. For one thing, they were northern Italians, and their culture was not radically different from the French culture already implanted in "Louisiana soil." For another, they were not so numerous as to threaten the dominant French Catholic and growing American Protestant Caucasian cultures that controlled life in the city. The other great cultural influence in the city came from the black community, which was richly multicultural. Blacks were an improbable mixture of slaves and freedmen, Africans and Caribbeans, as well as Catholics and Protestants.

It would be safe to conclude that prior to the Civil War, the cultural impact of the Italians in Louisiana was minimal as they were gradually being absorbed into the dominant French culture. The immigrants of the nineteenth century who were attracted to New Orleans were enamored of her climate and her Creole culture.[24] However, their main motivation was the business opportunities at the Port of New Orleans, with its role in supplying provisions for the Mississippi Valley. Their settlement was predominately in the old quarter (*Vieux Carré*). As this small community grew through immigration triggered by the political troubles of Italy, it evolved into a self-conscious cultural enclave within the city. The business and professional talents of its members were manifested in the way they carved out their economic and social niche within the city. Their activity gradually came to center on the export and import trade. The Italian community eventually became involved in every aspect of the food industry—exporting, importing, wholesaling, retailing, and, in the late nineteenth century, agricultural production.

Significant numbers of prominent Italian-American families can trace their origins to the business and professional people who developed and capitalized on the direct trade routes between New Orleans and Italian ports. The cargo arriving in New Orleans was citrus fruits, figs, tomatoes, olives, and other salted, preserved foodstuffs. The rapid domination by Italian merchants of this economic niche is a testimony to their business acumen and their visionary ability to recognize the importance of the port of New Orleans as the major supplier of the small towns, cities, and rural communities of the Mississippi Valley.

A case in point was the Vaccaro family. Alcée Fortier's account of Stefano Vaccaro and his family, although not typical, illustrates the talent found in the early Italian community in New Orleans.[25] Stefano Vaccaro was born in Contessa Entellina and aligned himself with Garibaldi's revolutionary cause. He was imprisoned for his political activities and in 1860 immigrated to New Orleans. At the outbreak of the Civil War, he moved to Louisville, Kentucky. Two years later, he returned to New Orleans and founded a fruit and produce business. In 1893, he returned to the town of his birth, leaving his business to his sons, Joseph, Luca, and Felix.

The original location of their business was Decatur and North Peters streets. They began importing bananas and coconuts from Spanish Honduras in 1898. In 1914, their firm employed 2,000 men in Honduras, 100 in New Orleans, and 200 on ships. They owned four ships, each of which had a capacity of 2,000 tons.

Whatever the Italian merchants' share of the economic pie in New Orleans might have been, it is clear that by the 1860s, the small but viable Italian community in New Orleans would pave the way for subsequent waves of immigrants from Sicily and elsewhere in the south of Italy.

TURN-OF-THE-NINETEENTH-CENTURY SETTLEMENT IN NEW ORLEANS

It was in New Orleans and its environs that the Italian community made its most significant impact on the state. It is easy to see why the French Quarter was attractive to the new immigrants. It was the center of a preexisting Italian community. The friends and relatives of the newly arrived immigrants resided there. There was the Italian church and Italian priests. There one could find the French Market and buy and sell fresh produce. In short, it was an island of Mediterranean life—a piece of Italy firmly planted in the middle of New Orleans.

Settlement was a product of ecological forces. To adequately understand the settlement of Italian immigrants in New Orleans, one must understand the city's unique topography and history. The Isle of Orleans was located by the French explorers at the intersection of two alluvial ridges on the east bank of the Mississippi.[26] The ridges are composed of sands deposited by repeated flooding of the Mississippi and a former stream, which roughly paralleled Esplanade Avenue. The otherwise swampy and poorly drained terrain is traversed by these ridges. The intersection was chosen as the site for the French colony on the lower Mississippi. The Isle of Orleans was indeed an island in a sea of swamp and marsh that flanked its east and west borders. To the north lay the shallow Lake Pontchartrain and to the south, the Mississippi River. Elsewhere, the swampy terrain is interrupted by the Gentilly Ridge, deposited by the bayou named for it, which no longer exists. The Metairie Ridge, also deposited by a former stream, parallels Metairie

Road. Before the advent of electrical pumps, settlement was confined to ridges paralleling streams or former streams. Settlement could and did occur up- and downriver but only on the narrow ribbon of alluvial sand that rose several feet higher than the swampy or marshy terrain that characterized most of coastal Louisiana. Maps of Louisiana as recent as 1920 show that much of the land within the familiar crescent carved by the river's bends was cypress swamp and therefore not settled.

New Orleans was not merely a physical island; it was also an island of French and Spanish culture in an Anglo-Saxon sea.[27] Whereas she has been successful in keeping out the waters of Lake Pontchartrain and the Mississippi River and expanding her inhabitable area, the city could only slow the inevitable tidal flow of Americans to her shores. Even before the Louisiana Purchase, the racial and cultural groups of New Orleans had established their niches. The French-speaking population was the cultural and social elite, while the Americans commanded the economic arena. The French-speaking or Creole population inhabited the French Quarter, and the Americans were building the economic hub of the city west of Canal Street. The cultural distinction between the Creole and the American cuts across racial boundaries. Blacks who were culturally French resided in the Creole section and are still known by locals as Creoles of color. Blacks who were culturally American resided upriver in the American section.

This division between the Creole and American population has been captured in the peculiar name New Orleanians use for the land that divides avenues. Everywhere else they are called medians. In New Orleans, however, they are called neutral grounds. They were, so to speak, demilitarized zones. Canal Street's neutral ground separated the Creole and American sections. By extension, all medians were subsequently called neutral grounds.

The distinction between Creole and American still persisted when the Italian immigrants arrived. It is easy to see how they could have found the Creole section more compatible. As we have stated, not only did an Italian community reside there, but it was also the location of the French Market. The immigrants who arrived after 1880 swelled the population of Italians in the French Quarter.

The census of 1900 indicates that the greatest concentration of immigrants was located between St. Philip Street and Esplanade Avenue.[28] From west to east, the streets involved were St. Philip, Ursuline, Hospital (Governor Nicholls), Barracks, and Esplanade. When population pressure required it, the Italians, like the Creoles, moved north into Treme and beyond. In this northward movement, St. Philip and Hospital streets appear to have been important paths.

Hospital Street ran north to Broad. It recommenced at Metairie Road and terminated at the lake, traversing what today is City Park. Some Italian immigrants settled at the southern tip of City Park, far from the hub of life in the French Quarter. They worked along the waterway that ran from Lake Pontchartrain to Bayou St. John and the Carondelet Canal, which constituted an alternate route to New Orleans from the gulf. They were riggers, luggermen, and laborers who kept the ships moving from the Rigolets through the lake, down Bayou St. John, thence to the canal and the back side of the city.

Italian settlement also proceeded along St. Claude Avenue and other streets east of Esplanade Avenue that parallel the river. This followed in general the Irish and German pattern. The area, known to New Orleanians as Marigny, was once an Italian immigrant truck-farming section.

Elsewhere, smaller pockets of immigrants could be found in 1900. Along Dryades between Clio and Jackson a cluster of immigrants settled, no doubt attracted by the farmers' market there. Along Magazine, in the old town of Carrollton, in Algiers, and in Amesville (Marrero), pockets of immigrants could also be found.

By 1940, notable changes had occurred.[29] The French Quarter

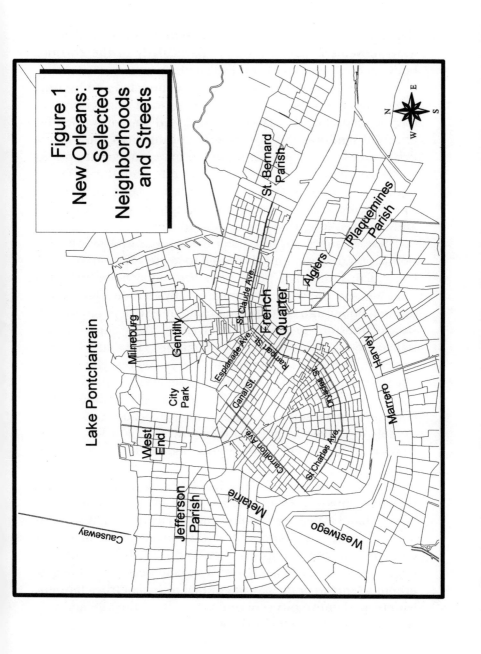

Figure 1
New Orleans:
Selected
Neighborhoods
and Streets

remained the area of greatest concentration, but a more northward movement was discernible, particularly in the corridor between St. Philip Street and Esplanade Avenue.

The St. Claude Avenue cluster had contracted and become more solidified. The largest concentration of immigrants was located between St. Claude Avenue and the river. Gentilly attracted significant numbers as one of the city's earliest suburban areas. Carrollton continued to have immigrants, particularly between South Carrollton Avenue and the Jefferson Parish line from Washington Avenue to Claiborne Avenue. However, by 1940 the pocket of immigrants along Magazine and the one along Dryades had dwindled.

These changes suggest the further decentralization of a population that was fairly dispersed to begin with. Not only was the Italian immigrant population beginning to be redistributed but also the general population. By 1940 this movement was well under way, though it was quite small compared to what was to transpire in subsequent decades. As a consequence, Italian populations emerged in Metairie, Harahan, Kenner, upper St. Bernard, and across the river in Algiers, Harvey, and Marrero. These enclaves were increasing at the expense of the Italian population in the city. There were preexisting Italian communities in some of these outlying locations, the most notable of which was in the little country town of Kenner just northwest of the city. Immigrants had settled in that area before 1900.

In the outlying districts, the Italians bought up land, which they developed into truck farms. Early in the twentieth century, Italian farmers were supplying the city with its fresh fruits and vegetables. As important as this was, it paled in significance to what was to happen after World War II, when the city began to suburbanize in earnest. The land needed for the geographical spread of the city was owned by Italian truck farmers, who reaped enormous economic gains from the sale and subsequent redevelopment of the land.

Comparatively speaking, New Orleans' Italian colony was never very segregated. Typically, Italians in other American cities were considerably more segregated.[30] Cities like St. Louis, Pittsburgh, Philadelphia, New York, Cleveland, Boston, and Chicago had Italian communities anywhere from two to four times more segregated than the Italians in New Orleans. What is significant about these findings hardly needs emphasizing. The strength and persistence of an ethnic colony depends on residential propinquity. It is easier for ethnic groups to maintain social and cultural distinctiveness when they share an area of residence and interact as neighbors. In short, neighborhood relations and institutions contribute to and reinforce the immigrants' identity. This is not to say that residentially dispersed ethnic groups cannot have a strong sense of ethnic identity. History has presented a number of examples that strongly argue they can—the most notable are the Jews. But history has presented an even stronger case for the converse, and the examples of this would be many indeed. The absence of a tight-knit, geographically segregated, residential community fostered a cultural environment conducive to the breakdown of Old World customs and institutions and to the Americanization of the Italian immigrants in New Orleans.

SETTLEMENT IN THE SUGAR PARISHES

The Italians who worked the plantations in the sugarcane parishes of South Louisiana and the cotton plantations of North Louisiana came from three main streams of migration. One stream was international with the immigrants coming from southern Italy, mainly Sicily. The other two streams originated in the United States—the first from Italian colonies in Midwestern and Northeastern cities, principally Chicago and New York, and the other from the small Italian colony in New Orleans.

It is impossible to get an accurate assessment of who went where, from where. In some instances we know the facts, but in far too many cases we simply have no information. This was an immigrant population that initially consisted of temporary, part-time workers who went from job to job in the cities, or they were migrant farm laborers. Both categories of workers are occupational nomads. The only comprehensive, systematic record we have of them is information obtained by the Immigration Service at their port of entry and census data compiled every decade. Once they got to Louisiana, we know they moved about a great deal in the early years of their arrival, going from job to job. When they had enough money to buy a home or a piece of ground their geographical journey came to an end, and their journey toward *rispetto* began.

Jean Ann Scarpaci has reported several methods of recruitment into the plantation system.[31] One important method was the use of agents. Some agents were brokers acting on their own as intermediaries between the plantation owners and the immigrants. Other agents were employed directly by the plantation owners or worked for shipping companies. The agents may have been in the employ of a state, parish, or private committee or association whose interest was to support the plantation owners. Vincent Lamantia opened a private agency on St. Peter Street in the French Quarter. As the former consul to America at Catania, Sicily, he had contacts with other Italian colonies in the United States. By 1891, he was recruiting from New York and three years later from Chicago as an agent for the Louisiana Immigration League, which provided him with a commission of two dollars for each immigrant he delivered to Louisiana. Sometimes, instead of money, the agent was given a privilege or a concession that led to financial gain. An interesting combination of enterprise and family ties was involved in the arrangement obtained by one agent. Gaetano J. Mistretta, in Donaldsonville, Louisiana, recruited laborers for plantations in Assumption Parish through his brother in Corleone, Sicily. In return, he was allowed to sell groceries on those plantations that received immigrants supplied by him. It is not known how common this kind of recruitment was statewide, but it was significant in the Donaldsonville area.

Lamantia and Mistretta are examples of middlemen, or brokers, known as *padroni* who, possessing neither license nor office and acting either on their own or as agents for others, obtained immigrants for employers in the United States. Though not formally recognized in law, the *padrone* system was made possible by federal legislation passed in 1864 allowing the recruitment of immigrants under contract. It flourished between 1890 and 1900. By 1910 it had almost completely vanished of its own inertia. Although never a major source of recruitment, it did, nevertheless, contribute to the overall influx of immigration from Italy, Greece, Turkey, Bulgaria, Macedonia, and Mexico. The Italian *padrone* experience was somewhat unique because it was the most extensive and it caused the most widespread reaction to it among nativists.

For a price, not unlike the commissions and fees paid for referrals among professionals today or the fees charged by contemporary employment agencies, *padroni* found jobs for immigrants. They may have, on their own or with financial backing by employers, prepaid the immigrants' passage, found the laborers their jobs, collected their wages, written their letters, acted as their bankers, provided them room and board, and served as their go-between in dealing with employers. Upon their arrival in the United States, the largely illiterate, non-English-speaking immigrants were initially so dependent upon the *padroni,* they were easy prey for those among them who were unscrupulous. Once in the grasp of the *padroni,* the workers were vulnerable to a variety of schemes to separate them from their money. In some cases, *padroni* would charge first-class rates when the employer provided free transportation.[32] Often the employer would pay the *padrone* instead of the worker. The crooked *padrone* might then be able to short-change the unsuspecting immigrant worker. Unscrupulous *padroni* found other inventive ways to overcharge workers for

their services. The most abusive *padroni* were those who operated labor camps where they could overcharge for everything
from room rent and pocket-change loans to soup and bread,
and they could price-gouge the worker for commodities in the
camp store. Although not all *padroni* were thieves, enough
were to give a bad reputation to the entire group. The *padrone*
system was a factor in New Orleans and Louisiana, but it was of
lesser significance than in Chicago and New York. In these two
cities, the system acted as a clearinghouse for seasonal labor
throughout the entire country.[33]

Ostensibly because of abuses among *padroni* against those who
contracted with them, the United States enacted the contract
labor law of 1905, which forbade private citizens in the United
States from contracting foreign laborers and paying their passage
to this country; however, it did not forbid states from doing so.
Consequently, the Louisiana State Board of Agriculture and
Immigration, which previously had stationed its own agents in
Europe, continued to recruit immigrants for Louisiana's agricultural industry.[34] But in 1907 a new law extended coverage of the
old law and denied to the states the right of making prior agreements with or paying passage for the immigrants.

Louisiana tested the law almost immediately. The United
States attorney general's decision was swift and compromising.
His interpretation allowed payment of passage but not contract of labor. In short, immigrants could not be lured with a
promise (contract) that work was available; however, the price
of their passage could be paid.

This legal clarification notwithstanding, nothing could
reverse decreasing Sicilian immigration to Louisiana. A series
of social, economic, and political events in Sicily and America
caused the partial curtailment of immigration after 1907. The
immigration statistics are clear on this point. The majority of
Sicilian immigrants to Louisiana arrived before 1907. Thereafter,
though immigration continued, it did so on a declining basis.
The United States contract labor laws of 1905 and 1907 had

some influence on the diminution of immigration, but far more important were three other factors. First, there was an economic depression in the United States about that time that reduced employment opportunities, especially for foreigners. Second, by this time so many immigrants had left the south of Italy and Sicily, the pool of available potential emigrants was greatly reduced. Third, the Italian government became very concerned that the drain on its population in the *Mezzogiorno* was threatening the future of the region and, therefore, instituted more stringent emigration laws of its own.

But before immigration greatly declined, before the depression of 1907, and before the labor shortages in Sicily, significant numbers of Sicilians were already working the sugar plantations of Louisiana, from below New Orleans to above Baton Rouge and as far west as the Teche Country.[35] Sicilians worked at the backbreaking jobs of planting, cultivating, and cutting cane alongside former Negro slaves and their children.

One estimate places the number of immigrant laborers in the sugarcane fields anywhere from 13,000 to 68,000.[36] As rough as that estimate is, it would be difficult if not impossible to pin it down any closer. Furthermore, it is not known what proportion of these laborers represents temporary workers from New Orleans, Chicago, New York, and the railroad work gangs. Based on these figures, anywhere from 12 to 60 percent of the total number of workers during grinding season (when cane cutters are needed) were Sicilians.

Others in the Old Country heard about the work in Louisiana through friends and relatives, many of whom had been there and returned either permanently or temporarily to their homeland. Word of mouth among the people was doubtless a major impetus for migration. Historians assure us that all of Europe at that time was abuzz with the story of "the home of the free" and "the land of opportunity."

Still others came as a result of recruitment efforts by the Planters' Association. Working closely with agents of the State

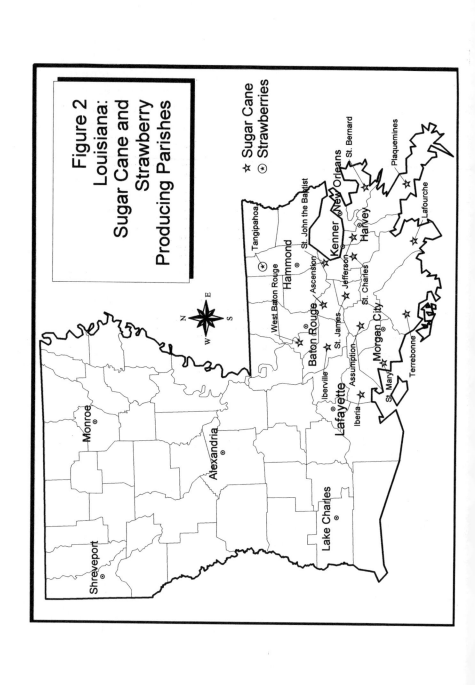

Figure 2
Louisiana:
Sugar Cane and
Strawberry
Producing Parishes

☆ Sugar Cane
⊙ Strawberries

Agricultural Department, they had people stationed in Sicily who negotiated with steamship lines to accommodate the expected influx of immigrants.

Immigrants were sought not just in Italy. They were also actively recruited from Italian colonies in the United States. As we have seen, Vincent Lamantia operated offices in Chicago and New York for the purpose of supplying Italian immigrants for Louisiana's sugarcane plantations.

In order to understand the settlement of Italian immigrants in the sugar parishes, some idea of sugar cultivation and production is necessary. "When seed cane was used to start a new growing cycle, laborers had to pull it out of the ground with great iron hooks attached to poles and load the material into carts." Thus begins Scarpaci's description of the cultivation and grinding of cane in the period 1880-1910.[37] Women called "droppers" would place piles of seed cane at intervals adjacent to the plowed furrows. A work gang would then chop the cane with cane knives and a machine hoe would press the soil near the sprouting "eyes" (nodes) of the cane. The first such crop of cane was called plant cane. After plant cane was harvested, the stubble was left in the field. The next spring, cane would sprout from this stubble (first ratoons). The following year, cane would again sprout from the stubble left after harvesting and was called second ratoons. The third year the stubble would be plowed under and the field planted with field peas to allow the land to recover. The spring work in the fields began with cultivation. The cane growing from stubble had to have soil removed from the roots to allow germination. This was done with plows and hoes. By mid-April, the soil had to be worked back toward the rows. During this period till about mid-July, the cane was constantly cultivated. The weeding was done by hand or hoe. Later the cane was thinned and deeper plowing was used. The soil so removed was thrown on the growing cane to cover weeds. The deeper ditches that resulted were necessary for drainage. From August to September the cane matured. In October or November, the cane was harvested before the first frost. The cane was cut, loaded onto wagons by hand, then hauled to the sugar mill for grinding.[38] A strong laborer could cut about three or four tons per day.[39]

Based on the amount of acreage in sugarcane cultivation during the period 1890 to 1910, the following parishes were investigated by Scarpaci: Ascension, Assumption, Iberia, Iberville, Jefferson, Lafourche, Plaquemines, St. Bernard, St. Charles, St. James, St. John the Baptist, St. Mary, Terrebonne, and West Baton Rouge. These parishes are situated along the major streams of South Louisiana—Bayou Teche, Bayou Lafourche, and the Mississippi, all of which flow south into the Gulf of Mexico. For thousands of years, they have traced their way to the gulf, not always following the same routes. Each year they would carry literally tons of silt and sand, which were deposited in the shallow waters where they emptied into the gulf. When rain in the Mississippi Valley was exceptionally heavy and snow in the upper valley melted, the floodwaters would spill over the banks. Thus, by a process of delta building, new land was extended southward and older land was covered with silt east and west of the streams. As a result of these forces, rich alluvial soils flank east and west banks. The Teche, Lafourche, and Mississippi have built and enriched coastal Louisiana by carrying the topsoil from the entire Mississippi Valley and depositing it along the coast. By flooding periodically, they have deposited soil along their banks that is both richly suited for agriculture and high enough to remain dry under normal conditions. Everywhere in coastal Louisiana, settlement follows a river, stream, or bayou. The larger ones generally run north to south, and the high ground or alluvial ridge that flanks both banks can vary in width from a few to many hundred yards. These major streams and lesser ones made agriculture possible. The sugarcane plantations that developed in the eighteenth and nineteenth centuries were located along these waterways. In all, there were 128 plantations in sugarcane production during the period of mass immigration from Sicily.[40]

It is not at all surprising that some of the earliest Sicilian plantation workers were in Plaquemines Parish on John Dymond's plantation. He helped to organize the Planters' Association and served as its first president. Personally dissatisfied with black cane workers, he urged other planters to recruit Sicilians.

According to Florence Dymond's memoirs, her grandfather, John Dymond, decided to buy Belair Plantation in Plaquemines Parish[41] in the late 1860s after stopping over in Louisiana during a trip from New York to Cuba. He apparently fell in love with Louisiana and no doubt saw the business possibilities there.

The Dymond memoirs add to our understanding of the relationships between the plantations and New Orleans. The plantations along the river had regular boat service to and from the city. It took ten to twelve hours to make the trip from Belair, which is about thirty miles south of New Orleans. The ship moved back and forth across the river, stopping at each plantation picking up and letting out passengers. The same trip took five hours by a buggy and a team of horses.

The economic exchanges between New Orleans and the plantations were many, but some of the more quaint were noted by Miss Dymond. "Fruits, vegetables, and ice were carried on luggers on the river manned by Sicilians or Italians and were peddled from plantation to plantation. . . . They came from New Orleans and went as far as the oyster beds and would return with their boats laden with oysters."[42]

One Sicilian, Captain Tony, owned a lugger and peddled ice, watermelons, and oysters in season. The downstream trip for Captain Tony was easy, but sailing upriver against the current required skill, strength, and patience. One person had to pole the lugger and keep it from banking while another or others positioned on the bank pulled it against the current.

Miss Dymond's memoirs also add to our understanding of the physical layout and work routines on a large plantation. Belair had about seven hundred men, women, and children working at the various tasks that keep a sugar plantation going.

During grinding season the number rose to over a thousand, and work in the sugarhouse was around the clock in four shifts of six hours each. If immigrant women worked the fields it would have been during the grinding season, when as many hands as were available were needed. Oddly, census documents are largely silent about the work of immigrant women. After poring over numerous census records of immigrant households, we could find only a handful reporting that Italian women worked on plantations. It may well have been deemed dishonorable for the immigrant to admit his wife worked as a field hand. Perhaps too the activities of women were not deemed worthy of note. In any event, immigrant women worked in the field as well as attending to all the household chores expected of women of that period.

The layout of the workers' quarters at Belair was simple. There were forty-five double cabins for blacks located in seven rows separated by three streets. Larger houses were scattered from the black quarters up toward the sugarhouse. Italians resided in these larger houses; some of them could accommodate three families. There were ten or twelve such houses on Belair.

There appears to have been a concerted effort on Mr. Dymond's part to segregate blacks from Italians. On other plantations, this was not always done. It appears that it was not a violation of custom for Creole planters to have whites and blacks work as equals. In any event, the censuses indicate a good deal more racial mixing than reported in Florence Dymond's memoirs of Belair.

Although most Sicilians began their lives on the plantation as wage laborers, many became tenants. Some even managed to own land. As noted by a surveyor, Italians occupied the divided small tracts on the old Woodland plantation at Bertrandville in Plaquemines Parish.[43] Farther downstream on the right descending bank (west), a similar situation held. On the Merritts' Plantation, formally known as the Repose Plantation, a surveyor noted that the estate was occupied by

Italians and planted in vegetables.[44] These notes were dated 1892-93. The surveyor did not explain what he meant by the word occupied. It usually implies tenancy or ownership. There is a legal usage that denotes ownership, but this is really stretching the point. The most probable meaning here is simply that Italians were on separate small tracts of land. Nothing more was said because nothing more was known. Fortunately, the 1900 census can corroborate and amplify surveyor notes.[45] Eleven large Italian families were residing in Bertrandville. All owned the land. In all cases the head of the household's occupation was listed as farmer. Seventy-two individuals resided in the eleven households. The largest totaled eleven, including nine children; the smallest consisted of a father and son. The census also recorded the date of immigration. The most recent arrived in 1898, the earliest in 1844. None of the immigrants could read or write, but most could speak English. In every case, the family immigrated as a unit.

An analysis of 1900 census enumerators' handwritten schedules for Jefferson and Plaquemines parishes indicates that of 330 male-headed households of Italian immigrants, about one-third immigrated before their wives or other close kinsmen. This means two-thirds of the immigrant males came with their wives, children, and/or other kinsmen. This is an important consideration to which we shall return when we consider the occupational mobility of the immigrant generation. About half of all married males who immigrated prior to their wives did so four or more years before. Caution must be exercised in making inferences from these data because the information was pieced together by recording date of immigration and number of years married. Some error accrues not only from the method but also the inaccuracy of the data used. However, a general picture does emerge that is defensible. Immigrants, at least in these two parishes if not in Louisiana generally, departed markedly from their co-ethnics elsewhere in America. Around 65 percent of Louisiana's Sicilians immigrated as a family unit.

Nationally, it was more typical for the immigrant to be a single male or a married man unaccompanied by a wife or children.

Settlement in Plaquemines was chiefly in the north. Oyster fishermen from part of the old Austro-Hungarian Empire resided in lower Plaquemines (the Tenth Ward). They were originally from the Dalmatian Coast, a region in western Yugoslavia along the east coast of the Adriatic Sea. They listed their nationality as Austrian, though their ancestry is Slavic. Colloquially they are known as Tockos. Along with Germans, Irishmen, Spaniards, and some Italians, they settled in lower Plaquemines. There is some evidence from the 1900 census that the "Austrians" and Italians intermarried. Particularly noticeable was the intermarriage of "Austrians" and first-generation Sicilian immigrants. Italian and Slavic names are still proportionately overrepresented in the oyster industry in and around New Orleans.

In other sugar parishes, three settlement patterns are discernable. The largest grouping of Italian immigrants was found living on the plantations and smaller farms. There, they worked as itinerant day laborers or resident field hands. These settlement clusters are generally located on the high and rich alluvial ridges along the Mississippi River, Bayou Lafourche, and Bayou Teche.

The second settlement pattern represented fewer immigrants and was confined to the railroad lines, often traversing both forest and farmland. Besides farmer, farm laborer, and day laborer, the most frequent occupation was sawmill worker. This settlement pattern was largely due to the recruitment practices of railroads, which often promoted settlement along their lines to increase the sale of railroad lands and to augment passenger use. Many of the immigrants who settled along the tracks worked in railroad gangs.

The third settlement pattern in the sugar parishes was found in the small cities and villages. Here, the hardy immigrant filled the niche of bartender, fruit peddler, produce dealer, grocer, fishmonger, teamster, shoemaker, barber, and the like. This settlement pattern was by far the least representative of the period 1880 to 1900.

The Italian immigrant population in Louisiana peaked in 1910. By then, a trend was in evidence that would see the plantation worker and farm laborer leave his first home in the state and either return to Italy, relocate to another state, or migrate to cities and towns elsewhere in Louisiana. With this out-migration, the slowdown in the flow of immigrants after 1907, and the normal death rate, the numbers of Italian immigrants in Louisiana fell.

Table 4

Foreign-Born Italians Living in Louisiana's Sugar Parishes, by 10-Year Intervals, 1880-1930

Parishes	1880	1890	1900	1910	1920	1930
Ascension	27	529	1,332	578	273	196
Assumption	9	270	770	460	181	66
Iberia	15	41	355	275	178	149
Iberville	13	273	886	865	645	472
Jefferson	139	380	1,012	1,209	919	804
Lafourche	6	149	830	343	102	71
Plaquemines	143	324	362	135	116	71
St. Bernard	2	15	123	238	190	102
St. Charles	4	323	626	254	137	113
St. James	8	317	1,218	699	162	73
St. John	3	249	450	144	70	88
St. Mary	17	207	1,639	1,246	593	304
Terrebonne	6	17	550	294	142	80
West Baton Rouge	5	199	120	210	106	66
Total	397	3,293	10,273	6,950	3,814	**2,655**

Sources: Figures for 1880-1910, Scarpaci, 100. Figures for 1920-30, compiled by the authors from Bureau of the Census.

The changes in the immigrant population throughout
Louisiana were uneven. The sugar parishes experienced the
largest decreases. A review of table 4 reveals an unmistakable
pattern in which movement of Italians into those parishes
began in about 1880, greatly gained momentum in 1890,
peaked in 1900, began to decline precipitously in 1910, and
continued its dramatic decline in 1920 and 1930. The declines
in 1910 are the result of out-migration, which is also probably
largely the case for the figures in 1920. But by 1930 the
declines are due to some unknown mixture of relocation and
death. After all, many of the Italian immigrants, especially
those who did not come to the United States in their youth,
were by that time in their sixties. They were beginning to die
off, though it took another thirty years before the immigrant
generation of that era completely vanished from Louisiana.

The parishes adjacent to cities seem to have experienced
smaller decreases. For example, West Baton Rouge Parish,
across the river from the city of Baton Rouge, held on to its
Italian population somewhat better than did the other sugar
parishes, as did Jefferson and St. Bernard parishes, which are
contiguous to New Orleans.

St. James best illustrates the decline of Italian plantation
workers in the sugar parishes. In 1900, there were 1,218 immigrants.[46] A decade later that number decreased to 699, then to
162 in 1920, then to 73 in 1930. The parish generally experienced a number of population increases and decreases as a
result of the ups and downs of agricultural prices. In ward 1,
which contains the town of Convent, Louisiana, diversified
occupations were found among Italians. Shoemakers, other
craftsmen, grocers, merchants, and numerous sawmill laborers
had settled to cut the oak and gum hardwoods, and the cypress
were harvested during the 1890s. In wards 2, 3, 4, 5, and 6,
farm laborers predominated among Italians. In ward 7, plantation workers were in the majority among Italians, with jobs
like plowmen, hoemen, and stablemen. By 1900, the shift from

plantation worker to tenant farmer was already well under way. Remarkably, many immigrants escaped the poverty of farm tenancy. Consider the case of the Panzeca family.

George Panzeca emigrated from Caccamo, Sicily in 1894. He worked as a farm hand in St. James Parish for two years, then returned to Italy. He later came back to the parish with his wife and three children and worked on a sugar plantation for less than a dollar a day. Eventually, four more children were born—the youngest, John George Panzeca, in 1906. At the age of twelve, John left to live with an older sister so that he could attend St. Philip School in the New Orleans French Quarter. John was much older than his classmates and his formal education ended at the age of eighteen after the eighth grade. He continued to pursue his education informally. He read the dictionary almost daily and later the *Wall Street Journal.*

John was emancipated as a teenager (the legal change of status from minor to adult) so that he could buy and sell real estate. His father entrusted John with the family's life savings ($3,000) and instructed him to buy a grocery store in the French Quarter. After the death of both parents in the 1930s, John purchased the store from his siblings and converted it into an upscale nightclub. La Luna, located on Bourbon Street, opened immediately after Prohibition ended and featured Latin music. La Luna's policy was coat and tie for gentlemen and escorts for ladies.

John Panzeca had both a love for music and acumen in business. He served the New Orleans Opera Association for more than fifty years. He was a real-estate investor and developer. He also started his own mortgage business. He served on the board of directors of a local savings and loan company that later became State-Investors Bank. Later in life he demonstrated his knowledge of the stock market and was very successful until his death at age ninety-three.

His son Salvatore Panzeca recalls, "When my father was about to borrow a large sum of money, he told the bank director that when he was 18 years old he applied for a teller's job at the Whitney Bank, but he was refused because he did not possess a high school diploma. He proceeded to thank the director, who was to lend him almost a million dollars and joked that had he gotten the job then, he would still be a teller; and he wouldn't be able to make the loan he just made."[47] With more modest levels of success, numerous former plantation workers were able to save and leave for work in towns and cities.

In St. Mary, settlement was confined to the alluvial ridges along the Teche. Farm laborers predominated in the entire northern part of the parish. Franklin, Louisiana revealed the typical town pattern of more diversified occupations. The same pattern was in evidence in Paterson, Berwick, and Morgan City. However, there were only ten Italian households in Morgan City in 1900.[48] Fourth Street was the original nucleus of the Italian community there. Franklin had a mere fifteen Italian households in 1900.

Boarding was particularly conspicuous in St. Mary Parish. Settlement was typically a male phenomenon. Boarders usually, but not exclusively, resided within the homes of Italian families. Were it not for the relatively rapid population increase of towns like Morgan City, more of St. Mary's Italian population would have resettled elsewhere. But the Italian colony in Morgan City not only survived but also swelled with the growth of the city. The Italian influence in that city can still be seen today.

The parishes that held their original Italian populations best were the suburban parishes. Jefferson is a good example. Around 1,012 immigrants were recorded in the 1900 census and increased to 1,209 in 1910.[49] On the West Bank of Jefferson Parish in what is Gretna they settled on First, Second, and Fourth streets. Immigrants settled also on Lavosier, Newton, and Copernicus streets. As one moves farther west, here and there immigrants could be found. The largest concentration was located in Amesville, subsequently renamed Marrero. Eugene Marrero served as the census enumerator in this area. Three hundred and thirty-two immigrants and their children, many of whom were born in Louisiana, resided in Amesville. This contrasted markedly with other West Bank communities, which had few Italian families—for example, one family in Westwego, four in Fairfield, and eight in Waggaman. They were primarily farm laborers and day laborers, but a sprinkling of merchants and grocers could also be found. In coastal Jefferson (Sixth Ward), three families of fishermen resided. In two of these families, the wives were Filipinos. In the other, the husband was a Filipino. This pattern is common wherever ethnic populations are sparse and comparatively isolated, as we have noted in lower Plaquemines Parish, where Italians and Yugoslavs intermarried.

On the East Bank of Jefferson Parish, where Italian settlement largely occurred in the 1880s and 1890s, truck farmers predominated. In the small town of Kenner, farmers frequently owned their farms and homes. Some 415 immigrants and their children resided in Kenner in 1900, making it the most Italian community in Louisiana at that time. Kenner would not enjoy that distinction very long, for by 1910 the town of Independence in Tangipahoa Parish would surpass it in the concentration of Italians within its city limits.

SETTLEMENT IN TANGIPAHOA PARISH

The best documented settlement of a parish in Louisiana by Italian immigrants is Tangipahoa.[50] Its terrain is totally different from the other parishes where most Italians settled. Situated north of Lake Pontchartrain, its sandy soils are forested primarily by pine. Except for the swamp and marsh below Ponchatoula, it is generally higher and drier than coastal Louisiana. It experienced a rapid settlement of Italians from 1900 to 1910. The 1900 census recorded only 97 immigrants, but in 1910 the immigrant population swelled to 1,621.[51] By 1920, 1,805 Italian immigrants lived in the parish; the number settled back to 1,550 in 1930. Italian-Americans remain a highly visible ethnic population in Tangipahoa Parish to this day. Settlement generally followed the route of the Illinois Central Railroad, which connects New Orleans to Chicago and runs north and south through the entire length of the parish. Immigrants could be found in 1910 from Ponchatoula, the southernmost community, to Kentwood, in the northern end of the parish. However, the greatest concentrations of Italians were at Independence and Tickfaw, where they comprised a majority of the population.[52] Amite, Natalbany, and Hammond also experienced significant settlement.

John V. Baiamonte noted several reasons for the settlement of Italians in Tangipahoa.[53] As early as 1894, a group of prominent Tangipahoans interested in encouraging immigration met with state immigration officials and sugar planters. The idea was primarily to attract Italian migrants to pick strawberries beginning in March, when the cane season had already ended. From March to May, the harvest months, the idle cane cutters were recruited by American and Italian strawberry farmers, with the assistance of the Louisiana Bureau of Immigration.

Other immigrants were recruited from the New Orleans Italian colony. At the turn of the century, every Monday morning some five hundred Italian berry pickers made their way from New Orleans to the strawberry fields of Independence. The Illinois Central Railroad supplied extra coaches on their trains to accommodate the additional passengers. On Friday, they would make the return trip to New Orleans.

The Sicilians already in Tangipahoa Parish did the most to encourage further immigration.[54] They wrote to friends and relatives back in Italy, and they sent word to other Italians they knew elsewhere in Louisiana, the Midwest, and the cities of the Northeast about the opportunities to pick berries and own their own farms. Considering the wages for other kinds of work, berry picking was somewhat more profitable. A worker could get anywhere from $1.50 to $1.75 a day.[55] Moreover, the nature of the work was such that a man's wife and children (about eight or nine years of age and older) could also pick berries.

In the Old Country the Italian peasants lived in a village surrounded by woods, pastures, and farmlands. They would leave their homes early in the morning, work the fields and tend the animals, and return in the evening. They had neighbors separated by nothing more than a wall or a lane just wide enough for a cart. They were always within walking distance of the church, the well, and the piazza, and they were always within earshot of their *paesani*. When they came to rural North America, they were confronted with a completely different agricultural settlement pattern. In this country, the isolated farmstead typifies the layout of rural farms. Because the farmhouse is situated on the farmstead, which in North America is rather large, the farmer is indeed isolated. His nearest neighbor may be miles away.

The immigrants showed little fondness for the isolated farmstead, preferring instead the Old World settlement pattern of a village surrounded by farmland. The physical layout of the Italian strawberry farms is very suggestive of this arrangement. "Generally the farm houses were built in the middle of the strawberry fields. Not far from the houses were the barns, sheds, and packing houses which also served as lodging for the berry pickers."[56] The farmhouses were on the farms, but since a strawberry farm's size rarely exceeded five acres, farmers were never very far from their neighbors on the adjacent farms. Frequently they could shout to one another from porch to porch across their fields. The original farmhouses were poorly constructed and unusually small, having no more than two or three rooms with precious few homemade furnishings. Some farmers had iron beds, but for many, straw on the floor served as beds. Most cooking, particularly bread making, was done out of doors in "Italian ovens," beehive-shaped structures of brick, clay, and stone.

The immigrant settling in Louisiana was often praised for his industry and frugality. While the accolades were deserved, it was not the kind of honor the immigrant sought. The respect he hungered for was not satisfied by being a good beast of burden.

Furthermore, everywhere he settled, and Louisiana was no exception, he found whatever praise he received tarnished by criminal labels: *briganti,* Black Hand, *Mafiosi.*

While settlement in Louisiana frustrated the immigrants' hopes to gain their brand of *rispetto,* the paths of settlement taken did open doors to the kind of respect that eventually comes with economic success. Italians came to Louisiana in small and unthreatening numbers. They encountered a mild climate, a responsive soil, an open economic niche, and a congenial culture. They settled as family units and because they did, they made it possible for their children, and especially their grandchildren, to realize their economic dreams. In the process, over the generations, the Old World idea of honor was Americanized, eventually becoming nearly synonymous with material success.

CHAPTER FOUR

Fortune (*Fortuna*)

LUCKY MATTEO

Old Matteo paused for a moment and wiped his brow. Only a few of his neighbors bothered to plant a garden. Matteo shook his head in quiet disapproval. He simply could not understand why they couldn't see the stupidity in wasting land.

The land on which he currently hoed was only part of his original truck farm. He had given some of his property to his children and some he sold to strangers. Now in his old age, he found the backyard sufficient to grow his vegetables.

Matteo resumed hoeing. He counted himself lucky. For a brief moment he took inventory of his blessings. He had his health. His wife and children were in good health. He owned his home. It was early March; soon, he would celebrate St. Joseph Day and his eightieth birthday. There would be family, music, and eating. To top it all off, he would be among the first to coax ripe tomatoes from late winter vines.

His thoughts were dispelled by the arrival of his favorite nephew, Angelo. As Angelo maneuvered his truck in position to load the trash from his uncle's yard, Matteo put down his hoe to assist.

"Angelo—oh, you're here already! You wanna mange?*"*

"No. I don't want to eat now. I have come for the trash."

In a few minutes, Angelo and Matteo had moved the larger branches into the bed of Angelo's truck and had placed the twigs into the compost pile.

"*Now, you wanna* mange?"

"*No, thank you.*"

Angelo was not hungry but thirsty for advice. "*My father is a hard man to work for. He pays me so little to help him build houses; I can do the same thing for a friend who will pay me more. I don't know what to do.*" *Matteo stood motionless, staring at the tidy rows of tomato plants.*

"*My son, so you wish for* Fortuna *like your uncle Matteo. Tell me; will this friend give you his business one day?*"

"*No, of course not!*"

Matteo fixed his gaze on Angelo and said, "*I'll tell you this. Work for no man but yourself. You have no brothers, only sisters. These sisters of yours are all well provided for, but they don't know how to build houses. Work for your father or start your own business. But don't you see? You already have a business; you are just not finished paying for it!*

"*Maybe you want to be like the Americans and take it easy. Watch others work.*"

This reproach prompted a response from Angelo. "*No! Uncle Matteo, I work. I work hard.*"

"Buono! *Let me tell you the truth. When I was a young man in Cefalu, I worked the baron's lands. The* contadini *must always work. Whether I stay or go to America, what will I do? Three things: work, work, and more work. So, I say to myself, 'Matteo, better to work for yourself.' I come to America. I worked a sugar plantation in St. James. Then, I leased some land here. You are standing on it. Later, I bought the land. I had nineteen pieces of property before I gave it all away to my children. You think maybe old Matteo is lucky? The first year I try to get the tomatoes early. The cold she kill everything. Next year, the same thing. Then, I planted late. I got plenty tomatoes but had to sell cheap. I made no money. I say to myself, 'Maybe I go back to Cefalu and work the baron's land. Maybe I will always be a* contadino *and work to make someone else rich. No! Matteo will never work for another man!' I stayed. The next season, I planted early and the cold she kill the tomatoes. The next year, the same thing. Three times the cold she kill the tomatoes. Ah! But the next time. I watch the plants like the mamma watch the* bambini. *I make good money. You wanna do good like Uncle Matteo? You gotta kick* Fortuna *in the* coglioni!"

As he wiped the tears of laughter away, Angelo knew what he must do.

Fortune, or as the Italians would say, *Fortuna,* is a boisterous, recurrent theme in the imaginations and conversations of Italians.[1] Its roots run deep in the history and culture of the Italian peninsula. Fifteen hundred years ago Boethius began his search for consolation in the face of abiding misery by observing that faithless Fortune had favored him with her worthless gifts. He was referring in this instance to the despair that accompanies old age. Fortune had turned something valued, a long life, into something presumably worthless, an old man. Boethius's larger quest, of course, was "the unending search for human happiness and the possibility of achieving it in the midst of the suffering and disappointment which play so large a part in everyone's experience."[2] Why do we not simply surrender to misery? Why not despair? What is it about the human condition that, with comparatively few exceptions, will not permit people to be utterly conquered by fate? Boethius's answer is the "Consolation of Philosophy," which properly conceived "allows us to stand above good and bad fortune, serene in the strength derived from self-mastery."[3] For Boethius, life is an endless struggle between the forces of Fortune (*Fortuna*) and moral philosophy. For a thousand years, from its publication in 524 until the end of the Renaissance, *The Consolation of Philosophy* shaped medieval thought. Its doctrine, inspired by Plato, Aristotle, and Augustine and consistent with patristic theology, was embraced by prince, peasant, and pope alike. Whether they knew it or not, everyone in Italy and everywhere else in the Christian West fell under the sway of Boethius and Fortune.

A millennium later, *Fortuna* was very much alive and prominently featured in the writing of Niccolo Machiavelli, the most influential Italian writer of the sixteenth century. In *The Prince,* originally published in 1532, Machiavelli was not specifically concerned with *Fortuna* in the lives of peasants. Instead, his observations concerning *Fortuna* apply to the wellborn who serve the prince and to the prince himself. Nevertheless, it is plain to see that *Fortuna* is no respecter of social rank. Observing that the Italy of his time embraced the view that things of this world are controlled by Fortune and by God and therefore could not be remedied by the actions of people, Machiavelli pondered the place of free will in human affairs. Somewhat contrary to the opinion of his day, to make room for free will, Machiavelli posited that Fortune has an ironclad grip on only one-half of our actions, therefore leaving us control of the other half. Without foresight and preparation, we will be overrun by Fortune as if flooded by a river. Where foresight and preparation have constructed levees, Fortune may be influenced to remain within her channel. Foresight and preparation indicate good judgment if not downright shrewdness. Machiavelli's term for these qualities is ingenuity. His advice to the prince who desires to attain and retain power is this: if the prince must choose between ingenuity and Fortune, he is best served by relying less on Fortune and more on ingenuity.[4] Here we see *Fortuna* as powerful but not all powerful. As difficult as it is, it is possible, under the right conditions, to tempt fate and get away with it. Ingenuity can prevail over Fortune. Or, what amounts to the same thing, Fortune may be enticed by ingenuity to be on our side rather than against us.

It appears the Italians of the *Mezzogiorno*, like Matteo, held a concept of fate in line with Machiavelli's views. They believed, to varying degrees, that it was possible to influence Fortune. The ancient Latin expression *carpe diem*, seize the day, comes close to the attitude of the Italian immigrant: be willing to take a risk at the right time, but be shrewd about it!

For the *contadini*, *Fortuna* was more than mere luck but not exactly a blessing. For good or for ill, *Fortuna* was one's unpredictable appointment with the gods. While the origin of such a belief was chiefly pagan, it has been modified under centuries of Christianity. Weigh, for instance, the interesting parallel between *Fortuna* and grace. Grace, like Fortune, is granted gratuitously. Neither is earned nor deserved for that matter. Grace comes from God; Fortune comes from only God knows where! The biggest difference between them has to do with their outcomes. The result of grace is always virtue or something highly prized. The greatest beneficial effect of grace for the Christian is, of course, salvation; but there are other consequences, like health, success, happiness, and honor.[5] *Fortuna,* on the other hand, is as likely to bring trouble as contentment. For that reason, the wise person is fearful of bad Fortune and wary of good Fortune. Sicilians, for example, look over their shoulders when things are going "too well," dreading that something bad is sneaking up on them!

The *contadini* often combine the pagan concept of luck (fortune) with the Christian idea of a blessing (grace). A Sicilian tradition, the St. Joseph Day celebration, includes blessing dried fava beans, then distributing them to the faithful for good luck. Could this be a pagan superstition baptized and made holy? Keep the blessed fava bean on your person and in your house, car, or purse so as to ward off evil and harm. Is this not a sacred version of a secular superstition, more or less equivalent to a lucky charm, like a rabbit's foot?

The search for *Fortuna* is reflected in a number of ways, but its chief element is excitement and pleasure in acquiring what has been neither worked for nor earned. It is intrinsic in games of chance where the players stake money or anything of value. As is obvious, such an activity is called gambling and presents the players with the enticing possibility of unearned largesse. It is the attendant excitement that keeps the players' interest. For Italians, the prize involved need not be great or majestic. Even when the game is played for a pittance, the excitement level is high. Anyone who has ever watched Italians play *boccia-ball* or cards for penny stakes knows how high the emotions can run and how quickly tempers can flare. Why so much emotion over so little? The American misses the point. When the gods smile on you, the joy is also in having been singled out. A certain honor or renown can be claimed by those who receive even a small gratuity. The Christianized version of this sort of good fortune is the prayed-for blessing from God or the saints.

Fortuna and the excitement that comes from gambling echo the dominant Italian value of dramatizing and embellishing life. But games of chance are widespread;[6] belief in fate is commonplace.[7] What makes the Italian version different is its intensity and pervasiveness. In Sicily, everyone gambles and, need we say, everyone prays for a blessing. A grown man cursing his fate or literally jumping and screaming for joy over losing or winning a trifle speaks loudly if not eloquently of *Fortuna*.

Over many generations in Italy, the constant search for *Fortuna* by the *contadini* contributed to the pervasive practice of gambling, which in turn helped the peasants acquire some skills useful in the marketplace. In the United States, until its relatively recent legalization, gambling was defined as a vice. It was associated with prostitution, political corruption, and family problems. Before the advent of state lotteries, off-track betting, slot machines, and casinos, gambling was considered a deviant activity. Of course, it still has its opponents. But gambling, like other games of chance, may be viewed as an essential element in socialization.[8] Undeniably, gambling can be problematic, but it can also have unintended, unrecognized advantages.[9] The favorable commentary on gambling calls attention to its value as fun, excitement, financial reward for the winners, and a source of taxation for communities,[10] but it ignores its worth in the world of business. After all, both gambling and establishing a business involve speculation and risk. Both require a spirit of adventure in the face of uncertainty, at least as far as decision making is concerned.

Widespread gambling cultivated a kind of pleasure in risk taking even among Italian truck farmers in the New Orleans area. They frequently planted crops in early winter, tempting fate with the hope that mild weather would bring a large return. Because the earliest crops brought to market commanded the highest prices, it was not uncommon for the immigrant farmers to plant and replant after repeated frosts killed the seedlings. They wanted to be among the first to sell their produce in the market.

Gambling also helps develop mathematical skills. Desiring to win at games of chance, French noblemen in the seventeenth century persuaded mathematicians to apply their knowledge to gaming. The result was the development of the mathematics of probability, which has become the cornerstone of modern science. Although a less lofty consequence of gambling, the sharpening of arithmetic skills is far more useful to the average person.

A noticeable attribute, especially of Italian immigrant males, was the considerable difficulty involved in cheating them. They could, of course, be cheated in love and other kinds of social relationships, as can anyone; but when it came to money and the marketplace, that was another matter. In the marketplace, they demonstrated an extraordinary sense of value and good judgment. The argument here is that, in combination with the other attributes discussed, gambling skills served these Italian merchants well. Even though many were illiterate, gambling gave them competency with numbers. Owing to their facility with figures, the immigrants could add and subtract, if not multiply and divide. Consequently, they could make change, figure stock, and run a small business. It must be emphasized that the age-old tradition of gambling in southern Italy and Sicily is universal. There everyone gambles—the men with each other, the women among themselves, and the children in their own games of chance. We have personally known many Italian immigrants who could neither read nor write but could easily handle arithmetic problems. Jerome Salomone, Sr., was one of them.

Born in 1904 in a wagon on a Tensas Parish cotton plantation in North Louisiana, Jerome was the eldest son of Italian immigrants who eventually had six other children. When the family left St. Joseph Plantation, where they were itinerant farm laborers, they relocated to a farm south of New Orleans, where the old man became a sharecropper for the remainder of his long life. Jerome, who was illiterate, went to work on the Mississippi River as a water boy at the age of thirteen. As a man, he made his living building and repairing steam boilers, mainly on tugboats. He worked for the Federal Barge Lines from before the Great Depression until the mid-1950s, when the U.S. government sold the company during the Eisenhower presidency. The Federal Barge Lines then became Saucer Marine Incorporated. Jerome worked for Saucer until his retirement. Because he could not read or write except to sign his name, Jerome was unable to read a blueprint. Nevertheless, he was so good with numbers he could figure the materials needed to build a Mississippi River barge. It was also near impossible to beat him at cards! Jerome's ability to calculate was impressive, but it was not unusual. For his time, Jerome was rather typical of the Italian immigrants and many of their children.

The significance of *Fortuna* and gambling is that they affected the immigrants' adaptation to life in America. Mindful of the bad pun, we are inclined to say they were fortuitous survivals of the Atlantic crossing. The Italian immigrants' attitudes toward *Fortuna* and their penchant for gambling played some significant yet immeasurable part in their economic success in America. Indeed, at the present time, Italian Catholics enjoy higher average incomes than all native Protestant groups.[11] Only Jewish Americans and Irish Catholics have higher average incomes. While on the national level contemporary economic achievement of Italian-Americans is impressive, the advancement of Italian-Americans in Louisiana is even more enviable. They seem to have achieved economic success much sooner than their ethnic counterparts around the country. Why that was so can best be explained if we take up a related topic, their intense desire for economic independence.

The dream of the Italians was to come to America, but that dream included more than passage across the Atlantic Ocean.

With their feet finally on American soil in Louisiana, they aspired to be their own bosses. This was a theme common to many immigrants, not just to those who came to Louisiana, but the potential for realizing that dream was greater in Louisiana than elsewhere. For one thing, the Italian immigrants in the big cities of the Northeast and Midwest found employment in factories or on construction gangs with large companies. They were more likely to become employees in emerging industrial and corporate bureaucracies, where they sought economic security. Rather quickly, within a generation or two, many of them became a boss (supervisor) without becoming their own boss.

The Louisiana experience was different. There was no industry to speak of—certainly no factory system comparable to the Northeast or Midwest where advancement through a series of graded steps was the norm. There were agricultural jobs on the plantations, but these were dead-end jobs. There was very little or no room for advancement for field hands on somebody else's farm. Moreover, unlike the Northeast and Midwest where the agricultural land was already well established in family farms, in Louisiana there was much swamp land and cut-over timber land thought to be unacceptable for agricultural production that was available for purchase. In effect, in Louisiana, if the immigrant was ever to become a boss, he had to become his own boss. There were only two ways this could be done: own a business or own a farm. That is precisely what happened over and over again. Merchant and farmer became the two most conspicuous occupations pursued by Louisiana's Italian immigrants.

Joseph ("Joe") DeMarco of Hammond, Louisiana combined both of these occupations—farmer and merchant—to become one of the most prosperous immigrants in the Florida Parishes.[12] Joe DeMarco was born in Villafrati, Sicily on September 15, 1884. He came to the United States when he was twenty years old, arriving at Ellis Island in 1905. From there, Joseph made his way to Louisiana. He married an immigrant

Italian woman named Anna Deliberto in 1912. Together they had eight children: five sons and three daughters. Before coming to Hammond, where he initially was a strawberry picker, he worked as a laborer in a sawmill in Des Allemands, a bayou village between New Orleans and Raceland. Joseph DeMarco died in 1958. Without the benefit of education and consequently unable to read and write, this resourceful man had at the time of his death accumulated what amounted to a fortune. At different times in his life, Mr. DeMarco was a strawberry farmer, dairy farmer, leader of a strawberry farmers' cooperative association, grocer, trader, timberman, broker, and real-estate developer. He left an estate of about a thousand acres of land, which is located almost entirely within the current boundary of Hammond. Possessed of both vision and nerve, DeMarco was an entrepreneur in every sense of the word. His son and namesake, Joseph DeMarco, says of his father:

> He always was thinking ahead about business. My father could not read and write, but you couldn't beat him at figures. He worked hard every day of his life, and he was a deal maker. Most of the time he came out on top. He was a gambler, not with cards and dice, but with nature and people. He knew when to take a chance on the weather and when to lend money to people. My father's philosophy of business was to buy all the land he could, always with trees. Then he put cattle on the land because he said, "Trees grow and cows multiply while I sleep."[13]

Once, in the 1950s, when asked by a friend how much he was worth, Mr. DeMarco replied in thick, broken English, "I don't know how much money I got, but I got over a million pine trees. If they are worth a dollar apiece, I got more than a million dollars!" Joseph DeMarco's business successes cut across ethnic and racial lines. In the 1920s and 1930s he owned a grocery store. His ledger for the two-year period 1929-30 shows that he had 312 customers to whom he extended credit. Of that number, 207 were Italians and 105 were non-Italians. In our interview, the son identified from the ledger the names of families he knew were black. Mr. DeMarco was extending credit and making loans to blacks at a time when it would have been highly unlikely that they could have gone to a Hammond bank to obtain loans. An especially interesting account in the ledger is that of Allen Brasfield, a black man, which indicates one fifteen-dollar and one thirty-seven-dollar credit by labor.[14] Instead of paying off his debts in cash, Mr. Brasfield worked them off.

OCCUPATIONAL CHARACTERISTICS

In order to understand how immigrants made their living, we examined the census of 1900.[15] The previously unpublished, originally handwritten documents became available on microfilm in 1978. This census contains names and addresses as well as social and economic data on each individual in every household located by enumerators. From these we compiled data on five immigrant settlements. Based on a broader overview of all Italians in Louisiana, it was evident that the great majority of immigrants in 1900 were either in cities, in farming villages, or on plantations. Accordingly, we examined Italian households in urban New Orleans, two farming villages in Jefferson Parish (Harvey and Kenner), and two settlements of sugar plantation workers (in St. James Parish along the Mississippi and in St. Mary Parish along the Teche).[16] From the rather large Italian population in New Orleans, a 10 percent sample of Italian-headed households in the most populated wards was taken.[17] Elsewhere, a complete enumeration of the households in the ward in which the settlement was located was used.

The study areas were selected primarily on known and expected community variation, so the important occupational differences among the five settlement areas shown in table 5 are not unexpected. The distribution of occupations in New Orleans is remarkable in two respects: first, in the extraordinarily *high* proportion of heads of households who had white-collar jobs, the majority being merchants, and second, in the extraordinarily *low* proportion who were laborers.[18] Fifty-two percent of the New Orleans sample held white-collar jobs, which included merchants and professionals. Many of the merchants were street peddlers who went around the neighborhoods in horse-drawn wagons selling produce, while others were grocers and fishermen. Most were functionally illiterate, petty merchants. Yet all of them were self-employed, independent entrepreneurs struggling to entice *Fortuna* to bless them with *pane e rispetto*.

Overall, 46 percent of the New Orleans sample fell into the category of laborer, evenly divided between skilled/semiskilled and unskilled workers. But that is an exaggeration, because many of the skilled workers were self-employed craftsmen like bakers, barbers, butchers, and shoemakers who owned their shops. When the self-employed laborers (who are properly considered employers) are distinguished from those who worked for someone else (employees), then the resultant figure reveals that only one in three (about 33 percent) Italians in the New Orleans sample was in the laboring class in 1900. By contrast, half (50.4 percent) of New York's Italians in 1916 were laborers.[19] Nearly half (47 percent) of Rhode Island's foreign-born Italians were either laborers or factory operatives and only 21 percent were self-employed.[20] The point is that the New Orleans enclave of immigrants was conspicuously successful in entering the middle classes. Elsewhere in American cities, the Italian immigrants were concentrated in the working class.

Table 5

Occupations of Italian Immigrants in Five Louisiana Settlements in 1900

Occupation (in percent)	New Orleans (N=108)*	Harvey (N=58)	Kenner (N=85)	St. James (N=81)	St. Mary (N=92)
Farmer	0	37.9	37.6	0	4.3
White collar	52.4	0	1.2	4.9	19.6

Skilled and semiskilled	22.3	0	3.5	4.9	12.0
Unskilled laborers	23.3	56.9	24.7	12.3	0
Farm laborers	1.9	5.2	32.9	77.8	64.1

*N=Number of cases

The occupational characteristics of Louisiana's rural Italians were, of course, different from those found in New Orleans. At the turn of the twentieth century, the Harvey area (also called Amesville or Marrero) was the site of extensive levee and canal construction. This explains why over half (56.9 percent) of the immigrants there were laborers. However, over a third (37.9 percent) were farmers. Just across the river, the small farming village of Kenner was more homogeneous. Over 70 percent of the immigrants there were either farmers or farm laborers. Laborers constituted about a quarter of the work force. In St. James Parish, upriver from New Orleans, not surprisingly the majority of immigrants were farm laborers (plantation workers). A small but significant population of white-collar workers resided in St. James Parish in 1900. In St. Mary Parish, as expected, the great majority of Italians were plantation workers (64.1 percent). However, substantial numbers of white-collar workers (19.6 percent) were residing in St. Mary. It was around this small nucleus of entrepreneurs that an autonomous Italian community eventually developed in the Morgan City area. By contrast, immigrants in Harvey, Kenner, and St. James Parish were part of the New Orleans community. The reasons for this are complex, but geography may well have had the most important role in determining community development.

In coastal Louisiana, east-west transportation has always been more costly and time consuming than north-south travel. Extensive and often-impassable swamps separate coastal river systems.[21] In any event, the general path of development was similar to what occurred in New Orleans and elsewhere in the state. However, the growth of the Italian community in St. Mary Parish was somewhat distinct from that pattern.

THE GROWTH OF IMMIGRANT ENTREPRENEURS

The occupational distribution of foreign-born Italian heads of household in New Orleans in 1900 is depicted in table 6. As can be seen, self-employment was commonplace. Merchants constituted over one-fourth of the total (28.8 percent). Laborers comprised a mere 22 percent, far less than their counterparts in other American cities. Craftsmen (17.8 percent) and the semiskilled workers (11 percent) collectively accounted for another 28.8 percent. Inspection of the city directories for the period strongly indicates craftsmen were typically shopkeepers. The conclusion we draw is that entrepreneurship was more common than a quick glance at the data might suggest. Table 6 also reveals that businesses in the food industry were prevalent. While every phase of the food industry in the state has been impacted by Italian merchants, their concentration in the retail grocery business is most impressive. Estimating from the city directories, an estimated 7 percent of all retail grocers in the city in 1880 were Italians. In 1900, Italian grocers constituted 19 percent of the total, and an astounding 49 percent in 1920. The percentage remained relatively stable until the 1940s, when corporate grocery chains were introduced into the New Orleans market. Since then there has been a decline in the figures, although the presence of Italians in the retail food business remained impressive at 36 percent of all grocers in the city in 1970. They continue to be the single largest ethnic group in the food industry.

In 1940 in Upper Algiers, a West Bank[22] neighborhood, there were corner grocery stores with names like Catanese, Sunseri, Sinatra, Columbo, Benninatti, Mele, Centino, Domino, Rouse, Manali, Callo, Labella, Talluto, Tripolina, Chifici, Luigi, Calderone, Tripiano, and Arnone. There were more. It seemed as though every other block contained a mom-and-pop food-related establishment whose owner's name ended in a vowel. Nearly every neighborhood in New Orleans could make the same claim in the twentieth century between the two world wars.

Table 6

Occupational Distribution of Foreign-Born Italian Heads of Household in New Orleans, 1900

Occupation	Number	Percent in Category
Professional (4)		3.4
Artist	2	
Engineer	1	
Priest	1	
Various Merchants (34)		28.8
Produce dealer/peddler	11	
Grocer	7	
Merchant	3	
Oyster Dealer	5	
Miscellaneous peddler	3	
Truck farmer	1	
Other	4	
Clerical (5)		4.2
Clerk	4	
Inspector	1	
Craftsmen (21)		17.8
Baker	2	
Barber	2	

Blacksmith	1	
Boat builder	1	
Bricklayer	1	
Butcher	2	
Carpenter	4	
Florist	1	
Lugger captain	1	
Shoemaker	6	
Semiskilled (13)		11.0
Bartender	1	
Cook	2	
Drayman	1	
Fisherman	1	
Game dealer	1	
Grinder	1	
Leather dyer	1	
Plasterer	1	
Sailor	2	
Ship watchman	1	
Wagon driver	1	
Laborers (26)		22.0
Farm	2	
Nonfarm	24	
Occupation Unknown	11	9.3
Female Headed	4	3.4
Total Households	118	99.9

The rapidity with which the New Orleans immigrants entered the business community cannot be explained on the basis of earlier and more affluent arrivals. Whether they arrived before 1870 or after 1890 made no difference in the extent to which they entered the business community. In each cohort, approximately half of the immigrants surveyed were in business of some kind but chiefly in the food industry. The New Orleans tradition of eating out, even among the working classes, presented an opportunity for the immigrants to enter the restaurant business. Immigrants have played a conspicuous role as owners and operators of restaurants, and many of these establishments have reputations that have grown beyond their neighborhood boundaries.

Casamento's is one of those restaurants. Joe Casamento came to New Orleans from Ustica, Sicily. In a few short years, learning the restaurant business, he opened his own at 4330 Magazine Street. Casamento's Oyster Bar and Restaurant is known by locals and outsiders alike as a place worth the wait to be seated. When Stella Pitts of the *Times-Picayune* interviewed Joe[23] he was celebrating his ninetieth birthday working in the restaurant. His attitude about being your own boss reflects the attitude of many immigrants. "My pleasure is work—working for myself, not for others. If you want to get anywhere in this world, you must be your own boss."

Preference for entrepreneurship seems to have been statewide. In Shreveport, Monroe, Alexandria, and Baton Rouge, a similar occupational distribution can be discerned. Shop owners, merchants, and peddlers, particularly in the food industry, were most conspicuous. Even in the more rural parishes, this tendency was evident. A survey of late-nineteenth-century European immigrants in Northeast Louisiana reported biographical sketches of eleven Italian-born immigrants from Tensas, East Carroll, and Ouachita parishes.[24] Of the eleven, five owned mercantile-grocery stores. There were also two saloon keepers, one wholesale fruit dealer, one shoemaker, one barber, and one mechanic. Of those listed in Ouachita, three were brothers who operated a family-owned barroom. They left an estate of over one hundred thousand dollars. In Tensas, two brothers operated a mercantile-grocery store. Their estate included Hollywood Plantation and a plantation near Lake St. Joseph, as well as other real estate in Tensas Parish. Places of origin mentioned for the eleven Italian immigrants were Sorrento, Trabia, Cefalu, and Chiavari.

In small and large towns alike, the immigrant tended to abbreviate his tenure as farmer and opt for the business opportunity when conditions permitted. In central and north Louisiana, he became a shoemaker or builder but more often a retail grocer, wholesaler of produce and seafood, or restaurateur. In more recent times, as family businesses have been replaced by corporate chain stores, he has become a conspicuous landlord, particularly in areas that once were white or racially mixed.

Quite often, Italian-owned businesses were located in or near black neighborhoods. Particularly in cities, Italians played the role of merchant to black customers. They were well suited for this kind of symbiotic relationship with black Americans. The special racial relations between them found expression in three different settings. They worked side by side as field hands on plantations, they played music in the same bands in the development of jazz in New Orleans, and Italian merchants owned many businesses frequented by black customers.

Italians and blacks, even in the Jim Crow Deep South, seemed to relate well to each other. Among the Italian immigrants, there was a noticeable absence of racism toward blacks. This might have been expected, since very few of the immigrants had ever seen a black person before, or ever thought about one for that matter. After all, there were none in the villages from which they came. Consequently, Italian immigrants knew nothing of racism as it was expressed in America at the time of their arrival. They had to learn about racial prejudice and discrimination after they settled in America. It was not a lesson learned very well by the immigrants. As a group, they never embraced racism enthusiastically. Indeed, they resisted it, if for no other reason than they found themselves in a similar predicament. They were a minority as well and so were their children! It took three generations (the grandchildren of the immigrants) for Italian-Americans to become, more or less, indistinguishable from other white Americans in their racial attitudes toward blacks.

Scarpaci found some conflict and violence between Italians and blacks on Louisiana's sugar plantations, but the trouble did not appear to be racially motivated. Rather, it was more likely inspired by the same kinds of personal differences that boil over into hostility everywhere. Even though they worked together in the same fields performing similar tasks, neither group perceived itself to be in competition with the other for the simple reason that they were not. Neither blacks nor Italians were likely to find themselves in supervisory positions, at least not beyond the lowest field-gang level. Furthermore, during the time of the large-scale Italian presence on the plantations, there was a continuous shortage of labor, so that Italians were not edging out any blacks. They replaced those blacks who had already departed the plantation and who very probably had moved out of the South.

The legacy of black and Italian contact in turn-of-the-twentieth-century Louisiana has endured primarily in two overlapping arenas, music and economic relations. First and foremost, blacks and Italians were drawn together by New Orleans' food and music. This twin seduction of New Orleans played well for both groups, who, separately and collectively, contributed to that distinctively American invention, jazz. Largely within but sometimes even outside the limits of what Jim Crow allowed, blacks and Italians shared their love of music and explored new sounds. Their creative musical instincts could be discerned from the sounds coming from the streets and from many of the unsavory establishments for which the Big Easy is famous. We address the music connection between blacks and

Italians in chapter 6. For the moment, we will focus on the economic ties between them.

The relationship between blacks and Italian immigrants and their descendants was shaped by their respective positions in American society. Blacks by law and custom were required to pay homage to the dominant white class. In the South, relations between the races evolved into a hierarchical structure of dominant and subordinate castes modified by a code of civility followed at least by highborn whites. Outside the South, the relationship between the races was more impersonal and indirect. Generally, the wealthiest whites encountered blacks only through an intermediate class of white foreigners generally from Europe. Jews in Northern cities played this mediator role between blacks and whites and were intermediate in status between the "subordinate" class and the white elite.

Southern cities generally did not receive many immigrants from Europe, but New Orleans was an exception. The close contact between blacks and Italian immigrants that was first experienced on the plantations in rural Louisiana and on the streets in New Orleans lacked the castelike quality commonly found between blacks and whites. In time, the Italian immigrants, their children, and especially their grandchildren would learn the racial prejudices of America, but not before a cultural amalgam of sorts had developed.

On the streets, in the restaurants, in the marketplace, and elsewhere, the contact between blacks and Italians contributed to a uniquely American popular culture. The late University of New Orleans professor Joseph Logsdon was among the first to call attention to the popular culture that tied New Orleanians together in their taste for jazz, a unique cuisine, and a body of traditions that made "The City"[25] a very different place. No doubt, it was from black Creoles that the Italian immigrants learned the cuisine of New Orleans. Many Italian restaurants still depend upon black chefs. But no matter how many close personal relationships developed between Italians and blacks,

Jim Crow ultimately exerted a profound influence. By the 1940s, neighborhoods that were once racially mixed were becoming predominately black or white. Suburban flight after World War II sped the process. Many Italian-Americans owned businesses and real estate in areas that were rapidly becoming all black. The result was that by the 1950s many Italian-American merchants had largely, if not exclusively, black customers. Italian property owners were becoming landlords to black tenants. In short, Italian-Americans had become a middleman minority not unlike the role played by Jews in Northern cities.[26]

THE PATHS TO OCCUPATIONAL SUCCESS

The most conspicuous path to occupational success was from migrant plantation laborer to sharecropper to independent truck farmer to peddler and merchant. The second most conspicuous path was through the trades: baker, butcher, barber, tailor, shoemaker, carpenter, and mason. As previously noted, these trades typically involved self-employment. In brief, tradesmen were shop owners and therefore small businessmen.

Obviously not all the immigrants were peasants, and even a few were successful before immigration. Chiefly before the Civil War, the Italian immigrants in Louisiana were more likely to be from northern or central Italy and much more likely to have come seeking a business opportunity than their counterparts who arrived later. There are numerous examples of economic entrepreneurs in the New Orleans area, but not all of them remained in the city. Some of these adventurous spirits sought their fortunes in other parts of the state.

A case in point was Lorenzo Casso.[27] He arrived in Louisiana in 1859 with the then-tidy sum of $1,000. He purchased a sloop and sold oranges and produce on Bayou Lafourche. He operated a grocery store with sails and eventually got into the oyster business. By contrast, the life of Salvatore Noti and family was more characteristic of the later immigrant.[28] He arrived in Louisiana in 1897 with his sons. Salvatore worked on a plantation, saved his money, then sent his savings to his family in Chiusa Sclafani, Sicily. Eventually, he returned to Italy, collected the remainder of his family, and came back to Louisiana with them. His sons, having stayed in Louisiana, worked on the railroad and the roadbeds in Missouri and Kansas in the spring and summer. During the sugar harvest (fall), they moved back to Louisiana and worked on a plantation. They finally settled in Churchville, a suburb of Donaldsonville. Their experiences closely parallel those of the great majority of the Italian immigrants to Louisiana. Yet there were immigrants like Dr. Edward C. Greco of Shreveport whose experiences in Louisiana were very different.

Dr. Greco was born in Marsala, Sicily. His family settled in Natchitoches when he was only two. He received his early education there and was interested in science. As a chemist and a specialist in the corrosion of metals, he enjoys an international reputation. A former professor of chemistry at Northwestern State University, he has received numerous awards. Until his retirement, he served as science advisor to a variety of organizations, including the U.S. Army and DuPont.[29]

On occasion, one encounters the immigrant account that shifts attention from the person to the place. Dr. Nick Accardo is a well-known physician in New Orleans and in wider medical circles. Besides developing innovative surgical procedures, he is considered an important civic leader in the city. Dr. Accardo's grandfather emigrated from Salaparuta, Sicily in 1892 and settled in the Patterson-Morgan City area. In eight years, he had enough money to bring his family to America. At the time of his arrival in Louisiana in 1900, Dr. Accardo's father was thirteen and worked on a farm in the same area. Later he married a native of Patterson of Italian ancestry, from the Cognata family. Dr. Accardo could identify four physicians in Louisiana whose ancestors came from Salaparuta: Giorlando, LaRocca, Saniglia, and Signarelli.[30] We might note, Nick LaRocca, the jazz musician, would have been added to that list of doctors had he only listened to his father, but that's another story.

THE LOGISTICS OF SUCCESS

The unskilled male plantation laborer working from sunup to sundown made about 75 cents a day depending on his ability. A first-rate cane cutter received about $1.25 a day; old men and young boys were paid less. During cultivation, old men, women, and boys received 25 to 60 cents per day. The cooperation of family members and their incredible capacity to endure backbreaking work is described in this account given by a visitor to a Louisiana plantation:

> A family of five Italians, the father, the mother, and three children, arrived on a cane plantation from Italy all set to work. Even in a depressed labor market, the father by working three watches of six hours each, at 50 cents a watch, could earn $1.50 a day. The mother could earn $1.00 and the children even if only 5 years old, could manage to earn 10 cents a day. So that the aggregate of such an average family's work per day was about $3.00.[31]

Sacrifice was the supper served; frugality was its guest at the table. Money earned was not spent; it was saved. The immigrants' needs were few, for they made or grew nearly everything they used, and often existed on bread and cheese.[32] The immigrant, no doubt with the usual amount of Sicilian hyperbole, said he and his family ate only bread and onions. In two seasons, a cane worker could save enough money to open a fruit stand or grocery. In four or five years he could save enough to be a landowner.[33] When he made the transition from plantation worker to truck farmer or entrepreneur, family cooperation was centered around the new economic activity. On the strawberry farms in Tangipahoa Parish, "all of the

able-bodied members of the family were expected to participate."[34] They transformed their meager earnings into a profit
because they systematically exploited every avenue to maximize income and minimize expenses. They tended garden
plots along with their strawberry farms, kept goats and cows,
and in some cases produced enough vegetables for retail.[35] On
the plantations, immigrants were frequently given access to
small gardens, which the entire family worked.[36] The harvested
vegetables would be sold to other plantation workers and to
the planter families on adjacent plantations.[37]

Likewise, the Italian peddler unashamedly mobilized all his
relatives and welded them into an efficient production unit.
Typically, these new entrepreneurs marshaled members of the
family and assigned them specialized roles. They did not forsake the land. Many peddlers grew vegetables—if not for retail,
then for their own consumption. As on the farm, the family
contributed to this endeavor. When the peddler was prosperous enough to be a shopkeeper, relatives were expected to do
their work in the family business. Young and old, male and
female, were expected to work.

Cooperation regularly extended beyond the nuclear family
to include a much larger network of blood and fictive kin.
Scarpaci has pointed out that in Louisiana's plantation
parishes, economic cooperation was established among persons who were already related by the multiple bonds of blood,
marriage, friendship, and community. Married siblings, their
spouses, and their children participated in certain cooperative
ventures. According to one account, four brothers, their wives,
and their children collectively cleared swamp land, tilled the
soil, harvested the resultant crop, and in a short period of time
were able to own the land free of mortgage.[38] In Tangipahoa
Parish, Italian-owned strawberry farms were about five acres on
average. They were frequently adjacent to farms belonging to
kinsmen like brothers, close cousins, or nephews. In such
cases, members of separate farms commonly combined their

resources to purchase mules, farm implements, and farming supplies, in effect creating a limited farming cooperative. Later, these same arrangements were made in buying a communally owned tractor together with equipment like a middle buster, disk, cultivator, and other tractor tools necessary for mechanizing the agricultural process. Moreover, joint, extended families could be seen preparing their fields, planting, then harvesting together on a rotating basis. Strawberry farming lent itself naturally to this kind of routine since berries are picked every third day. Three families could join together to harvest each family's field on successive days. A similar pattern of cooperation is reflected in family businesses in New Orleans. Groceries, meat markets, produce warehouses, and import businesses frequently bore the names of two or more brothers or of father and sons. Kinsmen also extended credit, lent stock, offered advice, and gave other forms of informal support to each other.

Thomas and Angela D'Gerolamo left Sicily in 1888 and became agricultural laborers on a plantation in St. James Parish in what is now the city of LaPlace. Ten years later they had saved $1,500, enough to purchase a farm in the village of Kenner. Eventually the farm encompassed part of what is now the New Orleans International Airport. Thomas and Angela raised their family on that farm, and when his parents died, the eldest son, Victor, started a modest vegetable-packing business. Victor would buy shallots, turnips, beets, carrots, cabbage, bell peppers, and corn from local farmers, pack the produce, and ship it to markets in Chicago, New York, and other eastern seaboard cities. As the business grew, his brothers Thomas, Anthony, Joseph, and Paul joined the company. The enterprise flourished until the economic depression of the 1930s; then, to keep it going, the D'Gerolamos were forced to mortgage some of the other properties they had accumulated during more prosperous times. World War II revived the company, as the United States military became one of its leading customers.

Then, after the war, when the partners got old and farm land disappeared as Kenner was transformed into a full-fledged suburb of New Orleans, the business once again went into decline. But the farm and the business had already provided the platform for the D'Gerolamos' entrance into politics and the professions of law and education. Family members have served Kenner, Jefferson Parish, and Louisiana in various elected and appointed capacities over the past four generations. Victor D'Gerolamo was an alderman for the village of Kenner in 1913. Two of his brothers, Nick and Joe, were also aldermen. Victor later was elected to serve successive terms as mayor of Kenner from 1930 to 1942. A generation later, Eddie D'Gerolamo became a city councilman (1954-62) and mayor of Kenner (1962-70); then he was sent to the Louisiana House of Representatives (1972-86). Family members were also attracted to the classroom, as nine of Thomas and Angela's grandchildren were teachers.[39]

How is it that the Italians of Louisiana were able to make such a rapid ascent up the occupational ladder? Six specific, interrelated factors stand out as being most significant: (1) the important role food, cooking, and culinary pleasures play in both Italy and South Louisiana; (2) negotiating and retailing skills acquired in Italy and brought with the immigrants to their new home in Louisiana; (3) the many generations of experiences of near famine and want; (4) the absence of an Italian ghetto in the Louisiana or New Orleans colonies; (5) the predisposition toward risk taking promoted by a belief in *Fortuna*; and (6) the strong family ties and loyalties that gave the immigrant entrepreneur a competitive edge.

Almost since its founding, New Orleans has had a reputation for being the most sensuous city in the United States of America. Its sensuousness is reflected in its climate and music, its linguistic styles and literary traditions, and its cuisine. More than in any other place in America, people in New Orleans have a proclivity for talk, especially small talk (gossip), and a nearly constant concern for food. Some would say these two oral inclinations border on the pathological. As a consequence, immigrants from Italy found South Louisiana, especially New Orleans, very receptive to their emphasis on eating, drinking, and sociability. Fine food and wine occupy an important place in both Italian culture and in South Louisiana, with its Mediterranean culture. Therefore, immigrants who became fruit peddlers, grocers, restaurateurs, and tavern keepers, who sold as much as food as alcohol, found ready customers besides Italians for their goods and services.

In Italy, particularly in the poorest sections of Sicily, people survived by virtue of their ability to negotiate prices. Additionally, the shrewd *contadino* would dedicate a small piece of land to mixed vegetables for personal consumption and for sale to local customers. Thus, the hard experiences of the Old Country tutored the immigrant in some valuable survival skills that are also essential in the marketplace.

The Sicilian peasant is an expert in calling upon heaven to ward off famines. Much folklore and popular poetry expresses the familiar theme of famine. The widespread devotion to St. Joseph altars, with their fava beans, a fertility symbol, is a case in point.[40] Not only did the fear of famine reinforce the place of food in the life of the immigrants, but it also cultivated in them habits of thrift, even hoarding. The concern for having enough food can be illustrated by the newspaper accounts of U.S. Customs officials finding bread hidden in the bosoms of immigrant women. Thrift is a requisite virtue for future economic success. The merchants or truck farmers in New Orleans in 1900 were the plantation workers of a decade earlier who had saved their money. Their frugality was the product of their age-long fight against starvation. Rudolph Vecoli has described it as an example of economic individualism, by which he meant that family units learned over the generations to be self-sufficient in the face of dire hardship.[41]

The Italian colony in New Orleans, the largest in the state, was never a ghetto. Unlike other Italian enclaves in the United States, it was not very segregated.[42] This fact facilitated assimilation and consequently occupational mobility by forcing the Italian immigrant to speak English, mingle with non-Italian neighbors, and learn American customs and folkways sooner than if he had lived in an Italian ghetto.

Fortuna predisposed the immigrant to risk taking. The willingness to take a chance that spring frosts would not materialize prompted early planting and increased the possibility of higher returns. Similarly, every business is a calculated gamble. The immigrants were often willing to risk all they owned to start a business.

The final point to be considered is how the Italian family and family loyalties helped the immigrant through the transition from farm laborer to merchant. Everyone in the family worked and contributed to the household. The business was a family business. Not only sons but also wives and daughters worked in it. They were petty merchants who opened businesses in the front rooms of their homes. The shops they owned, they operated! They did all the manual labor as well as whatever white-collar work was associated with the enterprise. The businesses they owned required little in the way of capital investment. This was fortunate, because they began with little money and great uncertainty, but with much cooperation among husband, wife, children, and kin.

CHAPTER FIVE

The Family (*la Famiglia*) and Security

The family is supreme. The Italian who has a family is never alone. He finds in it a refuge in defeat and an arsenal for his campaigns. The law, the state, and society function only if they do not interfere with the family's interests.[1]

The Italian family is a fortress protecting its members against the outside forces of indifference and hostility. For the landless peasant in 1900 and before, in the Old Country, the family was a refuge from the caprices of cruel rulers, landlords, and the vicissitudes of nature. It also served as the first and last line of defense against starvation. More than any other institution, indeed, more than all other institutions combined, the family satisfied the Italians' hunger for security.

In America, Italian immigrants relied on family for that same kind of protection. It was their greatest resource in the New World. The immigrants brought their families with them physically or they carried their kinsmen with them symbolically in their minds and morally in their hearts. The family was an ever-present reality from which the immigrants could not escape, even if they had wanted to. Of course, some immigrants abandoned their families, but the number of them who took that action was remarkably low. The literature is full of stories of great sacrifice by those who returned to Italy to retrieve not just spouse and children but parents, brothers and sisters, and extended kinsmen like uncles, aunts, nieces, nephews, and even first cousins. The enormous solidarity of the Italian family as a social institution in America provided the principal basis upon which the immigrants' economic welfare was built.[2] It helped them to realize economic security. This was especially true when the family's economic well-being was derived from the private ownership of a business or farm. In such cases, the head of the household could and did call upon the entire family, including extended kinsmen, for assistance, thereby reducing risk and lowering costs for credit, labor, and other services.

How did the Italian family satisfy the needs of its members for security in Italy and Louisiana? Were there any changes in domestic relations and family patterns between the immigrant generation and subsequent generations of Italian-Americans? As we shall see, the changes have been substantial, though remnants of the older form can still be seen in the families of the immigrants' grandchildren and great-grandchildren.

OLD WORLD PATTERNS

Despite the certainty with which the literature describes the Italian family, qualifications are necessary. One could argue there is no Italian family for the same reason there is no American or German family. In short, there is so much diversity in all societies that generalizations and categorizations are necessarily partial falsifications. While recognizing the danger in overgeneralizing, we can nevertheless make some broad and defensible descriptions.

The Italian family has been praised and damned! As a tight-knit organization bound by a pervasive sense of domestic fealty, the Italian family has often been envied by those bewildered by alienation in modern society. Others level numerous charges against the Italian family, particularly the variant found in southern Italy and Sicily. The *contadini* are said to be quintessentially parochial (*campanilismo*), exclusively oriented toward family goals and completely bound by a sacred allegiance to old values. As a consequence, so the argument goes, the family system is unprogressive, pathological, authoritarian, sexist, and amoral.

The fact that this family system transported to the New World could at times give the immigrant the competitive edge in the Louisiana marketplace is hard to reconcile with its reputed backwardness. In the literature on the subject, southern Italy and Sicily are unquestionably identified as the most backward areas of Europe. As the theory of modernization goes, the parochialism and traditionalism of peasants are barriers to progress.[3] The rationality, individualism, cosmopolitanism, and openness to change so characteristic of modern societies are blocked in societies organized as agricultural villages. The core component that makes backward societies backward is familism.[4] In simple terms, familism is the hardening of the boundaries between family members and nonmembers. Family loyalties supersede the interests of individuals, and the circle of interest and trust is confined entirely to kin. Familism is also expressed as a preference for large families, extensive family cooperation in the economic sphere, and family stability.

THE SHAPING OF THE FAMILY

The Italian family was molded by centuries of exploitation and caprice. In a seemingly endless procession, foreign rulers came to rape the pearl of the Mediterranean and the breadbasket of Europe. Even after unification, Sicily and southern Italy were treated as stepchildren by the Italian government. For centuries, Sicily and southern Italy were scorned and drained of their resources. Most importantly, the callous rulers left a legacy of contempt, mistrust, and neglect. The centuries of foreign rule tutored the *contadini* to cope with the corruption of both

foreign and domestic rulers. From these seeds, an entirely innovative organization, the *Mafia,* emerged. The *Mafia* performed
those functions that corrupt legitimate authorities were unwill-
ing or powerless to carry out and, thus, bandits policed bandits,
dished out justice, and kept a semblance of order. In time, these
"protectors" would themselves become instruments of injustice
and they, too, would exploit the *contadini.*[5]

In such a world, the *contadini* placed their trust in their small
circles of family and friends. Ultimately, they developed a reasonable response to a terrible condition. For their own security
they trusted no one outside the village. They were suspicious of
all strangers. Even fellow villagers, *paesani,* could be treacher-
ous. They could at times be agents of foreign rulers, or police
who were the hired lackeys of noblemen. Indeed, they could
also be members of that invisible empire of murder, extortion,
and thievery, the *Mafia.* Burned by such experiences, the *contadini* were reluctant to extend open hands of trust to anyone
outside the family. Family honor and loyalty became virtues
instilled in every member, by word and by rod.

No serious student of Italy and the Italians can escape from
the conclusion that the family is supreme. Francis Ianni simply
says, "Italy is a nation of families, not of individuals."[6] Richard
Gambino echoes this sentiment: "The unique family pattern of
southern Italy constituted the real sovereignty of that land,
regardless of which governments ruled it."[7]

In the Italy of 1900, the family was indestructible. Family solidarity was supported by forces of law and custom. The Catholic
Church soundly and unequivocally condemned divorce. This
canonical ban was supported by the state, which also prohibited the legal dissolution of marriage. Community norms reinforced the immutability of marriage. No quicker or more
certain pathway to ostracism could be found in the community
than by traveling the road to family dissolution. Neither unhap-
piness nor infidelity could challenge a marriage's permanence.
Those who ignored or contradicted the mores lost not only

social status in the community; they also felt compelled to leave it. They had to live elsewhere. But what the church dictated and what the community required through its collective conscience, the family absolutely insisted upon. Married men and women who refused to live as husbands and wives suffered the wrath of their own families. And they suffered this animus not merely because of their real or imagined personal immorality. Far more was at stake. Such a contemptible violation of God and nature was considered a mark against the good name of the whole family—the larger, extended family of parents, grandparents, and great-grandparents, including deceased members.

Faced with such formidable cultural requirements, it is no wonder that the family withstood every challenge put to it. It was not that Old World Italians dismissed divorce as an unworthy temptation; they could not even contemplate it. There simply was no alternative to marriage and the family in their secular world.

An important part of family life among Old World Italians was the practice of godparenthood. The godfather entered into a special relationship with the child and the child's parents. He became the parents' *compare*. In like fashion, the godmother became their *comare*.[8] Two sets of godparents were involved, one for baptism and the other for confirmation. The two sets could be the same, but that was not always the case. The relationship was a spiritual one, though frequently godparents were consanguineal kin, thus creating the double family bonds of religion and blood.

Il comparatico (godparenthood) created the need to exercise special care in selecting one's best man and maid of honor for a wedding, because these witnesses automatically became godparents to the couple's firstborn. Another consideration in this selection was the extraordinary power the godparents would enjoy.

It was believed that children inherited personality from their spiritual parents. The Italians firmly believed that the spiritual as well as the actual daughter of a bad woman never turned out well, that a madman's child could never be sane, and that the offspring of a thief was inherently dishonest. As the old ones put it, "The cat's daughter either bites or scratches." In the case of godparents, their sayings typically pointed out, "From the godparents come the blood," and "A slice is taken from the godfather."[9]

Godparents were expected to keep an eye out for their god-children's moral well-being, but their duties went beyond that. They were also expected to provide financial and other material aid in emergencies. And, of course, godparents were expected to assume the responsibilities of parenthood in the event of the untimely death of the parents.

Perhaps it is best to illustrate some of the essential qualities of the Italian family by briefly sketching the experiences of an immigrant family that faced what most observers would consider severe hardships. While divorce was rare in the nineteenth and early twentieth centuries, death of family members was not. Gioachino (Jake) Montalbano was born on July 18, 1900, in Bisacquino, Sicily.[10] A brother, Giuseppe, eight years Jake's senior, came to America as a young man. Jake's twin sister, Michela, died shortly after birth. Tragically, his mother, Vincenza Latino Montalbano, and father, Vito Montalbano, would also die. That left their lastborn, Jake, in the care of relatives who were cruel, so he departed to live and work on a ranch on the opposite side of the mountain. Despite these tribulations, Jake chose to tarry on the sunny side of life. Until the day he died, Jake would remember tending the goats, sheep, and cattle on the ranch. He would savor sweet memories of the nuns whose convent, the *Monastero di Santa Maria del Bosco,* was next to the ranch; of his beautiful and beloved village, Bisacquino; and of the friends and relatives he left behind.

From March 1918 until October 1921, Jake served in the Italian military. World War I came to an end shortly after his military stint began, so he did not have to fight. The army did, however, provide young Jake with the opportunity to travel to other Italian cities and towns.

By this time, Giuseppe was residing in New Orleans and sent for his younger brother. Jake paid the 252-lira fare[11] and boarded the SS *Providence* on October 29, 1922, arriving at Ellis Island some three weeks later. After processing, and with only a few dollars in his pocket and a slip of paper bearing his brother's address, he boarded the train to New Orleans.

Jake's marriage to Giuseppina (Josephine) Latino followed Sicilian traditions. Josephine's father immigrated to New Orleans in 1896 and eventually settled in the Hammond area as a strawberry farmer. Her mother, Rosa Di Chiara, immigrated originally to Plaquemines Parish, where she worked in the sugarcane fields. Josephine was born in Hammond in 1908. When she was four, her mother died. Her father subsequently married a widow with children. In this regard, both Jake's and Josephine's childhoods were crossed by tragedy. In both cases, parental death forced them to accommodate unbreakable Sicilian traditions.

Jake and Josephine were married in St. Mary's, the church for the Italians in New Orleans. It was a double wedding including Josephine's older sister Lena, who married Jake's cousin, Vincent Cataldo. In Sicilian fashion, the wedding brought two families closer. Furthermore, each was the other's best man and maid of honor, which meant they would become godparents to the firstborn in each household. The choices the two couples made further strengthened the ties between the two families. Further demonstrating that marriage unifies families and provides economic cooperation, the couples shared a residence for a short time after the wedding. In this case the two couples were bound together as kinsmen in three ways: by blood, by marriage, and spiritually as *compare* and *comare*.

With few independent resources, Jake and Josephine Montalbano supported themselves by making and selling hot tamales at two for a nickel on the streets of New Orleans, particularly in the uptown section of the city. Eventually, Jake would apprentice as a shoe repairman through a godparent connection. During the depression, he worked on WPA projects in Audubon and City parks, digging lagoons and canals.

The couple settled for a while in the Hammond area, where they grew strawberries. When not farming, Jake worked in Hammond as a shoe repairman for Leone Monteleone. The Monteleones were godparents of Jake's son, John.

In 1945, the couple and their growing family (eventually eight children) moved back to "The City," on Bienville Street, subsequently moving to a larger place at 2835 Bienville. Jake worked in his own shop and later for the Arrow Shoe Repair shop at 8114 Oak Street, where he had first learned the trade. He subsequently bought it and worked as a shoemaker. Upon his retirement, he sold the shop to his half-sister's son, Michael Governale.

Jake Montalbano, like most Sicilians of his generation, knew and loved opera music. He was also an accomplished musician who could play a number of instruments. Jake played for the *Band Di Roma*. He was active in a number of Italian organizations and was an officer in the *Societa Italiano di Madonna del Balzo*. Like so many immigrants, Gioachino Montalbano dedicated himself entirely and untiringly to his family and work, and drew strength and a sense of dignity from both.

THE ITALIAN FAMILY IN LOUISIANA

The Italian family appears to have made the transatlantic crossing virtually unaltered. Immigrants set up households and lived family life essentially as it was lived in the Old Country, but with different results. Old World traits that perpetuated backwardness in Sicily became a progressive force in Louisiana. Familism created a curious set of paradoxes. Out of the fabric of *campanilismo*, cosmopolitanism was fashioned. From the threads of traditional values, economic shrewdness was woven; and from the collective family orientation, an economic individualism took shape.[12]

The Italian immigrants' *campanilismo* taught them to trust no one but family members. Those outside the family were viewed equally—one is like all others. No matter how "close" they approach, they never are allowed to penetrate the inner boundary of the family. So close is the circle, so unambiguous the individuals it envelops, that outsiders pose no threat. They are nonpersons or abstract entities like customers. Tenaciously clinging to traditional family values and loyalties, the *conta-dini's* collective front against a cruel, uncertain, and untrust-worthy world becomes a rational plan in the economic sphere, a shrewd calculation of costs and benefits for long-term gains. The product is a domestic "corporation" based on blood and marriage ties, with lifetime loyalty to the "firm."

Because family loyalties and responsibilities take precedence over all other duties, the family encourages economic individu-alism for the male heads of households. Self-employment becomes the family's guarantee of freedom and protection from outsiders. Business activity and family life are merged. Long hours working at the family business are not stolen from family time. By contrast, the salaried worker must make excuses for not meeting employers' demands. Thus, conflict between work and family life, a constant source of tension in contempo-rary America, is escaped through self-employment.

Other forms of individualism are supported by Sicilian familism. Each family member is encouraged to be a *prima donna* in matters of personal taste and style. In fact, idiosyn-cratic personalities are cultivated. Is this reflected in the art and drama characteristic of Italian culture? Does this cultural trait, a flair for the theatrical, have anything to do with the fact that Milan is the fashion center of the Western world?

Ironically, what ensured the persistence of Old World family patterns eventually transformed them. As the immigrants sought security, they applied familism to the economic arena. This frequently gave them a competitive edge in the market-place and helps explain their rapid economic success particu-larly in Louisiana. Such success, however, resulted in greater acceptance by the larger community, thereby weakening the very values that helped win that success. It was not until the

next generation[13] that the effects could be seen. The immigrant generation typically maintained Old World family patterns. They immigrated as families, and they found a receptive
culture in Catholic Creole Louisiana that reinforced their
familism.

The period of mass immigration from 1880 to 1910 saw
large numbers of Sicilian immigrants working on Louisiana
soil. While they may have originally conceived of themselves as
sojourners, they soon gave evidence of other intentions.

In the five settlements first reported on in chapter 4 (New
Orleans, Kenner, Harvey, St. James Parish, and St. Mary
Parish), there was variation in year of immigration and age on
arrival.[14] Over one-fourth (27 percent) of the immigrants in
New Orleans in 1900 arrived prior to 1880. One consequence
of their comparative early entry was that by 1900 many of them
had children of marriageable age when later Italian immigrants arrived. Additionally, only in New Orleans was there a
significant number of immigrant heads of households in 1900
(8.7 percent) who had previously arrived as children (under
nine years of age). By contrast, the immigrants residing on
plantations in St. James and St. Mary parishes arrived somewhat later—over 80 percent of them after 1890. The two settlements of largely independent farmers in Harvey and Kenner
of Jefferson Parish contained both early and late arrivals. In
each settlement, over one-tenth arrived before 1880; however,
over 70 percent of Harvey's immigrants arrived after 1890,
whereas only 41 percent of Kenner's immigrants did so. This
figure is closer to the 38 percent for the New Orleans settlement and consistent with the fact that Kenner is the second
oldest settlement of Italians in the state. In each settlement,
the typical age of the immigrants at the time of their arrival was
between twenty and thirty-nine.

Though immigrants arrived as family units, there was considerable variation across the settlements. The majority of
household heads in Harvey, Kenner, and St. James arrived the

same year as their spouse. The patterns in New Orleans and St. Mary Parish were quite different.

The New Orleans community, as already noted, was old enough by 1900 to have begun the next generation. It was not uncommon for single immigrants to find spouses among the adult children of immigrants. In the case of St. Mary Parish, there was a considerable time lag (2.7 years on the average) between the immigration of husbands and wives, nearly three times longer than in New Orleans. However, when husbands came without their wives, they nevertheless were not without kinsmen, because there was a decided tendency for fathers and sons, brothers, uncles, and nephews to immigrate and build a household around the segmented family. Later, wives and the other children would rejoin their husbands and fathers. Reflecting this fact, over 78 percent of the households in the St. Mary sample were nuclear, illustrating that solitary, single, young, male immigration was not typical in Louisiana. This pattern of migration as a family unit indicates a desire to settle in quickly rather than jumping around indefinitely from city to city or job to job. Unattached males, even those with family obligations, are likely to do precisely that if left to their own temptations. Males who immigrate with their nuclear or extended families are far more likely to work at establishing themselves economically. Long ago, Pitirim Sorokin showed the enormous power of bondedness in social relationships. The more bonds we have, and the greater frequency and intensity with which we exercise those bonds, the more likely we are to comply with group pressure.[15]

Immigration did not disrupt marriage and fertility patterns. Old World cultural values favoring marriage and large families were transplanted in Louisiana. Fertility levels for Italian women in Louisiana have been reported to be considerably higher than native American women and comparable to the high fertility levels of Irish women.[16] In Louisiana, fertility levels were high and marriages do not seem to have been delayed.

Age at maternity for immigrant women was 22.6 years, comparable to the figures reported for Sicily and southern Italy at the turn of the twentieth century.[17]

Financial success did not result in smaller households in New Orleans in 1900. On the contrary, merchants and craftsmen had larger households than did laborers. The high fertility levels of Louisiana's Italian immigrant women speak favorably for the retention of large-family norms and reflect, although indirectly, a familistic orientation.

Immigrant family patterns faced few cultural impediments in Louisiana. Italian and Creole family patterns were similar. Owing to their common Catholic background, both groups practiced a system of godparenthood. Creole families tended also to be large and, like the Italian immigrants, they expected loyalty. In addition, Creole culture placed a premium on living the good life—eating, drinking, and celebrating within the context of the family (an argument can be made that Creole planters were an exception). The immigrants found a hospitable soil in Creole Louisiana. This rich supportive cultural environment nourished and sustained Italian Old World family patterns.

Economic success ushered in changes in the family, and not just the family composed of a husband, wife, and children. Changes were also taking place involving the extended family—grandparents, aunts, uncles, cousins, and spiritual kin (godparents). However important the nuclear family might be, among Italians it is typically woven into a larger kinship web. These relationships are activated on special occasions and in times of uncommon need.

Reunions, feasts, marriages, funerals, anniversaries, and other celebrations are examples of special occasions. The Italian sponsor of such an event is obligated to invite everyone in the family, or not have the event at all. Those who are disliked, those who are hardly known, and those who are loved must all be invited. To leave out a despised uncle is to insult his brother, the host's father. Conversely, when invited to an event, there is a strong compulsion to attend. Invitations from Italian kin are qualitatively different from those received from friends and acquaintances. Within the circle of the extended family an Italian is never forgotten. Absence is more obvious than actual attendance. That simple fact is strong enough motivation for most to be drawn to the event. Accounting for the missing is an inevitable topic of conversation. "No, Annie is not here, but her three daughters are." Or "None of Tony's family is here. Where are they?" Once the accounting is rendered, it is not left at the statistical level. Elaborate conjectures follow as to why this one or that one is not here. It does not matter that so and so never attends; the same ritualistic accounting is always rendered. Unlike in the cocktail circuit, the missing are never forgotten.

In times of crisis or uncommon need, the extended family, even without petition from the one in need, feels obligated to take matters into its own hands for the good of the family. In the 1950s a widow in Tangipahoa Parish remarried several years after the death of her first husband, who was of Italian descent. The second husband was an American outsider who proved to be a scoundrel. He squandered the widow's money surreptitiously and secretly sold some of her valued possessions to pay off his gambling debts. Later he wrecked her car, ran around with other women, and then impregnated her. One evening, four of the woman's brothers, carrying shotguns, called on the man. They informed him that he was to leave town without turning back, not even for a glance, and that he was never to return. The man was never heard from again. In the eighteen months of their acquaintance with the man, the brothers had not once referred to him as a brother-in-law. The essential fact is that throughout these episodes the sister was neither scorned nor condemned; the larger family showed compassion and concern for one of their own who had made an unfortunate mistake.

Much more frequently, the extended family is called upon to keep a potentially wayward child in line, help find employment, and assist in getting loans. A relative well established in business or in the professions is frequently called upon to aid an aspiring nephew with his occupational ambitions. The assistance could take many forms, from personal encouragement to financial support to aid in obtaining a place in medical or law school. Once established, the physician or lawyer is expected to continue the service to the extended family by attending to the medical and legal needs of his or her kin, even if they are unable to pay for those services. And the physician or lawyer in turn is to help aspiring nephews and nieces.

Serious illness is an event that calls forth the solidarity of the extended family, and typically it responds. Everyone is expected to get involved in one way or another. The women who can do so offer nursing aid. Others prepare food for the household of the sick, and the remainder of the family is required to run errands and visit, visit, visit.

The long, slow death of one Italian immigrant, Salvadore ("Mr. Sam") Macaluso, illustrates these facts. Mr. Macaluso was a strawberry farmer in his eighties at the time. His daughters and some of his granddaughters took turns assisting their stepmother, Mary, in nursing Sam and in keeping the kitchen well stocked in food, wine, and coffee. The pantry was stretched thin during this time because the many visitors Mr. Sam received "needed" to be served something. Mr. Macaluso, who loved to play cards, made it known he wanted to play for a while every night. In response to his request, which was received by his grown sons as a command, the men in the family organized themselves into groups and took turns visiting on a particular night of the week to play Mr. Sam's favorite card games, *Tresetta* and *Briscola*. This routine continued without open complaint by anyone for the better part of a year, until he finally died.

Another function of the extended family among Italians is advising. As in the case of some other kinds of assistance, advice is sometimes given against the wishes of those who receive it. Much has been made of the advice solicited from the head of the family—especially by his grown sons—and, in his absence, from the oldest son. Less publicized but of equal importance is the advice given by the mother to her daughters. Fathers advise their sons about staying out of trouble, the kinds of girls to marry, the kinds of jobs to seek, the lands or houses to purchase, what to do with their money, and anything else that might enter their minds. Mothers likewise dole out advice with unending profusion. Their advice more often takes the form of admonitions. "Stay away from boys; they are only after one thing: your good name"; or "Do not wear too much makeup; you will look like a tramp"; or "Be careful about spoiling the child." Advice from mothers tends to stick to domestic and sexual affairs. It seldom spills over into areas beyond the home.

Parental advice to grown children is, of course, not exclusively an Italian proclivity. It is a universal theme in family relations. What does seem to be more prevalent among Italians, however, is the ease with which advice is offered beyond the limit of the nuclear family. Grandparents, uncles, and aunts show no disinclination to get into the act. Kin of whatever degree freely participate in the advising process. The only rules seem to be that those who give advice must be older than those who receive it and that women are not to counsel men. Men, though, may advise either sex, and in special circumstances may even advise their elders; but when they do, the advice must be solicited.

Among Louisiana Italians, parents have always preferred to have their married children live nearby. Modern America requires mobility and what anthropologists call neolocal residence: the establishment upon marriage of a new household apart from the parents of either spouse. Following the American custom, the extended family over time has scattered, first to another neighborhood or town, then across the parish (county), and finally out of the state and across the country.

As a consequence of such dispersion, the Italian family in Louisiana remains only nuclear in form. In this regard,

Louisiana's Italians resemble the Italians living in Boston's West End, whom Herbert Gans described as urban villagers. The term Gans uses for the Italian family type in Boston is the expanded family, referring to the frequent presence in the household of a relative other than parents and their children. The Italian family in Louisiana has followed the same pattern.

Boarding practices among Italian families are vestiges of the extended or expanded family. Boarding was an especially important American feature during turn-of-the-twentieth-century immigration. It allowed the recently arrived Italian a friendly haven in a foreign land. This temporary lodging represented a kind of domestically based settlement house so frequently encountered in the cities of the Northeast. Boston, New York, Philadelphia, and some of the other cities receiving large numbers of immigrants all used settlement houses to buffer the impact of America on the frightened immigrant newcomer.

As immigration declined and the Italian community became more self-sufficient, boarding declined. It was on the verge of disappearing altogether when World War II resurrected the practice. The stepped-up economic activities accompanying the war attracted large numbers of small-town and country residents to the big cities, where industrial manufacturing was concentrated. Boarding was reinstituted to accommodate the newcomers, who easily found jobs but not much unoccupied housing. Because the Port of New Orleans was the point of entry for Louisiana's Italians, those who lived outside the city usually had relatives living in it. And because of the extended family, when they came to work in support of the war effort, they found room and board with their "city cousins." With the end of the war, boarding declined once again, but it did not disappear altogether.

Beginning in the 1950s, boarding became associated with attending college away from home. Students from New Orleans lived with relatives in Hammond as they attended Southeastern

Louisiana University; those from outside the city lived with relatives in New Orleans as they attended the several colleges and universities located there. No matter what form it takes among Italians, boarding represents the perpetuation of the long reach of the extended family.

There has been, from the beginning, a network of relationships between New Orleans Italians and other Louisiana Italians, especially those who eventually settled in the southern part of the state. Nearly all of them outside of the city had relatives living in it. Early in the century and continuing through the 1940s, the Italians in Tangipahoa Parish, those living just upriver from New Orleans, and even those who settled in Baton Rouge periodically came to New Orleans to do some shopping. Sometimes it was for their domestic supply of flour, sugar, pasta, oil, and other items of the Italian diet; sometimes it was for a first communion outfit. These trips were made by train or, if the distance was not too great, by wagon and later by automobile. In most instances the trip required an overnight stay in the city with kin. Such episodes represented economic cooperation within the extended family, and they reinforced the social bonds between relatives.

Italians in the outlying parishes were fond of honeymooning in New Orleans. It was close enough to get to without much delay, and it was inexpensive. Rosalie, a woman from Tickfaw in Tangipahoa Parish, moved to Algiers, a West Bank district in the city of New Orleans, as soon as she was married. Her younger sisters spent their honeymoons in her home. Rosalie and her husband stayed with friends for several days to accommodate the newlyweds. This kind of wedding present was not unusual, especially for couples who could not yet afford to rent a hotel room.

It is perhaps unnecessary to say the older generation of Italians expected their children to marry Italians. The expectation was indelibly there but it was more often than not unstated. There was no need to "preach" about the matter. It was simply understood by all the parties concerned. First-generation

Italian-Americans overwhelmingly married within their ethnic group. Among the Italians in Louisiana, a distinction was made between Italians and Americans. The Italians and their families called themselves Italians; everyone else was referred to as Americans. An Italian marrying an American was unusual, and an Italian girl marrying an American boy was especially so, owing to the greater family control over the girl's behavior. When marriage took place across ethnic lines, as it sometimes did, it rarely crossed religious ones. In New Orleans the most frequent early interethnic marriages were between Catholics of Italian and French descent. Marriages between Italians and Irish Catholics and between Italians and German Catholics were less frequent.

Only through marriage could the woman assume her proper station in life as wife and mother. These were properly the highest hopes and ambitions of the daughter. Her parents' concern for her marriage was soon replaced by a concern for grandchildren, who were not only desired but desired in great numbers. Illustrating this point is an Italian shoemaker who had one of five children complete college and then go on to receive his doctorate. When asked about his Ph.D. son, the old man's reply was, "Oh, he is doing real good. He has eight wonderful children!"

Marriage for the son is equally important but for a different reason. Only through his marriage and paternity can the continuation of the family name be assured. If for no other reason, this has made males more important than females to the older generation. The concern of one immigrant in his early eighties was no doubt shared by other old-timers in a similar situation. He admonished one of his two grandsons to marry and have many sons because his own sons had not populated the earth with many sons themselves. The admonition was accompanied by a brief but pointed discussion of the overriding importance of keeping the family name alive.

Sicilian mothers and fathers act like grandparents with their very young children. When children are that age, parents are quite permissive. They hug them, sing to them, and otherwise make a fuss over them. However, in later childhood, the children are expected to work hard like an adult. A male immigrant reported that at the age of eight he worked on roads in Sicily. Leaving his family for two or three weeks at a time, he carried stones used to repair and construct roads. Walking to and from the construction sites, he would often arrive home in the middle of the night, when the family was asleep. The expectations for daughters were comparable. At the tender age of eight, the sole daughter of an immigrant truck farmer would cook for thirty, which included her father, brothers, and hired hands! This she would do outdoors with a beehive oven that Sicilians used throughout the state.

The relationships between men and women are difficult to summarize. So much nonsense has been written about the traditional roles of men and women that the reality is hard to resurrect. Very little of the textured nuances that develop between a husband and wife are present in the social-science literature on the family. Contemporary images of Sicilian husbands and wives are not much more than sterile stereotypes. Sicilian women were stronger, more independent, and far more assertive than the traditional feminine stereotype. Oftentimes, they insisted on using their family names. How does the conventional stereotype correspond to "The Game of Love" between Vito and his wife, Vita?

THE GAME OF LOVE

Vito sat on his front stoop, escaping the summer heat. Tiny rivulets of sweat flowed down his face, collected into larger streams, and dripped on the stoop. The hour or so Vito spent in the backyard hoeing his peppers and tomatoes and the intense June sun had forced him to temporarily retreat from his work. Despite the heat and the stiff joints, Vito preferred hoeing to delivering ice, even though he made what he called "good money" by selling ice. He owned his truck and through hard work and thrift owned his home and two little shotgun houses in his neighborhood. He didn't have to plant and hoe, but growing his own vegetables was like an ancient calling. Some men have to find a reason for waking each morning; Vito was not one of them.

Suddenly, Vito's peaceful thoughts were rooted from his brain by the screaming in the backyard. "Stupido, where are you hiding? This is what you buy? This is what you call meat? This is mule droppings!" Vita was a small woman with a big voice and an even bigger temper. Vito marched to the backyard and heard almost all his ancestors maligned.

"You paid good money for this? You just like your father, stupid. He bought that nanny goat that had only one teat." Vita continued to call attention to the acts of stupidity of Vito's kindred. She even suggested that poor Vito's godparents were stupid. Vito responded with a few choice adjectives for some of Vita's kin. But Vito's remarks were lame by comparison. He quickly ended his feeble diatribe with inaudible curses and then in silence picked up the hoe and resumed his work. Vita was still insulting his ancestors as she entered the house and slammed the wooden screen door.

A long while passed and so did Vita's fury. She opened the kitchen door and in a most angelic voice beckoned to Vito. "Vito, my little Vito, you wanna eat? You wanna pasta?" Vito's muscles stiffened and, in the same muffled voice as before, he cursed her. Vita redoubled her resolve to mend fences. She interpreted the inaudible curse as a sign that Vito's angry mood was almost over, like a flickering flame on a spent candle.

She retreated into her kitchen and prepared Vito's pasta. Moments passed and she reemerged, calling out with saintly confidence, "Vito, the pasta is ready." By now Vito's mood was almost completely changed. He dropped his hoe with a final flicker of anger and walked toward the kitchen with slow measured paces. By the time he had reached the kitchen, Vito's anger was buried under the heavenly cloak Vita had woven. The inseparable two sat down to an enjoyable meal, one that was blessed by a little more silence than usual.

The Italian family in Louisiana has undergone many changes since 1900. Fundamentally, these changes have been in the direction of accommodation with the urban and suburban middle-class family found in America. The changes have not totally eradicated its Old World characteristics. Instead, new values, attitudes, and behaviors have been combined with the old, producing "another American family type" with Italian flavors. Paul J. Campisi has argued that the most basic changes include those of size, family roles and statuses, interpersonal relations, marriage, fertility and child care, sex attitudes, divorce and separation, and psychological aspects of the individual.[18] He maintains that "complete" transformation of the Italian can be found in the grandchildren's families. By contrast, the immigrant generation was too rooted in Italy to change. The children of immigrants were marginal; neither Italian nor American, they often vacillated between the different values. It was in this generation that conflict within the family became evident. Furthermore, the children of immigrants were more often beset with problems of adjustment, as is reflected by the rates of mental illness, crime, and delinquency.

Campisi's analysis applies to the Italian experience in Louisiana. The grandchildren of immigrants have Americanized; the children of immigrants to a lesser extent. The immigrant generation retained its Old World patriarchy. The father was and remained *pater potestas*. His word was the first, last, and often the only one to be heard. For the most part, the sons of immigrants modeled their behavior after their fathers' but with much less success. On the other hand, the grandson has more rigorously accommodated himself to the democratic principle while retaining some vestige of a more patriarchal style.

The transformation of the Italian family was largely ushered in by the acceptance of successful Italians. Other factors were also operating. An educational gap between men and women existed. This was created by the immigrant generation's refusal to send their sons to school. In 1900, very few teenage sons of immigrants were enrolled in school. Fathers normally expected sons to work on the farm or in the business. They saw no useful purpose for school. While daughters were also expected to help, they were sent to school more readily than sons. This differential treatment exacerbated the second generation's conflicts. Husbands and wives had different educational backgrounds. While the wife of the second generation could normally write, frequently her husband could not. Under these conditions, the patriarchal form was harder to maintain.

Perhaps the best indicator of the Italian family's transformation in Louisiana is the statistics on exogamy, marriage across ethnic lines. New Orleans marriage records indicate that in 1925 only about one-third of all Italian marriages involved exogamy. Males were more likely than females to marry non-Italians (40 percent of males compared to 28 percent of females). Post-World War II, endogamous marriages shrank to roughly 10 percent of all marriages, which meant nine out of every ten Italians married a non-Italian. At the same time, the difference between male and female exogamy disappeared. Given these facts, it is not surprising that the extended family ties weakened, the family's functions dwindled, the number of children per family declined, and the place of reverence occupied by the aged noticeably lessened. In short, the very success Italians in Louisiana enjoyed hastened the Americanization of the Italian family. The grandchildren of Italian immigrants, the third generation, like those of other immigrant groups, have begun to realize that the culture of the Old Country is all but gone. It cannot be recalled by parades. It cannot be conjured up by ritual feasts and celebrations. It is as far away from contemporary Louisiana and New Orleans as the routine round of plantation work or the tidy stalls of the neighborhood fruit peddler.

The family satisfied the Italians' hunger for security in both Italy and Louisiana. It was a place of refuge from the uncertainties and cruelties in the larger world. It was a loyal ally and an army of faithful soldiers ready to do battle to the death against its enemies. It was moorings, an anchor, and a safe harbor in troubled times. Because of it, the Italians of Louisiana improved their economic lot more rapidly than they otherwise would have. Furthermore, because Louisiana's Italian immigrants, more than Italian immigrants elsewhere in the country, came with intact family units, their material success was ahead of the eventual economic gains made in other colonies. Because family solidarity ensured success, it quickened the process of Americanization. While remnants of the Old Way can be found here and there in the somewhat higher stability of marriages and the slightly larger average family size among Italian-Americans, the essential form of the Italian family has been largely replaced by an American variant.

Carts like this, made to be pulled by donkeys, were once the main mode of transportation and cargo handling in Sicily. At the height of their popularity as working wagons about 1900, more than 5,000 such carts could be seen in the streets of Palermo. This ornately decorated cart is on display in the American-Italian Museum and Library, New Orleans. (Courtesy American-Italian Museum and Library, New Orleans)

Located at 17 Decatur Street in New Orleans in 1900, the Dell Orto Arturo Italian Bank served as the agent for shipping lines whose ports of call included Palermo, Messina, Naples, and Genoa. (Courtesy Sidney Mazerat III)

Vito Scorsone, a successful Italian immigrant businessman, owned this New Orleans barroom located at 2259 Dryades Street, at the corner of Philip Street. Scorsone, who became an American citizen in 1904, owned three other bars and several residential properties. This 1915 photograph shows Mr. Scorsone serving two black customers. (Courtesy Sidney Mazerat III)

Italian-Americans in Louisiana gravitated toward businesses in the food industry. They can still be found in large numbers in farming, wholesaling, and retailing operations. Francisco Antonio Cristadoro is thirty-eight years old in this 1904 photograph. He is standing beside his son, Anthony Joseph, in front of his grocery store in New Orleans. By 1920, nearly half the grocery stores in the city were owned by Italians. (Courtesy Sidney Mazerat III)

The Battistella Sea Food Company was located on Decatur Street in the French Quarter in the 1930s. (Courtesy American-Italian Museum and Library, New Orleans)

Anthony Serio, owner of the French Market Ice Company on 1020 Chartres Street in New Orleans, is standing beside his delivery truck in this ca.-1940 photograph. (Courtesy Salvadore Serio)

The mule-drawn Roman Candy wagon was an institution in New Orleans neighborhoods in the 1940s. Children were drawn to the sound of the bell as the wagon approached their homes, and the long, chewy toffee was a delicious treat. (Courtesy American-Italian Museum and Library, New Orleans)

In 1950, in a four-block area in the heart of downtown Hammond, twenty-three business establishments were owned by Italian-Americans. This grocery store was typical of the small family-owned shops that were strung out along Railroad Avenue. (Courtesy Center for Southeast Louisiana Studies, Southeastern Louisiana University)

This grocery store on Railroad Avenue in Hammond was also owned by an Italian-American merchant. (Courtesy Joe DeMarco)

The Santa Maria Produce truck belongs to an Italian-produce wholesale distributor in Shreveport. (Courtesy American-Italian Museum and Library, New Orleans)

Italian immigrants were originally recruited as field hands to pick strawberries in Tangipahoa Parish, Louisiana. Eventually, they bought farms of their own and were instrumental in revitalizing the state's strawberry industry. Joe DeMarco, pictured here, established an association of strawberry farmers and served as their broker, selling berries to markets in Chicago and elsewhere. (Courtesy Joe DeMarco [son of the man in the picture]).

During the season, buyers and farmers or their agents would assemble at the auction house, where the price of strawberries would be set each day that strawberries were shipped. Seated in this ca.-1930s picture like birds on a wire are Italian-American strawberry farmers waiting to find out what price their berries would bring. (Courtesy Joe DeMarco)

These farmers are loading their strawberries in an Illinois Central Railroad car in Hammond. These berries are headed to Chicago. Before refrigeration, the berries would be cooled by packing them with 100-pound blocks of ice for the eighteen- to twenty-four-hour train ride to Chicago. Refrigerated railroad cars improved the process immensely. (Courtesy Joe DeMarco)

Nearly every Italian immigrant farmer in Tangipahoa Parish, Louisiana had an outdoor oven in the yard close to the house. It was used mainly to bake homemade bread, but anything that required baking could be cooked in the oven. None of these original ovens exists today, although one was recently con-structed on Konkle Hill Road in Tangipahoa Parish and is in use. (Courtesy Center for Southeast Louisiana Studies, Southeastern Louisiana University)

Many communities throughout the United States continue to celebrate Columbus Day (second Monday in October) with a parade and other festivities. The day has special significance for Italian-Americans, since they proudly claim Christopher Columbus as one of their own. (Courtesy American-Italian Museum and Library, New Orleans)

Comprised principally of Italian musicians, this Independence, Louisiana band performed for civic and religious events and on other special occasions. It participated in Columbus Day and Independence Day celebrations, as well as the St. Joseph's Feast Day Parade. The band no longer exists, though it did perform in the 1990s at the annual Italian Festival in Independence. (Courtesy Center for Southeast Louisiana Studies, Southeastern Louisiana University)

The St. Joseph Parade continues to be a popular, annual event on the feast day of St. Joseph, March 17. Frequently it is associated with St. Joseph altars and with special chapels in honor of the saint. St. Joseph processionals are conducted all over the New Orleans metropolitan area, in Baton Rouge, Hammond, Independence, Donaldsonville, and elsewhere. (Courtesy Center for Southeast Louisiana Studies, Southeastern Louisiana University)

Though the Sicilian custom of the St. Joseph altar is observed by Italians in other parts of the United States, its most elaborate and enthusiastic expression is found among Italian-Americans in Louisiana, where churches, religious sodalities, and private citizens prepare altars of food in honor of St. Joseph for favors asked for and received. The food is used to feed the celebrants, especially the poor and hungry. This small family altar in 1940 was in the New Orleans home of Victoria Caruso. (Courtesy Anna Mae Caruso Frommeyer)

Nick LaRocca founded the Original Dixieland Jazz Band, one of the first jazz ensembles to attain national recognition. Louis Armstrong credits LaRocca for influencing his own musical style. This 1917 photograph, with LaRocca in the center, shows the band performing in New York City. (Courtesy American-Italian Museum and Library, New Orleans)

Societa Italiana di Mutua Beneficenza Cefalutana *was founded on August 10, 1887. It is one of the oldest Italian-American organizations in the United States. Salvadore Serio serves as its current president. This photograph was taken in 1937 in front of Italian Hall, 1020 Esplanade Avenue, New Orleans on the occasion of the fifty-year anniversary of the society.* (Courtesy Cefalutana Benevolent Society)

This wedding picture symbolizes the importance of the family to Italians. Nothing could challenge its solidarity in 1900. The immigrant family was indissoluble. In Italy, the state outlawed divorce; the church would not permit it; and it was taboo in the family itself. (Courtesy American-Italian Museum and Library, New Orleans)

Next in importance to the family among Italian immigrants was their religion. Indeed, it could be said that the two most important resources they brought to this country were their family system and their religious values. This first communion photograph, taken in 1927, depicts Marie Teresa Lodato of New Orleans. (Courtesy Salvadore Serio)

As a general rule, the Italian immigrants in Louisiana were suspicious of education and did not consider it essential for their children. Perhaps as a reaction to their parents, the first-generation Italian-Americans emphasized it for their children. This graduation picture, probably taken about 1920, represents an outstanding accomplishment for this young woman and her family.
(Courtesy American-Italian Museum and Library, New Orleans)

Like thousands of others, Salvadore Macaluso and Frances Arnone Macaluso were Italian immigrants who came to Louisiana in 1900 to build a better life in America. They were strawberry farmers in Tickfaw and left the world sixteen children, many more grandchildren, and a few good stories. (Courtesy Jerome J. Salomone)

Founded in 1834, the Societa Italiana di Mutua Beneficenza a Nuova Orleans *was the first Italian benevolent society established in the United States. This mausoleum in St. Louis Cemetery No. 1 in New Orleans is the final resting place for over a hundred of the society's members.* (Courtesy American-Italian Museum and Library, New Orleans)

CHAPTER SIX

Drama, Art, and Spectacle

Anthropologists have always insisted that culture is more than a mere assemblage of traits. It is integrated or unified in some fashion. Within societies, cultural traits coalesce around a central theme or related themes. The search for drama is a central theme that unifies and integrates Italian culture. It is no surprise that Louisiana's Sicilians have brought drama to their otherwise mundane pursuits on this soil.

While food and security are basic to life, everywhere people desire more. There is more to life than mere existence. At some point, we forsake life itself if we believe it is not worth living. Every society identifies the spiritual ingredients necessary to sustain life and defines the life that is worth living. In the case of the Italian immigrants to Louisiana, it was not sufficient to avoid starvation and gain a small measure of respect. More was required.

Italians in general and in Louisiana have elaborated upon these basic needs,[1] adding a desire to dramatize and embellish life. Their aspiration to add lace to the fabric of life is hard to miss. Through their art, cooking, religion, and folklore, Italian immigrants have made a consistent statement about the quality of life worth living. To them, life unadorned is unpalatable, unbearable, and unlivable. Their task is to take the ordinary and humdrum aspects of life and transform them into something larger than life. In everyday affairs, the individual hopes to realize the dramatic moment by the skillful use of exaggeration, gesticulation, vocalization, and touch. The techniques are simple, but their effect is rich.

Exaggeration sets the scene for a dramatic moment. For example, an Italian immigrant may refer to a high-school teacher as a *grand professore!* A religious person is a saint! One who acts without scruples is a devil! An immigrant rarely understates things. Through aggrandizement, an ordinary event becomes extraordinary. The stage is set for further drama.

One of the better known methods of stretching the truth is bragging, a habit that defies the virtues of honesty and humility. Both Italian men and women succumb to the great temptation of bragging. It is much more dramatic when a small victory can be made into a huge conquest. This has its limits, though, as the braggart must always be prepared to be outboasted, as is revealed in this humourous fifteenth-century story:

> A certain young man from Parma, who had been married only a few days, was at a window with his bride when he saw a beautiful young woman going to mass. He turned to his bride and said: "I want to make you laugh. See that young woman who is passing below our window? Well, before she got married, I was intimate with her several times; but she was so harebrained that she went and told her mother everything, and we narrowly missed a big scandal."
>
> Then, his wife replied: "What a fool, what a scatterbrain she is! I was intimate over a hundred times with the cart driver, with the manservant, and with our sharecropper, and I never told my mother a word about it!"[2]

Exaggeration is aided and abetted by animated body language, which often accompanies everyday conversation. Gestures are used for emphasis and to express or evoke feelings—joy, sorrow, despair, contempt, disgust—the full range of human emotions. It is said, not without some justification, "Tie their hands and Italians can't talk!" Gestures are assisted by a wide range of vocalizations. Loudness, pitch, and tempo are varied to heighten the dramatic moment. *"Bravissimo!"* shouted at the limits of the vocal chords while the hands are raised and vigorously shaken is an unambiguous sign of approval. Conversely, holding a quivering hand in the teeth in a kind of biting gesture while making a kicking movement is the absolute limit of disapproval. Usually this complex gesture is accompanied by words of contempt. Many gestures and vocalizations merely express excitement and amusement. A grandfather who reacts to a Western on TV by jumping up and down and saying, "Ai yi, you got 'im; shoot 'im," is much more amusing to a child than the script itself.

Finally, touching contributes to the dramatic moment. The immigrants not only exaggerated, gesticulated, and shouted; they constantly touched, embraced, squeezed, pinched, and slapped.

It is no mystery why Italians have come to be associated with the artistic spirit and the feelings or emotions inherent in aesthetic experiences. Indeed, painting, sculpture, music, opera—all the arts—are emphasized in Italian culture. Here are a people who are not only unafraid to show emotions, they are quite incapable of concealing them. Of course, there are differences among individuals and social classes in their response to high or low art, to drama or spectacle. We leave artistic evaluations to those qualified to make them. Instead, we choose to focus on the everyday aspects of culture among ordinary immigrants, not the *prominenti*. Reflecting their dramatic approach to life, what was fundamentally Italian about the immigrants of Louisiana was their cooking and eating habits, their rich oral traditions handed down for generations, and their use of leisure.

FOOD

We wish to compare the food values of contemporary Italian-Americans to those of the immigrants. Did Old World culinary

habits eventually die out? Or did they find novel expressions in
the United States?

It is said that in one part of Louisiana, people live to eat,
while in the other, they eat to live. In South Louisiana a
Catholic, largely French, culture existed at the time of immigration. The good life, including gustatory pleasures, was
already highly valued there. By contrast, in Anglo Saxon,
Protestant North Louisiana, a more Spartan and puritanical
approach to life was prevalent. Above Alexandria, a more utili-
tarian attitude toward cuisine was apparent, but that evidently
made no difference whatsoever to Italian immigrants who settled there. They did not adapt differently according to region.
In Shreveport and Monroe, as everywhere else in Louisiana, the
immigrants' dominating orientation toward the production,
distribution, and consumption of food eventually led them predominately into occupations related to it—production (truck
farming), wholesale, retail, export, and, of course, restaurants.

Food is so basic to human existence it hardly seems necessary to underscore its importance. But beyond sustenance, its
acquisition, preparation, and consumption reflect important
cultural values and tell us a great deal about the life of a people. Food simultaneously provides nourishment and social
interaction. It is acquired collectively. Its consumption is
almost always social, as one experiences family meals or community feasts. Because every society is at least minimally integrated, every part of that society will be affected by its systems
of food production, distribution, preparation, and consumption. As the proverb has it, "You are what you eat."
Furthermore, in Catholic societies food appears as a symbol of
the Divine presence. Therefore, an examination of the part
food plays in Italian culture is an examination of one of the
most fundamental concerns of that culture.

Louisiana's Italian immigrants' hunger and quest for bread[3]
and the significance they attached to it is a product of three
primary factors: experiences of food shortages in Italy, cultural

factors, and their experiences in Louisiana. Unlike most Americans, Italians of southern Italy and Sicily were frequently threatened by inadequate food supplies. Poor harvests and poverty had been endemic for centuries. Thus, they were conditioned to hoard and to endure adversity. They came to Louisiana with collective memories and fears of starvation. Those memories hardened their spirits to cope with shortage. In Italy, they developed both the psychological and practical skills to deal with deprivation. They learned how to entice crops even from poor land and wisely conserved what they produced as insurance against still leaner times. The Sicilians claimed they could subsist on bread and onions alone. For some immigrants, this bit of overstatement was not far from the truth. It expresses the confidence and determination to endure the hardest of times. Food shortages may not only produce patterns of hoarding and thrift but may also give rise to overindulgence under certain circumstances. The abundance of food is cause for celebration—celebration Italian style.

At another level, Louisiana's Italians have had their attitudes toward food shaped by values embedded in Italian culture. Major cultural themes direct attention to food, its preparation, and its consumption. It is lavishly prepared and richly garnished. There is a sublime enjoyment associated with its consumption. It would not be too far off the mark to suggest that Italians hope to achieve a state of gustatory ecstasy. However, there is no evidence that ostentation drives the love of fine food. Italians are not inclined to engage in "conspicuous consumption" as Thorstein Veblen, the originator of the phrase, understood it. Veblen was appalled by the *nouveau riche* who lavishly overspent to enhance their social standing. Italian immigrants would never even think of promoting their status by "dropping" names of expensive foods and drink they seldom consumed. Furthermore, not all meals were feasts; peasants do not have deep pockets. Still, their approach to food was very different from other groups. For example, an Anglo-American might have an egg poached, fried, or scrambled. An Italian will take the egg, combine it with an assortment of vegetables (perhaps leftovers), and cook the ensemble in olive oil and garlic to produce a colorful and tasty omelette.

What was conspicuous about the preparation and consumption of food in Italian households was its elaborate preparation and presentation, not to mention its delicious smells and tastes. An Italian housewife's kitchen of yesteryear, from all outward appearances, was the antithesis of efficiency. She was not a time-and-motion engineer whose ambition in preparing a meal was to minimize input and maximize output. Every pot and pan in the kitchen may well have been involved in making the main meal for the day from scratch, very likely using vegetables grown in the backyard. She probably used most of the day to accomplish her task.

The meal was elaborate also in the quantity of food set before those who were to eat it. To run out of food while "hungry hands" were reaching for more was the equivalent of a mortal sin. Naturally, when family finances did not permit it, less food was presented. Less expensive cuts of meat and cheaper vegetables might have been used. Besides, pasta was never costly. The trick was to cook meals that could be "stretched"—make the sauce a little thinner, add some potatoes to the gravy, or serve the main course over rice. This strategy guaranteed leftovers, which, of course, were used in subsequent meals or as side dishes.

Conspicuous as well, at least to the discerning eye, was the manner in which the table was set. This was particularly true of the main family meal in the evening, typically called supper. Middle-class Americans now call this dinner. The table was not considered set unless everything required for the meal was in place. Paramount in importance was bread! No meal was complete and no table was considered set without it—not ever. The absence of bread was unheard of; that would be a sign of some kind of culinary defect. Wine, when available, accompanied the main meal. All were invited to have a glass with their meal, children included. Butter, salt, pepper, and other condiments were set in place, preferably atop a linen tablecloth with matching napkins, although cotton would suffice. Paper towels were taboo, as well as plastic dinnerware, which by the grace of God had not yet been invented. Setting the table completely, without omitting anything thought to be necessary for the meal, was a sacred ritual required before the meal itself could be served. Contemporary Italian-American families, like all others, are likely to set the table in this fashion only on very special family occasions, or when they formally entertain guests at dinner. Not so for the old ones. As a matter of fact, it is an adjustment that more than a few Italian-American male traditionalists still find difficult to make.

One other element of conspicuousness associated with Italian cuisine is its aesthetic presentation. The Italian meal is intended to be a thing of beauty. No matter how inexpensive the ingredients or how impoverished or unlettered the family, every effort is made, usually with great success, to have the food look appetizing. The meat must be cut just so, the vegetables scalloped or diced a special way, or the fish presented attractively. Also, the meal must be colorful. In short, it must look beautiful and delicious, reflecting and reemphasizing the search for drama and spectacle in Italian life.

There is little patience and absolutely no palate for unadorned food. Each meal is prepared with intense concentration and attention to detail. The Italian housewife desires to achieve excellence that will bring her personal satisfaction and the accolades of others. Because her standards are so high, her goal is not always reached. When she does fail, she blames someone else, cursing her fate and often the saint who failed her. Many a saint's ear has been burned by an otherwise puritanical Italian housewife whose pasta was not *al dente* or whose *sugo* was not *perfetto*. However, her concept of failure can be peculiar. When an Italian housewife says her food is ruined, she means it is mediocre. On the other hand, when she has achieved perfection, she smacks her lips, cocks her head, and moves about the kitchen like a schoolgirl. It is impossible for her to conceal her delight. By contrast, when an American housewife says she has ruined the food, it is best for all concerned to hasten to the nearest restaurant.

These preoccupations with food are reflected in the persistence of St. Joseph Day celebrations among the Sicilians of Louisiana. Symbolizing both famine and feast, these celebrations artfully and dramatically use food as an object of prayer. Without food and shelter, the Holy Family goes from door to door seeking aid. After suffering two rejections, Joseph and Mary are welcomed into a house where a lavish feast has been prepared. Like Joseph and Mary, on St. Joseph Day, the poor of the city are invited to eat the food prepared for the St. Joseph altar. The foods prepared—today these preparations take weeks—often have symbolic meanings. The fish is an ancient symbol for the resurrected Christ. The bread, of course, is the symbol for the broken Body of Christ.

Food also represents unity. The "communion" of an Italian family is around the table. It is hard to convey the emotions the immigrants felt when surrounded by kinsmen at a table groaning under a mountain of artfully prepared food. The sight of the intense enjoyment of the food and the interaction of the family members brought great joy to everyone, especially to Mamma and Papa as they watched many children devour the bounty. The word *abbondanza,* abundance, may be uttered to capture the moment in memory.

Finally, experiences in Louisiana also had an enormous impact on how the immigrants produced, prepared, and consumed food. Louisiana's fertile soil, and the familiar Old World culture in South Louisiana, helped to shape the immigrants who arrived at the turn of the twentieth century. How traditions from Italy and new experiences in Louisiana played out is often interesting and unpredictable, as is illustrated by the Perrone family.

In 1908, Bartholomew Perrone, whose father operated a grocery business in Palermo, left Sicily to work in a relative's wholesale business in New Orleans. In 1910, he married Gaetana Bova, a New Orleans native; they had four children. In 1924, with the assistance of a partner, Bartholomew opened his own business on Decatur Street. Upon the partner's death, the Progress Grocery was owned exclusively by the Perrone family. Bartholomew's experience in sales in his relative's business, which required travel to neighboring states, served him well in his own business. The Progress Grocery specialized in imported products, especially Italian, French, Spanish, and Middle Eastern foods. The Perrone family (Perrone & Sons, Inc.) still operates the business at their new location at 512 Zenith Street in Metairie. Today, as in the 1920s, olive salad is one of their specialty items, which they ship around the world.

According to Andrew Montalbano, the Progress Grocery played its part in the evolution of the muffoletta sandwich. As the story goes, poor working men would go there to buy ham and cheese sandwiches for their lunch. Usually, the customers would ask the Perrones to add olive salad; thus the famous muffoletta sandwich was born. Since a number of Italian establishments are co-claimants to the invention, including the very credible Central Grocery claim, it is best to treat the muffoletta as a case of parallel evolution. Prof. Carlo Di Maio marvels at the wondrous taste of this culinary creation and also at its many spellings. He says, "I have seen it written as *muffoletto, muffoletta, maffaleto, maffaletta,* and only God knows how many other ways!"

Historians, if left to themselves, may well have only recorded the greatest achievements of the most celebrated and powerful figures, but thanks to ethnography, we have gradually come to appreciate also the significance of the common folk. It is only through the study of everyday culture that the story of the overwhelming majority of people can be told. Among them are the Italian immigrants to Louisiana. The items they chose to bring with them reveal what was meaningful in their culture. They brought what they thought was irreplaceable as they reconstructed their lives on foreign soil. In a figurative sense, this process was a transplantation.

The immigrant attempted to reassemble his life across the Atlantic just as he had lived it in Italy. We have previously claimed that this partially explains the emergence of ethnic colonies in American cities. It was through these intimate neighborhood relations as well as through family relations that the Italian culture was preserved and nourished. The ethnic colonies in America made the transition less disruptive than it might have been. They also served as bulwarks against the Americanizing forces and provided the immigrant with the sights, sounds, and smells of his native Italy. It was a piece of Italy reconstructed in America. Not only was Italian spoken, but specific regional and village dialects could be heard as well. Immigrants were drawn to their *paesani* and often segregated themselves according to village allegiances. Vecoli has described this provincialism along village lines in the case of the Italian settlement of Chicago.[4] Also, items that could not be made or grown in America were imported, like special foods or articles of clothing.

There are many examples of transplanted items, from cheese to statuary, but the most enduring of these have been the plants. All the plants we are aware of are edible, but they are best considered food for the soul. Four of these are considered here: the fava bean, yard-long bean, fennel, and *cocuzza*. The fava, *Vicia fava*, which figured so importantly in the Mediterranean region in ancient times, is the only Old World edible bean.[5] It is eaten all over Italy, usually raw after dinner like a fruit. Because of its large size, it is known also as the horsebean and was used as a staple that replaced bread during famines. Many immigrants kept the dried beans in their purses, the way four-leafed clovers or rabbit's feet are kept. They were considered "lucky" but also were associated with St. Joseph altars. The dried beans, like all the food at the St. Joseph Day celebrations, are blessed by the priest. Therefore, they are also considered "blessed" beans. Immigrants seem to be divided about whether they are primarily "lucky" or "blessed." The coexistence of pagan and Christian elements reflects the unclear boundaries between *Fortuna* and grace. As already stated, fava beans are not exclusively Italian or Sicilian, for they have been used throughout the Mediterranean world. The dried beans as well as the green pods are used either as food for man or fodder for animals.[6]

The yard-long bean, *Vigna sesquipedalis,* was probably first domesticated in Africa.[7] It was introduced into Asia and Europe through Egypt or Arabia. It reached the West Indies by the sixteenth century and North America by the seventeenth century. It is most widely cultivated in the Far East. Since it is a tropical plant, its range is limited. It grows well in the New Orleans area, but without plenty of attention, encouragement, and warm weather, it does not do well north of Lake Pontchartrain. The pod, which grows to thirty inches or more, is consumed. The dried beans are small, black, very hard, and usually not eaten. The plant is a climbing vine; it does well on fences, where it is still grown by New Orleanians of Sicilian ancestry as well as by those of Chinese ancestry. The plant is very productive, and with frequent rains, six to ten feet of fence covered with the vines will supply more beans than one family can consume. Unlike the fava bean, which can be purchased in season throughout the metropolitan area, the yard-long bean is rarely found in grocery stores.

Fennel, *Foeniculum vulgare,* grows wild in Sicily; it is the wild form that is most highly prized. This aromatic plant has always been used as a flavoring. The Italian immigrants prepared the sliced bulbs with vermicelli. The dish was simple but tasty and afforded a real Lenten treat. Fennel currently finds its most popular use among traditional Catholic Italian-Americans during Lent in a meatless tomato sauce served over pasta. To this day, it is the required sauce for the pasta served at a St. Joseph altar anywhere in Tangipahoa Parish. Fennel is not as popular today in Louisiana as it once was in Sicily, perhaps because the tastiest variants, the wild ones, do not grow in Louisiana. However, it is routinely sold in local grocery stores as anise.

The *cocuzza*, or *Tagenaria siceraria*, is a bottle gourd and is the only domesticated plant known to both the Old and New World. This long, often crooked, gourd probably originated in Africa.[8] It is one of the most ancient and widespread crops known. Besides its obvious use as a container, the fruit is also eaten. Sicilian immigrants sauté garlic, onions, and tomatoes in olive oil and add cut pieces of cooked *cocuzza*. Water is added to make a thin, slightly pink sauce. The tender shoots of the *cocuzza*, or *tenderumi*, are prepared after the fashion of fennel. The fruit of the *cocuzza* resembles a crooked baseball bat. When dried it is very hard. Its shape does not favor its use as a drinking gourd. The hardness of the dried *cocuzza* prompted Sicilians to draw a parallel between it and their stubborn mules, children, and spouses. A *testa cocuzza* is any hardheaded person; children and husbands most usually earn this label. It is ordinarily uttered with the word *testa* (head) emphasized while the fingers are drawn to a point toward the speaker and the arm moves up and down several times. We candidly admit to having been called the same by our mothers.

Although for the most part Sicilian cooking is simple compared to the more affluent regions of Italy, one can hardly miss its embellished quality, intended to lift the diner out of the ordinary, humdrum world. We are reminded of *Il Trionfo della Gola* (The Triumph of Gluttony), a cake filled with pistachio-flavored cream whose taste is not meant for a monk's palate.[9]

The persistent desire for similar delicacies in New Orleans has been satisfied by the Brocato family, whose Carrollton Avenue store is something of a landmark in the city. Their *biscotti, cannoli,* and a variety of other pastries, candies, and ice cream have delighted Italian and non-Italian palates for years. Some of their delicacies are also sold in supermarkets in the New Orleans metropolitan area and beyond.

The staples of bread and wine do for the Italians what they do for all the people of the Mediterranean Basin; they sustain the body. Each cultural group—Italian, Greek, French, Spanish, and others—has developed its own kinds. More than other food and drink, they are deeply connected with religious worship. Most obviously filling this role are the sacrificial bread and wine, which nourish the soul. But if these unite believers into the Body and Blood of Christ, the ordinary bread and wine taken daily in communion at the table can be said to unite the family.

In Louisiana, the making of bread and wine has all but died out. Today, there is very little wine making by Italians in the state. It had persisted until the 1940s but suffered the fate of many other unique cultural traits that were homogenized in post-World War II America. The great earthen jugs and funnels and other apparatuses of wine making have given way to the less time consuming task of selecting beer, wine, whiskey, and other hard liquors right off the grocer's shelf. However, in the first half of the twentieth century in Tangipahoa Parish, virtually every Italian strawberry farmer had a wine shed somewhere off from the house and barn. This housed the large wooden casks in which the juice from the strawberries was fermented to make strawberry wine. Nick Arnone of Tickfaw had four fifty-five-gallon barrels in his wine shed. Two were for fermenting and two for storing the finished wine. The wine was made from stemmed berries late in the growing season. Stemmed berries were usually sold at a greatly reduced price to canneries for processing into jams and jellies. The ones that were too small, spotted, or overripe could not be sold. Had they not been used to make wine, they would have gone to waste or been fed to the chickens. Besides, late-season berries were actually better for making wine because they were sweeter than those grown earlier.

The large, hard-crusted Italian bread garnished with sesame seeds can still be purchased in Louisiana supermarkets, but the Italian-American-run bakeries now actually sell more French bread. It is a curious fact that the best French bread in New Orleans is produced by Italian and German family bakeries. Italian bread is no longer baked in the traditional beehive-shaped oven. This outdoor brick oven was once a landmark of sorts in Louisiana and could be found almost everywhere Italian immigrants settled. It is all but gone now. However, in 1978 the *New Orleans Times-Picayune* ran a feature on it in its Sunday edition along with photographs of a surviving one in Independence.[10]

In 1990, Barbara Monteleone, a resident of Tangipahoa Parish, recorded her father's memoirs. Tony Monteleone, born in 1928, fondly remembered how special it was to be at his grandmother's house when she baked bread.

> Back then you didn't run to the corner store for bread; you made it at home. My grandmother would prepare the dough while my grandfather went outside to heat the oven. Their bread-baking oven, which was built of mud bricks, was located outside. My grandfather would fill the bottom of the oven with wood, light it, and wait for it to burn down, which took about two hours. While waiting for the oven to heat, my grandmother would place the dough in the baking pans made from olive-oil cans which had been cut in half. Money was not spent on luxury items such as baking pans.
>
> Once the oven was heated, the pans of dough would be placed inside on a board attached to a long stick and then removed once the bread was baked. Ten to twelve loaves of bread would be baked at the same time. The delicious aroma which filled the air near the oven and the beautiful golden-brown color of the bread are indelibly etched in my memory.[11]

In emphasizing distinctive Italian culture, it is easy to overlook the tremendous variation in cuisine, language, and customs found among the Louisiana immigrants. In Italy, each village was nearly self-contained, a small enclosed world set apart from other villages. Just as differences in dialect and customs endured, so have differences in cuisine. To cite but one example, in Trabia, a coastal town in Sicily, squid and other seafood were and remain an integral part of the diet. Farther inland, such items were abhorred. Also, a considerable Saracen (Arab) influence on cuisine existed and was transported to Louisiana. For example, cream-of-wheat dishes prepared with special Arab cooking ware are still eaten by families who hailed from the coastal villages of eastern Sicily.

FOLKLORE

One aspect of Italian culture that has largely disappeared among the Italians of Louisiana is oral tradition or folklore: proverbs, expressions, and stories. For the illiterate immigrants, the oral tradition distilled for them the essential elements of their culture. More than the written word, the spoken word utilizes a script, acting, and sound effects. Extend the script, add music, and you have opera. There is something operatic about the lively conversation of Italians. Interestingly, many oral traditions contain, if not songs, at least musical sound effects. Unlike opera, literature, and other celebrated art forms, oral traditions often go unnoticed and, therefore, unappreciated.

Immigrants who routinely use folklore are at a loss when asked to give an example. The reason is that these "packages of culture" are usually evoked only during a real-life experience. Thus, a father might say to a son who is frequently found in unsavory company, "He who consorts with cripples will end up limping." It takes the appropriate experience to awaken the memory. Furthermore, because the oral tradition is not written, there frequently exists multiple versions of the same proverb, expression, or story. Collectively, folklore represents the wisdom of the common people. It contains their science, religion, art, and literature.

In addition to using proverbs, the Italian immigrant would intersperse in everyday conversation terse phrases or single words that convey a strong emotion. Just as an English speaker might say, "My God!" or the French say, "Mon Dieu!" the Italian immigrant might say *"Segnuite de sconzo"* (the Lord deliver us)! But many phrases are truncated. *"Segnuite"* is sufficient to convey the proper emotion. Some sayings require choreography. For example, *testa* merely means head. Depending on the context and the accompanying gestures, it could either mean "You are crazy" or "You have a hard head." Unlike proverbs, one rarely hears these expressed in English. To express some tragic event, nothing can replace clapping the palm of the hand once against the forehead while loudly exclaiming, *"Madre mia!"*

Another vehicle of folk wisdom is the short story recounting an episode in the life of the legendary Sicilian buffoon, *Giufà (Juffà).*[12]

First Story

One day a friend visited the house of *Juffà.* "I like your house and want to buy it."

Juffà said, "No, I do not want to sell it." The friend persisted and *Juffà,* realizing his friend would not accept a refusal, agreed to sell. "I will sell it to you under one condition."

"Name it."

"Allow me to put a nail in the back door so that I might have a place to hang my coat."

"Sure, by all means," answered the friend.

Some weeks passed and the friend heard a knock at his door at nine o'clock one night. He asks, "Who is it?"

"It's me, *Juffà.* I want to hang up my coat."

"Okay, come in."

The next night *Juffà* knocked at the door at twelve o'clock. The nightly visitation was repeated several times until the friend could stand no more and sold the house back to *Juffà* at a considerable loss.

Second Story

In a small village in rural Sicily that depended on the vegetables grown for its livelihood, several bandits had been robbing the poor villagers blind by hauling off their artichokes before they could get them to market. The villagers asked *Juffà* to catch the bandits and retrieve the vegetables. Early one morning, *Juffà* saw the bandits stealing the artichokes and followed them to a mountainous region where they were dividing the spoils. At this time, *Juffà* had to urinate. The stream of urine fell on a rock and splattered in every direction. Amused by this sight, *Juffà* spoke to the splashes of urine out loud: "You go this way; you go that way." The bandits, believing they were surrounded, fled, leaving the artichokes behind.

The *Juffà* stories and others like them were intended to amuse and instruct. The proverb serves similar functions, but because of its brevity, flexibility, and frequency of use, the proverb best expresses the Italian culture of the *contadini*.

So as to give the reader a better understanding of the meaning associated with Italian proverbs, we place them in the context in which they might appropriately be used. Moreover, we have included some sayings that are exclusively a part of the oral tradition, as well as others that have been formally recorded. The selection of examples presented is obviously arbitrary. There is no claim for exhaustiveness. They simply highlight the cultural aspects often stressed in proverbs. Kinship, traditions, food and eating, practical advice for a virtuous life, and amusement or instruction are important concerns in Italian culture.

Marriage and the family are crucial in every society, but in Sicily they are said to be more essential than elsewhere. To stress the magnitude of the work of the family in protecting and rearing children, one might say: "Cloth is judged by its texture and a girl by her upbringing (WO)."[13] When family loyalty needs to be encouraged, no more cogent comment can be found than: "Defend your kin right or wrong (O)." Of course, one can never be reminded too often of the sanctity and permanence of marriage. Those experiencing either happiness or sadness in marriage are reminded that: "Marriages and bishops are made in heaven (WO)."

Family loyalty must be nourished through respect, particularly for one's elders. "Be a saint and be rich (O)" is not a proverb but a greeting that a nephew might give to an uncle. Wherever there is love and respect for family members there is home. To encourage this sentiment among the young, the elders might say: "Blessed is the bird that makes its nest where it was born (WO)." "There is no place like home!" exclaimed Dorothy in *The Wizard of Oz*. A Sicilian might echo the sentiment and say: "Every bird to its own nest (WO)" or "Home of mine, mother of mine (WO)."

Despite the high regard Sicilians have for marriage and the family, in Sicily as elsewhere the battle of the sexes continues. A very perplexed male when confronted with the inscrutable ways of a woman would say: "Women are long in the hair and short in the brains (WO)." By contrast, a mother might caution her daughter: "Keep away from husbands and mules (WO)." Nearly every society sounds a cautionary note regarding in-laws. "No girl gets on well with her mother-in-law (WO)."

In Sicily, one takes the advice of elders, the guardians of tradition. It is the elders' responsibility to remind the young that: "He who changes the old for the new changes for the worse (WO)," and one might add: "Be satisfied to do what your father did, or you'll come to no good (WO)."

While Sicilians are quick to give advice, like most people they find it difficult to follow their own. Who could disagree with: "The servant should be patient, the master prudent (WO)"? And yet numerous proverbs reveal the impatience Sicilians feel with slow-moving events. "By that time, either the donkey dies or the owner (O)" expresses impatience with slow business deals, in this case, the proposed purchase of a draft animal. "Long engagements turn into snakes (WO)" is used when the family longs to have a proposed marriage finalized.

There is much practical advice given with regard to food. The Sicilian believes: "An empty sack can't stand up (O)." Eating good food not only makes you healthy but beautiful:

"Little dove, little dove, it's your beak that makes you beautiful (O)." Always concerned about having enough to eat and drink, Sicilians recommend conservation: "Economize when your vat of wine is full; when you see the bottom it is too late to save (O)."

Advice about choosing a line of work seems to have been a priority among Sicilians who immigrated to Louisiana: "Do the job you know; if you don't make money, at least you'll make a living (WO)." "If you don't know your trade you should close your shop (WO)." "He who has innate ability will not fail in his undertakings (O)."

We must confess that our personal favorites are those proverbs intended to amuse. Oftentimes they are as honest as they are unkind, as the following proverb illustrates: "Ugly, ugly, don't wash your face; you'll only dirty the water (O)." There is nothing quite like laughter or dancing for lightening life's burdens. Sicilians believe that you can dance and sing your blues away. "When you are sad, dance and sing (O)."

It is fitting to terminate this discussion on folklore with a passage from Giovanni Verga's *House by the Meddlar Tree,* in which so many of the proverbs and other oral traditions of Sicily of the nineteenth century can be found. Old Master, N'toni (Verga's character who embodied tradition), remembered many sayings he had learned from his elders, because, as he said, "what the old folks said was always true."[14]

LEISURE

Leisure was not a familiar term to Italian immigrants because they had precious little of it to begin with, and when they were at leisure, it was hidden from them in plain view. In the cities, immigrants, as well as everyone else, worked long, arduous hours. The ten-twelve-hour day and six-day work week were commonplace for laborers. The merchants' workday was even longer. Out in the country, farmers were no less likely to work long hours, especially during planting and harvesting seasons. As a consequence of their extraordinarily heavy occupational burdens, when Italian immigrants were not physically engaged in their work, they were resting, which essentially meant they were regaining their strength for the next day's work. Such periods of rest were the necessary side effects of manual labor in America in the early twentieth century. There was nothing discretionary about it. That hardly could be called leisure. In contemporary America leisure means discretionary time off from work that frequently is used as a diversion, perhaps a vacation, from gainful employment. At the time of the immigrants' arrival in the United States, that alternative to work was available only to the affluent, who represented a very small fraction of Americans. Italian immigrants were not initially numbered among them.

When immigrants were not on the job and were rested, they used their spare time to visit their relatives. Visitation was by far their most popular pastime. It was inexpensive, which suited their meager pocketbooks, and it reinforced the obligations of familism. Visitation was not thought of as some discretionary, leisurely activity. That is why it was hidden from them in plain view.

Sundays were occupied by Mass in the mornings, at least for mothers and children, followed by the midday meal with grandparents. This ritual was repeated Sunday after Sunday, provided distances were not too far. Where the drive was rather long, weekly visitation was replaced by monthly visits. Sometimes family visitations among immigrants took place away from the family home, such as in a public park.

Leisure for the immigrants in Louisiana was different from what it had been in the Old Country. The promenade on Sunday in the *piazza*, the village square, with its conversation and the display of newly acquired clothes, was replaced in Louisiana by visits to the homes of friends and relatives. In Sicily such visitation, particularly if it involved elaborate preparation of food and entertainment, was rare among the *contadini*. In Louisiana, among the more fortunate where money, food, and possessions became gradually more abundant, Sunday afternoon visits sometimes involved elaborate preparations of foods and drink, lawn decorations, and the hiring of large bands. A family whose parents came from Trabia reported that such parties were common. On Sundays, their lawn was festooned with flowers and other decorations, a band was hired for the occasion, and the food that had been prepared the preceding day was served. Music, dancing, eating, and games went on the entire day and well into the night.

In New Orleans, where space has always been a precious commodity, the citizens could take their leisure at one of the city's resorts. In the late nineteenth and early twentieth centuries, New Orleanians could find their amusement at West End Park, Milneburg, and Spanish Fort. They flocked to these areas on Sunday afternoons, and in the crowd one could find the immigrants and their children. The immigrants were particularly attracted to those areas that supplied music. Many an immigrant family and later the second generation would go to Spanish Fort to listen to marching and concert bands, crowding around the pavilion and enjoying the lake's breezes.

Today, Spanish Fort is a historic site at the mouth of Bayou St. John. The once-popular resort area with its hotel and restaurants is now part of an upper-middle-class lakefront residential area. More of Milneburg and West End have survived. Greatly altered over time, West End today is a cluster of restaurants, a fishing pier, and a yacht harbor. The bandstand and concerts of West End, as well as the New Orleans and Carrollton Railroad that connected it with downtown, are now things of the past.

Milneburg survived in a sense as Lake Pontchartrain Amusement Park until the 1970s. The Pontchartrain Railroad that ran along Elysian Fields Avenue and whose terminus was Milneburg was the first railroad constructed in the city. In 1932, after 101 years, it ceased operation.

What most attracted the Italian-Americans to these resorts, and other amusement areas like the one in City Park, was undoubtedly the band concerts, although the food and open air were also appreciated.

Another entertainment for the immigrants was the friendship, food, and music supplied by Italian organizations. Each had its own band and somewhat parochial tastes in music. For example, the Roma Band played for the Italian Society, and the association of *Contessa Entellina* enjoyed the music of the *Abreshe*.[15] Marches and classical music were the most frequently heard sounds. Occasionally non-Italian bands would supply the music at the associations' socials.

In many immigrant homes, whether in the stately residences of the successful merchants or the more modest houses of the street vendors, a Caruso recording could be heard. No doubt Italian immigrants were among the patrons of the French Opera House, particularly when famous Italian opera singers such as Andelina Patti performed there. The Italian school of music met with great success in New Orleans. The works of Verdi, Rossini, Bellini, Donizetti, and, somewhat later, Mascagni, Puccini, Leoncavallo, and Ponchielli figured prominently among the offerings at the French Opera House. Elsewhere in the United States, Italian opera dominated the scene from the earliest.

"Things must change so they can remain the same" is an Italian proverb whose truth is confirmed by the musical tastes of the Italians of Louisiana. One thing is certain in the world in which we live today: the music of young men and women is not the music of their parents! That was true also of the Italian immigrants and their children in the 1870s. The popularity of opera waned in the twentieth century as tastes in music were transformed. New expressions of music and new styles emerged, and the Italians of Louisiana were as much a part of the new traditions as they were of the old. Considering the unique musical heritage of New Orleans and the Italians' love of music, it is not surprising that the sons of immigrants would contribute to the making of jazz, that very special, uniquely American art form.

Joy Jackson, a respected chronicler of New Orleans, speaking of the relationship between jazz and Italian musicians, said:

> As the nineteenth century gave way to the twentieth, classical music began to give way, in some Italian hearts, to the new music, jazz. Younger musicians of Italian descent, whose fathers may have played in local orchestras and brass bands, now turned to the syncopated music which was beginning to be accepted as respectable. It had started in local back street dives and bordellos. By 1919, a popular composer of New Orleans, Joseph Davilla, wrote 'The Axeman's Jazz,' which was a spoof of the axe murders that had occurred in the city in the early twentieth century. . . . This song was a piece of local folklore set to a jazz beat. As jazz became popular among the white population, some young Italian-American musicians on the local scene chose it as the focus of their musical careers. They included Irving Fazola, Louis and Leon Prima, Sharkey Bonana, and Tony Almerico. Dixieland Jazz drew not only from the heritage of black musicians, but from the classical training and ethnic musical background of first and second-generation Italian-Americans growing up in New Orleans. Their contribution to American jazz was profound in its richness and virtuosity.[16]

The role Italians played in the emergence of jazz in New Orleans is well known among musicians and jazz afficionados but was unfortunately ignored by the city when it commissioned the mural over the inside main entrance to the Louis Armstrong New Orleans International Airport. Among the nearly two dozen musicians pictured in the mural, not one of them is of Italian descent. Such an omission is more than an oversight; it is an affront to the entire Italian-American community.

Another Italian-American musician is equally deserving of praise for his musical talents and contributions to jazz. The evidence is increasing in support of the opinion that Dominic ("Nick") James LaRocca has not gotten the credit he deserves from jazz historians. There still is controversy surrounding the invention of jazz and the role played by LaRocca's Original

Dixieland Jazz Band. But "even if the Original Dixieland Jazz Band did not invent jazz, then at least through their immense success on phonograph records, they became a prime influencer of its subsequent style."[17] Louis Armstrong had no hesitation in saying that LaRocca's instrumentation in songs like "Tiger Rag" and "Livery Stable Blues" was different from anything that had preceded it. LaRocca, born in New Orleans in 1889, became a musician against his father's wishes. His father, Girolamo LaRocca, an immigrant shoemaker and amateur cornetist from Salaparuta, Sicily, wanted Nick to become a doctor. "All musicians are bums!" declared Girolamo. He even destroyed several of Nick's cornets in the hope that Nick might have a change of heart.[18]

It is easy to see why a love affair blossomed between the immigrants and the city, at least that part of the city that cultivated a love of good food, music, and good times. To a city that thrived on the good life, to a city "that care forgot," came a people predisposed to enjoy it.

In addition to the Sunday break from the work routine, the numerous public celebrations of both a secular and sacred nature have always been well attended by the Italian population of Louisiana. Saints Joseph, Rosalie, and Anthony of Padua have been honored on their feast days not only in churches but also in parades. Important secular events, like Italy's Independence Day, have been similarly commemorated. In most of these public celebrations, food, music, and games were standard fare.

A discussion of leisure, particularly one that deals with the ordinary people, would not be complete without mentioning card games. Though they have largely fallen into disuse today, *Briscola, Scopone,* and *Tresetta* were once enormously popular among Italian immigrants. The games themselves are not nearly as interesting as the way in which they were played. The drama, emotions, and lively conversations attendant to these games of chance defy adequate description. Even when there were only pennies at stake (the games were always played for money), the atmosphere around the table would be loaded with intense excitement. The size of the pot and the stakes did not determine the level of emotions. It was not uncommon to see a man curse his cruel fate after losing a thirty-cent pot.

Whether or not these games survive is less important than the cultural trait that is their source. The love of games of chance, to be pitted against fortune and the drama that it brings, is the essential element. Even among those Italian-Americans who neither remember nor care about these particular games, one can see the attraction to games of chance. And in New Orleans, with its Creoles, themselves lovers of games of chance, the Italian immigrant found almost limitless opportunities to satisfy his "appointment with the gods." Neighborhood card games, horseracing, casinos, sports pools, lotto, keno, bingo, and, in the nineteenth century, even a state lottery were but just some of the ways the Italians satisfied their cravings for games of chance, and in the process embellished the cultural ideal, the quest for good times, for which New Orleans and South Louisiana are famous.

In the immigrants' high and low arts, the dramatic ideal is hard to miss. It can be discerned in their organizations as well. These were formed for mutual aid, civic, political, religious, philanthropic, and social reasons, but they served other functions too. St. Joseph Day, Italy's independence, and political events called for theatrical parades put on by these organizations. We recognize this aspect of the associations but wish to call attention to their many other purposes.

The oldest Italian organization in Louisiana, and one of the oldest in the nation, the Italian Mutual Benevolent Society, was established on July 4, 1843.[19] It was organized to render assistance to incapacitated members and to widows and orphans of deceased members. Before the Civil War, it met semiannually at 61 Common Street in New Orleans. By 1857, the local Italian architect Pietro Gualdi had completed the society's burial monument. The officers for 1870 included Angelo Lanata, Angelo Socola, Efficio Trois, and J. B. Solari.[20] Lanata, Socola, and Solari were prominent New Orleans importers.

Another Italian organization, known as the second "Italian Society" in the city, was called *Tiro-al-Bersaglio* (Hit-the-Target). It was chartered in 1869 and was both a mutual aid society and a marksmen's club.[21]

In addition, a number of Italian immigrants joined Masonic lodges previously established by the French, Spanish, and Americans. In 1865, Italian Freemasons organized their own lodge and called it *Dante Alighieri*. It included a number of non-Italians.[22] Later in the century, the massive influx of largely poor, uneducated, and unskilled immigrants from southern Italy and Sicily increased the need for benevolent and social organizations. The associations that were subsequently established typically were named after the villages from which their members emigrated. Contessa Entellina and Cefalu are examples. The *Cefalutana* Benevolent Society concurrently celebrated its 108th anniversary and the feast of Jesus the Savior on August 6, 1995. The organization continues its long history under the leadership of its current president, Salvadore Serio.

By the beginning of the twentieth century, so many Italian religious, social, and cultural associations had been chartered that on July 1, 1912, the Baldwin Mansion at 1020 Esplanade Avenue, New Orleans, was purchased by the Italian Hall Association for $13,000. Subsequently, the *Unione Italiana* was organized to serve as a common meeting place for member organizations. During its more than fifty years of service, the Italian Hall was a symbol of unity in the New Orleans Italian colony. By the 1920s, there was an umbrella organization consisting of association presidents.

The building itself has had a long and interesting history. The property dates to the Louisiana Purchase. In the early nineteenth century, it was owned by the city but passed into the hands of a succession of private owners. Unfortunately, it remained empty until the consular agent of the Netherlands purchased it and commissioned architect James Gallier, Sr., to design an elegant home on the property. Thereafter, ownership passed through a succession of private hands, including political boss John Slidell and Civil War general P. G. T. Beauregard. In the late nineteenth century it was known as the Baldwin Mansion.[23] The main building was Italianate style and could be entered from Esplanade Avenue in the front or through a carriageway on Barracks Street. The first floor had two conference rooms. There was a courtyard, which had a mosaic dance floor. There were pool tables and a bar. Other buildings surrounded the courtyard, including a kitchen, dining room, classrooms, and a well-equipped gym. Stairs at the end of the courtyard led to the sleeping quarters and other rooms on the second floor. From the second-floor gallery one could see the courtyard. On the walls of the courtyard was a mural of a Sicilian village painted by Gaetano Montana, who also managed the hall from the early 1930s until his death in 1957.[24]

Throughout the early twentieth century, the organizations continued to play multiple roles. Mutual aid, burial, religious, social, philanthropic, and cultural goals were pursued not only in New Orleans but also elsewhere in the state. For example, Shreveport's Moderna Club was primarily a mutual aid society but served religious, social, and civic purposes as well.[25]

By the first decade of the twentieth century, the Italian organizations responded to the new wave of antiforeign sentiment sweeping America. During this period, they showcased their Americanization role, training immigrants for citizenship.[26] This is, of course, an extension of the mutual aid function. During the 1920s, it was not only a nice thing to do for one's fellow countrymen, it had become a matter of survival for Italians to spotlight their loyalty to America. Not only lessons in Americanism but American politics had become part of the new curriculum that immigrants were learning at their association meetings.[27] During this period the Italian Political Club was formed and served to politically socialize immigrants.[28]

By the 1940s, Italian organizations were depicted by the local press as organizations that sponsored religious celebrations. By the 1950s, fewer children and grandchildren of immigrants saw reason to join. In 1957, *La Voce Coloniale,* the local Italian newspaper, had ceased publication.[29] There was an eclipse of ethnicity after World War II. Italian-Americans, like Americans generally, were busy making and benefiting from the economic boom of the period. But because of the civil rights movement in the 1960s, by the 1970s, a new wind of ethnicity was blowing across America.[30]

The nationwide resurgence in Italian-Americans' concern for their ancestral heritage resulted in an enormous increase in the number of local, state, regional, and eventually national organizations. The spread of umbrella organizations was especially rapid. Associations of associations were formed.

In the 1970s, Joseph Maselli, a prominent New Orleans Italian-American businessman, used the umbrella organizing principle for the numerous Italian-American associations in the area. The organization he founded is now known as the American Italian Federation of the Southeast[31] and it covers Georgia to Texas. The organization spearheaded the construction of the *Piazza d'Italia* and the American-Italian Museum and Library on South Peters Street in New Orleans. Numerous able men and women worked on the these projects, chiefly through the Renaissance Foundation. However, Maselli was always there to organize, promote, and clear the path around obstacles. Also, in 1973, he began publishing the *Italian-American Digest* at his own expense. By the 1980s, he was holding leadership positions in a variety of national organizations.

Joseph Maselli and other leaders of the Italian-American community represent a new breed of ethnics created in the complex arena of American pluralism. They organize Columbus Day parades, St. Joseph altars, marching clubs, and other projects for business, social, cultural, and philanthropic reasons. At the same time, they cast a cautious eye on the claims of other special-interest groups. Always ready to announce their accomplishments, they are eager for Italian-Americans to get their share of the credit for what America is becoming. If one eye is on cultural pride, celebrations, and good times, the other is inspecting the American landscape for evidence of discrimination directed at Italian-Americans. If all the marching, celebrating, and cultural embellishment is evidence of their dramatic spirit, then contemporary Italian-Americans' readiness to rout anti-Italian sentiment reflects their enduring hunger for respect.

To be sure, the leadership of the new Italian-Americans has its detractors as well as its supporters inside and outside the Italian-American community. Those who preside over the boards, committees, and associations and who are charged with carrying their co-ethnics into the twenty-first century have floundered. They have been accused of touting the Italian-American cause with their words but not with deeds. At times, so the charges go, they have been roosters wasting their efforts in staging spectacle and show.[32] They have been shadow without substance. They have been quick to talk about Italian-American accomplishments and to promote festivals but slow to foster education and research. Their critics fail to mention the real accomplishments of the new breed of Italian-Americans who have emerged since the 1970s: vigilance and action against old and new forms of prejudice, establishment of museums and libraries to further research, and promotion of education and philanthropy through Italian-American foundations. While the *Piazza d'Italia* continues to have its critics, even they should agree that the museum and library on South Peters Street, local support for scholarships, and aid to victims of disaster are noteworthy causes. Nevertheless, the critics raise a good point. The love of drama and spectacle can overshadow and obscure more meaningful goals. Does what has always been an important cultural value run the risk of being a flaw?

CHAPTER SEVEN

Hunger for Justice

A specter is haunting Italian-Americans—the specter of *the Mafia*. All the manufacturers of American public opinion have entered into an unholy alliance to promote this ghost: journalists and their editors, politicians and their governments, writers and their publishers, filmmakers and their producers. Sometimes separately, sometimes in concert, they have succeeded in creating a *mafia* of the mind in our national consciousness.[1] It has taken a while for this to happen, and the route to this vision of Italian criminality has been circuitous. But despite all the evidence to the contrary, when it is convenient, the stubborn alleged connection between Italians and crime is called forth. It is not so bad that some Italian-Americans are said to have been gangsters, for some of them were; and some still are. What is both wrong and wrongheaded is the implication that all Italians are inherently inclined toward lawlessness, especially successful Italian-Americans, who "got that way" because of presumed *Mafia* connections.[2] This incorrect and unjust public perception has been promoted by those (Italians among them) seeking personal gain at the expense of law-abiding Italians in America. Nurtured by the alien scare, which gained momentum in the early 1900s, fear and hatred of the Italians was compounded by their association with organized crime in

America. The resulting animosity gave rise to the discriminatory legislation of 1924 that severely curtailed Italian and southern Mediterranean immigration to the United States.[3]

John F. Kennedy, who could turn a phrase better than most of our presidents, warned us that "the great enemy of the truth is very often not the deliberate, contrived, dishonest lie, but the persistent, persuasive, unrealistic myth." The association of Italians and organized crime feeds on the kernel of truth embedded in the myth. The truth is, some Italians have justifiably gained an unwholesome reputation for their involvement and leadership in gangland crime. The larger truth is that Italian-Americans did not invent gangland crime nor did they ever monopolize it. And the even larger truth is, only a minuscule percentage of Italian-Americans ever had any association with organized crime or any other kind of crime. The great majority have lived law-abiding lives. The reputations of the innocent have been unjustly tarnished by the persistence of the myth. A curious and perceptive Italian-American from Brooklyn raised a telling question when he remarked, "Sicilians have gone all over the world, Argentina, Brazil, Australia, all over and the only place where the *mafia* developed was here in America. Can you tell me why?"[4]

The origin of the gangster label is well known. In the late nineteenth century, Sicily bore the dubious distinction of having the highest homicide rate in Europe. At least since the seventeenth century, organized brigands circumvented legitimate but corrupt authorities and passed out their own brand of justice. In the nineteenth century, violence and lawlessness were deeply rooted in Sicilian and southern Italian society. They were outgrowths of political and social injustices. The *contadini*'s response to centuries of injustice was an abiding, inexhaustible desire for justice in the New World. In America, it was precisely the immigrants' longing for justice that helped perpetuate the criminal label assigned to them, which, in turn, made their adjustment to America problematic.

In chapter 5, we saw how the family protected the *contadini* from a capricious and unjust world. Callous rulers, arrogant barons, corrupt police: all helped to spawn that unique variation on the tight-knit family that is found in southern Italy and Sicily. That same family system also created the traditions of violence and lawlessness in the area. Specifically, these traditions were: acceptance of violence as a solution to injustice, suspicion of all authorities, reliance on the family to protect, avenge, and advance the individual, and the elaboration of that form of provincialism the Italians call *campanilismo*. These beliefs and values represent the hunger for justice—a hunger that springs from the well of justice denied. The *contadini* longed for justice but found none, neither in the courts, because they were instruments of foreign rulers in league with the aristocracy, nor from the police, because they were often agents of the barons. In this context, organized bands of brigands sprang up and administered their own brand of justice. Even when their hostility was directed at the police or the noblemen, the *Mafiosi* were never Robin Hoods. They quickly discovered the vulnerability of the peasants. To achieve their ends, they used intimidation, extortion, and murder. In the end, the *contadini* had one more reason to expect violence and injustice.

In this milieu, the *contadini*'s suspicion of authorities became deep rooted. Their reliance on the family nearly became pathological, their mistrust of strangers a barrier to real community progress. Their acceptance of violence as an instrument to combat violence became counterproductive, as the vendetta produced self-defeating results. These patterns would prove to be the main obstacles to adjustment in America.

It is impossible to deny that Americans looked upon Italians as a criminally inclined people, since the label persists. Over a century of living in America has not erased it. One case in point is the Italian-American Anti-Defamation League's attempt in the 1970s to force the U.S. government to cease using infamous labels: *Mafia* and *Cosa Nostra*. The league met with success in its first year of activity. It pressured the Nixon administration, the National Broadcasting Company, and the *New York Times* to refrain from using offensive labels. Unfortunately, at the second Unity Day Rally, Joseph Colombo, a reputed *Mafia* boss and organizer of the league, was shot. The incident had all the markings of a gangland slaying. The whole episode served only to confirm the gangster label in the public's mind.

The problems associated with immigrants in America—mental illness, poverty, and crime—have been viewed as byproducts of immigration and adjustment difficulties. A number of explanations have been proffered. Everett V. Stonequist has described the immigrants' problem as marginality. He argues that "the individual who through migration, education, marriage, or some other influences leaves one social group or culture without making a satisfactory adjustment to another finds himself on the margin of each but a member of neither."[5] This dilemma of occupying two worlds is the cause of the immigrant's problems. Even when he is willing to discard the ways of his ancestors, he is never assured of acceptance in America. Neither world has his absolute loyalty. No place can he be himself.

A somewhat different but related picture of the immigrant's problems has been described as an uprootedness.[6] Forced by political, economic, or religious difficulties to emigrate, the European immigrant of the late nineteenth and early twentieth centuries faced problems in American cities for which his peasant origins had not prepared him. Oscar Handlin, who advocates this position, sees the European immigrant in America as one who has been uprooted from a tight-knit peasant village and thrown into a chaotic, dirty, crowded, impersonal American city.

Handlin argues that the harmonious village life immigrants enjoyed in the Old Country was destroyed in urban America. This assumption has been soundly criticized by Rudolph Vecoli on a number of accounts.[7] Vecoli correctly argues that peasant villages in southern Italy and Sicily were not small country hamlets but "rural cities." Like cities, most had large populations and were socially complex. In some cases the populations reached twenty to thirty thousand. The inhabitants lived in "town" and walked to and from their fields each day. Furthermore, each village contained not only the *contadini* but the landed aristocracy, professionals, shopkeepers, craftsmen, and artisans. The peasants, no doubt, could and often did find something beautiful and meaningful in the seasonal cycle of planting and harvesting, but their enduring ambition was to rise above their peasant state. They wanted their sons freed from the drudgery of work in the fields and their daughters married to someone of higher status.

According to Vecoli, the Italian often emigrated with others from his *paese*, thereby preserving not only the customs of his village but the rivalries and feuds as well.[8] Many an Old World feud would be fought on the streets of American cities.

Vecoli's description of peasant society is far different from Handlin's assumption. The community solidarity and neighborliness of Old World Europeans (including Italians) depicted by Handlin contrasts sharply with the envy and hatred described by Vecoli. The *contadini*'s hatred of the aristocracy and the latter's exploitation of the *contadini* along with the general rivalries, feuds, and homicides described by Vecoli are hardly consonant with the spirit of village cooperation and the *esprit de corps* portrayed by Handlin.

In summary, the problems the immigrant faced in Louisiana have been explained in the literature as the transplantation of pathological Old World traditions, including distrust of the law and acceptance of violence; marginality, which is a byproduct of a desire to be accepted in America; and uprootedness caused by immigration and urban life.

Marginality was less destructive in Louisiana than elsewhere in America, particularly for the South Louisiana Italian immigrant, who found many similarities between his old and new cultures. Marginality was chiefly a problem for the children of those immigrants and was reflected in higher rates of personal problems, including mental illness, which almost all immigrant groups experienced in America. Marginality was, therefore, implicated in both the social and personality problems of the ethnic community. The identity crisis that comes along with marginality and with attempts at assimilation produced the problems.

Organized brigandage, the vendetta, the use of extortion and control through fear, a system of exploitation (*padrone* system), traditions of violence, and a distrust of government and law are just some of the Old World transplants that made life in Louisiana in some ways as problematic as it was in Italy. These Old World patterns were woven from the fabric of a weak state.[9] In Sicily, the government was unable to protect the *contadini* from the caprice of local officials and from the agents of the landed aristocrats who extracted ruinous contracts from the peasants. Essentially, the state and local governments were viewed as illegitimate and, therefore, did not earn the peasants' trust. The *Mafia* arose to fill this niche and operated primarily as a protective enterprise. It developed its own code of honor based on strength, violence, and silence before the police and the courts. It conducted its affairs as a private network sustained by payments from its clients. For a price, the *Mafia* could protect crops and business dealings, avenge personal and family insults, and mete out justice, which the government was powerless to do. The state offered the *contadini* empty promises. The *Mafia* gave and kept its word! But in usurping unofficial legitimate power, *Mafioso* became both constable (police) and judge. Without the benefit of scrutiny, the *Mafia* grew at the public's expense. In its use of intimidation and violence, the *Mafia* became one more agent of injustice and exploitation the peasants had to endure.

Adding to these Old World difficulties for the immigrant was the chronic problem of separation from family and friends.

Thousands of miles lay between brother and brother, brother and sister, mother and son, and husband and wife, although this problem was somewhat mitigated in Louisiana by the marked tendency to emigrate as family groups. For example, only 14 percent of immigrant households in St. James Parish in 1900 were composed of unrelated individuals. Comparable figures were found in other areas of Louisiana. It is difficult to say how typical this tendency was in America. Vecoli reports somewhat similar findings for the Italians in Chicago;[10] however, this family pattern of immigration was not typical of New York's immigrants.

Even though the majority of immigrants to Louisiana arrived with relatives, or were soon joined by them, other relatives were left behind. Usually the nuclear family emigrated. Sometimes other relatives joined this group. But all of the immigrants left behind large segments of their extended families. It would be at least three generations before Italians in America had more relatives there than in Italy. In 1900, less than 10 percent of immigrant households included kinsmen other than husband, wife, and their children. However, it was not uncommon to see related nuclear families living in close proximity. Immigration in Louisiana often separated segments of the family, rather than an individual from his family.

Separated by the ocean, the immigrants used every means at their disposal to keep in touch. For the fortunate who could write, the letters helped to sustain family unity. These letters were usually brief updates of family histories like reports of baptisms, school matriculations, confirmations, marriages, and deaths. Very often, correspondence contained requests for money, promises of money, or actual money.

Detailed studies of the correspondence between the immigrant and the family left behind, such as *The Polish Peasant in Europe and America,*[11] reveal the gulf of misunderstanding that existed between those who stayed and those who emigrated. The family members who remained behind usually believed

America was paved in gold. They could not understand why more money was not sent "home." The immigrants, for their part, found it difficult to explain their failure, when it occurred, in the land of opportunity. They constantly had to defend themselves against the hurt of their own deficiency compounded by the frequent charge from the Old Country that they were living a profligate's life.

For those who could not write, assistance from relatives, friends, priests, or lawyers was required, which necessarily resulted in the sharing of personal intimacies and family secrets. Messages and reports were also transmitted orally. Family news from Italy would frequently be obtained from newly arrived immigrants or from immigrants returning to Louisiana after a brief stay in Italy. This practice was quite common prior to 1900, when immigration was at its peak. Owing to the improvement in ocean transportation and the relatively low cost of passage, trips back and forth across the Atlantic were not uncommon at that time. There is clear evidence that many Italian immigrants came to Louisiana in the fall, harvested cane, then returned to Italy. Some of them repeated this itinerary for several years. Undoubtedly, the news of the money they made in the sugarcane fields motivated fellow villagers to make the trip. This would help explain why the majority of Italian immigrants in Louisiana hailed from a handful of Sicilian towns. While other areas and villages of Sicily contributed very few immigrants to Louisiana, these same places experienced heavy migration to other parts of the United States.

In addition to the separation of families, the problem of finding shelter and work is worth noting. This problem was further aggravated by the language barrier and, for many, the lack of skills. Those who worked the plantations had both house and job assured, at least during harvest time. Considering the number of children immigrant families had, the quarters supplied on the sugar plantations were inadequate and overcrowded. On some plantations, the owners supplied larger and nicer quarters to the immigrant families than to blacks. This seems to have been true of the Dymond Plantation in Plaquemines Parish but was by no means a general rule. In St. Mary Parish, no distinction was made and the immigrants occupied former slave quarters.

In the cities, the situation was not much better. In New Orleans, the immigrants inhabited the areas in and around the business district. These areas were typically crowded and run-down, but slums comparable to those in Northern American cities did not exist in turn-of-the-century Louisiana. There were of course many exceptions, but the typical immigrant in Louisiana cities lived in some of the oldest and therefore most deteriorating sections. There was a bright side in the New Orleans area. For those contented to engage in truck farming, the noise, dirt, and density of the city was avoided by living down-river as far as St. Bernard, or in Algiers, Harvey, or Carrollton, or upriver in Kenner.

The most precarious immigrant job was day labor. This constituted less than 10 percent of immigrant occupations in New Orleans. The most typical employment in Louisiana was farm labor. Low wages and uncertain prices were typical for farm laborers and farmers in the South. But the immigrants' industry, thrift, and knowledge of farming gave them an edge over other farmers. Many were able to cut out the middleman by selling their produce as well as growing it.

Some immigrants were fortunate enough to have skilled trades, but they had to compete with native whites and blacks. In New Orleans the free men of color virtually monopolized some of the crafts, but Jim Crow laws undermined their control over traditional crafts.

Despite their small numbers in the skilled trades, it did not take long for the immigrants to carve out their own economic niches in Louisiana. Certain occupations were more accessible. All over the state, in every town of any size, by 1900 one could find Italian cobblers, grocers, fruit peddlers, produce dealers, merchants, and stevedores. Many became materially successful and eventually sent their children to business, law, and medical schools. We hasten to add there were also many who returned to Italy with broken spirits and withered hopes.

Returning to the theme presented earlier, the transplantation of Old World traits must be considered in relation to crime. The well-traveled road to crime is not particularly Italian. Indeed, it is frequented by natives and immigrants alike. A casual review of international crime statistics easily supports this. The road to crime is as American as apple pie and the flag. Furthermore, nowhere has it been so glamorized in the press as in the United States. Nowhere have there been so many opportunities to pursue it. Crime has always been one avenue to success in America, and the Sicilian immigrant, so well prepared by his history, was easily tempted by it. In Sicily, the law, police, and the government were often on the side of injustice. Attitudes and values favorable to law breaking were deeply ingrained, and the association between law breaking and injustice was not easily made. In fact, the outlaw often seemed to be working on the side of justice, since he often thwarted the efforts of the police, politicians, and landed aristocracy to exploit the poor. One could never tell for whom the police worked, so the peasant was usually too afraid to report a crime to authorities.

The grooming of the immigrant for a life of crime can be correctly ascribed to his social and cultural experiences in southern Italy and Sicily, but this is only the initial push toward a criminal career. The upheaval that accompanies immigration further pushed the new arrival in the direction of crime. Additionally, he found in America a land of opportunity, with a government ready to enact ill-advised laws and a populace ready to make celebrities of big-time gangsters.

Native white Americans were generally ambivalent about crime. On the one hand, in the name of morality, they condemned it. On the other, they praised the successful gangster for his resourcefulness, intelligence, and conspicuous display of wealth. It can be said that a career in crime is not unlike a career in business; both rest on the desire to succeed and acquire. Like the corporate executive, the gangster believes in free enterprise. Both take risks, and each in his way draws the attention of the courts. The crimes committed are different; corrupt executives are less visible and rarely resort to violence, at least in contemporary times. Both individuals succeed precisely because of their knowledge of the rules that govern men's actions. Both are creative and willing to try the untried. If we find it easier to excuse the excesses of the executive, it is only because we too have made mistakes from time to time and find it easier to call greed by another name.

The twilight of analogies must eventually yield to the full light of facts. What evidence is there for the foregoing? The immigrant's involvement in crime as both victim and offender must now be examined.

ITALIAN IMMIGRANTS AS VICTIMS AND OFFENDERS

The Federal Bureau of Investigation did not establish a uniform crime reporting system until the 1930s. Coverage for earlier periods can be obtained, but the quality of the data is poor and the extent very limited. Furthermore, the ethnic identities of the offender and victim normally were not ascertained. The popular press throughout the period of immigrant settlement reported crime committed by immigrants. Even when ethnicity was not reported, it can usually be inferred from the names of offenders and victims. By itself, this kind of information would not be much better than the early police statistics. It can be used along with demographic facts, particularly estimates of the size of the young male population, to give a more realistic assessment of the immigrant's involvement in crime.

Newspaper accounts of crime were notoriously prejudicial

and given to stereotyping, particularly in the late nineteenth and early twentieth centuries. For example, the major newspaper in New Orleans during the period of peak immigration, the *Daily Picayune*, seemed to go out of its way to connect criminal activity with the Italian community. One of its more offensive labels was "Dago." In the late nineteenth century, an account of a fight between two Italians appeared under the prominent headline, "The Crime of Dago Pete."[12]

The blatant prejudice of the press assures that immigrant crime was not underreported. It should, however, sensitize us to the possibility of overreporting. There is the temptation to ascribe these early accounts to the desire to blacken the name of Italians. Yet one must admit that the early history of Italians immigrants was a stormy one. The notoriety that Italians got from being associated with violent crimes in the late nineteenth century must be judged—in part, justified. Because of renewed interest in ethnic identity and heritage, it is popular today to uncritically praise one's ancestors and explain away all apparent failings as products of prejudice. We, however, eschew such blind loyalty to our heritage.

Our conclusions about Italian criminality and the reputations of Italians derive from a content analysis of the *Times-Picayune (Daily Picayune)* for selected years between 1880 and 1920.[13] All daily issues for each year chosen were analyzed, with the expectation that the press would both shape and reflect the attitudes of the general population of New Orleans.

The issues were scanned for articles dealing with Italians. Once located, these were categorized into two broad classes: those covering crime and misconduct both actual and alleged and those covering all other topics. In the years covered, there were thirteen homicide offenders (one involved the assassination of the police chief in 1890), twenty-two homicide victims or attempted homicides on Italians (including the Italians lynched for the assassination of the police chief), fifteen fights, two suicides, four attempted suicides, and twenty-five other crimes including arson, attempted bombings, and illegal flight from the law. What is most striking about these accounts is the extent of violence. Furthermore, the homicides or attempted homicides involved the most gruesome methods—bomb, fire, ax, knife, and the sawed-off shotgun. The noncriminal topics included stories of immigration, facts concerning the Italian colony in New Orleans, religious and civic activities, and human interest stories. The following table depicts the salient facts gathered.

Table 7

Reports of Crime and Misconduct Among the Italian Population in New Orleans for Selected Years (1880-1920)*

Articles Reporting	1880-82	1889-91	1900-1901	1913-15	1919-20
Crime and Misconduct	14 (78%)	10 (67%)	10 (31%)	10 (30%)	30 (32%)
All Other Themes	4 (22%)	5 (33%)	22 (69%)	23 (70%)	65 (68%)
Total Articles	**18**	**15**	**32**	**33**	**95**

*The tally in this table does not include follow-up articles.

In the 1880-82 period, 78 percent of the articles reported crime and misconduct. The percentage declined in the subsequent periods to about 30 percent. These results reveal both objective and subjective facts. For example, one could conclude that the amount of criminal behavior had declined over the years covered. Although the reporting of crime in newspapers rarely gives a true picture of the actual amount of crime, we do know from other sources that the above conclusion is reasonable. The more relevant fact revealed is the subjective one. Religious, social, civic, and other themes became more common, not necessarily because more of these activities were taking place, but because the newspaper chose to report them. Likewise, crimes committed by Italians became, in time, crimes committed by citizens. These facts indicate that the newspaper, like the larger society, gradually began to define Italians as citizens rather than as a foreign criminal element.

If the period is characterized as a violent one, it was not solely because the immigrants were criminal offenders, for they were also very often victims of violent crimes, as reflected in the Italian immigrants who were lynched in Louisiana. Although the Hennessey case is the best known, it was not the only lynching incident involving Italians in the state in the 1890s.

1890S LYNCHINGS OF ITALIANS

The last decade of the 1800s was the peak period of "lynch law" in the United States, when 1,665 persons died at the hands of lynch mobs. Black Southerners were the primary victims of these human atrocities, but others suffered as well, including Italians. There were six incidents of Italian lynchings in America during this time. As hard as it is to believe, three of them took place in Louisiana. Of the three incidents, the Hennessey Affair in 1890-91, in New Orleans, was the most serious, provoking an international incident between the United States and Italy, but the other two events were no less tragic. One occurred in South Louisiana in St. Charles Parish in 1896, the other in North Louisiana in Madison Parish in 1899.

Three Italians Lynched in Hahnville: A Dramatic Miscarriage of Justice

Leaving the Hennessey Affair aside for the moment, we turn to the Italians who were lynched in Hahnville, a sleepy river town on the West Bank of the Mississippi River in St. Charles Parish, a sugarcane-growing area. On August 9, 1896, a triple lynching of Italians in Hahnville was the first of two consecutive *Daily Picayune* stories covering the preceding dramatic week. The Italians found swinging from the rafters in a shed adjacent to the courthouse were Lorenzo Saladino, Decino Sorcoro, and Angelo Marcuso. The trio was awaiting trial on charges of murder in separate incidents.

It was Saladino who, as the *Daily Picayune* put it, "so foully assassinated Jules Gueymard," a well-known merchant and planter of Freetown. It was this incident that so inflamed the local population that Sheriff Ory took special precautions to protect his charges. The other victims were being held for robbing and beating to death an old Spaniard, Don Rexino.

The murder of Mr. Gueymard was accomplished by a single shotgun blast from an assailant who hid behind a tree near Mr. Gueymard's store. Apparently, the victim was playing cards with friends as he awaited a shipment. When the ship's whistle sounded, Mr. Gueymard stood up and walked toward the river. It was then that the single blast loaded with "all sorts of charges" nearly decapitated the unfortunate planter and wounded one of his friends. Whoever shot the planter vanished in the nearby thick brush. However, suspicion pointed to the Sicilian who had threatened Mr. Gueymard after Gueymard accused him of attempting to defraud some New Orleans creditors. Mr. Saladino was arrested on a charge of murder. His wife and son were also arrested as accessories. The evidence against Saladino was a double-barreled shotgun allegedly found in his home with one recently discharged chamber and a belated confession from his wife. Initially, she denied knowledge of the incident but subsequently gave the police a very incriminating account. According to the police, Mrs. Saladino said that when her husband returned home the day of the murder, he declared, "I got him!"

As for the other two victims, Sorcoro and Marcuso were accused of the wanton beating death of Don Rexino on the Ashton Plantation near Boutte Station. According to the *Daily Picayune,* nearly every bone in the old man's body was either broken or cracked. The body was found in a field with a rope tied to one foot. According to the police, the victim was a successful moss gatherer and had secured most of the trade formerly controlled by the two Italians.

The drama surrounding the triple lynching would have been comical had it not been for the tragic fact that three people were hung by a mob and their bodies riddled with bullets.

The whole affair was a series of poorly staged acts in an ineptly directed theatrical production. Consider that on the day of the arrest of the accused, the sheriff places Saladino, his wife, and his son under strong guard and moves them to the nearby woods. After the alleged confession of Mrs. Saladino, he returns them to the jail. Upon being promised by the townspeople that they will make no interference, the sheriff removes the armed guards. That night 100 masked horsemen gather near the jail. Because a country ball is in progress, suspicions are not raised.

What follows seems to be in imitation of the worst movies to come out of Hollywood. A midnight whistle is used to start the drama. A newspaperman happens to be in the right place and takes a shortcut through the woods to the jail so that the readers of the *Daily Picayune* can be assured of full coverage. The sole guard separating the mob from the accused is an old, unarmed black watchman. He is powerless to prevent the inevitable. Descriptions of the accused seesaw between cowering and violently resistant. Pleas for mercy and declarations of innocence are made in broken English. The accused are given a chance to pray. Through it all Sheriff Ory is asleep, unaware until morning of the gruesome happenings, and is said to have been "more than surprised." He promises to investigate the matter but is convinced that the masked riders will never be identified, even though some were reported to have come from St. Gabriel, Mr. Gueymard's hometown. The *Daily Picayune*'s attitude was that justice was done and the triple lynching was a protest against *mafia* methods.[14] No one was ever fingered for this breach of justice.[15]

Goats, Guns, and Italians

In 1899, Tallulah, a delta town just across the Mississippi River from Vicksburg, Mississippi, was the site of another tragic miscarriage of justice against Italians. Five immigrants were hanged by a mob of 250. The five Italians were the chief suspects in the

shotgun death of Dr. J. Ford Hodge.[16] Three of the men hanged
were brothers, Joe, Charles, and Frank Defatta. Frank had been
warned by Dr. Hodge to keep his goats off the doctor's porch.
Hodge shot one of the goats presumably because Defatta failed
to curb the beast. At this point, the story gets extremely mud-
dled. One account has Dr. Hodge and a friend walking past the
Defatta store, where Frank Defatta and two friends were armed
and waiting. According to this account, Dr. Hodge drew his pistol and fired in self-defense but was felled by shotgun blasts.
Frank Defatta and his two friends were arrested immediately by
the sheriff. The other two Defatta brothers were later found hiding in their home.

Citizens who had gathered at the courthouse took the two
Defatta brothers who had been captured last and hanged
them. They then got Frank Defatta and his two friends from
the jail and did the same. The grand jury investigating the
lynchings concluded that the five were guilty. According to the
New York Times, the grand jury said: "It is evident from the facts
brought to our knowledge that the men who were lynched had
formed a conspiracy to assassinate Dr. Hodge, and the mob,
learning of the facts took the law into their hands. After diligent inquiry we have not been able to learn the names or identity of any of the men composing the mob."[17] This "diligent
inquiry" lasted less than twenty-four hours, and Italians all over
the country were outraged by this mockery of justice.

The episode was so much like the infamous New Orleans
lynching of 1891 (see below) that the secretary of the Italian
Embassy, Marquis Romano, initiated an investigation of his own.
In the meantime, Gov. Murphy J. Foster, grandfather of the
1990s governor of Louisiana of the same name, tried to defuse
the situation by claiming that three of the five victims were nat-
uralized citizens.[18]

Romano's investigation declared the shooting of Dr. Hodge an
"act of self defense." It indicated that Charles Defatta punched
the doctor, whereupon Hodge, realizing he was no match for

Defatta, drew his pistol and delivered a nonfatal wound. Frank Defatta then shot the doctor to prevent his brother's death. The mob, which had already gathered around the affray, lynched Frank and Charles Defatta. They later got Joe Defatta and two friends, who had been arrested and jailed, and lynched them also.[19] Law enforcement generally accepted the *Mafia* stereotype and therefore assumed that Italians did not act alone. It was, therefore, not uncommon to arrest relatives and friends who were not present at the crime scene.

A third account, Governor Foster's, not surprisingly supported the grand jury's position. This account was accepted by neither the Italian community nor the government of Italy. Two years later, after much effort to have justice done, indemnities were paid to Italy by the United States government. The lynchers, however, were never punished for their crimes.[20] Incidents like this in Louisiana, Mississippi, Arkansas, and elsewhere in the South, plus reports of low wages and poor working conditions, convinced the Italian government to advise its citizens not to immigrate to the American South.

The Hennessey Affair

David Hennessey, the chief of police of New Orleans, was gunned down on the night of October 15, 1890. Mortally wounded, before he lost consciousness, he reportedly said, "The Dagoes did it," thus precipitating a chain of events that culminated in the most infamous lynching of Italians ever to take place in the United States. Eleven arrested, but not convicted, Italians were dragged from their prison cells by an angry mob and killed. So serious was this atrocity that, for a while, diplomatic ties between the United States and Italy were severed, and it seemed likely that some kind of armed confrontation between the two countries would occur. The affair was eventually settled, but only after the U.S. government had offered financial reparation.

It seems incredible, but the incident is still remembered

with bitterness in and around New Orleans. Contemporary Italian-Americans continue to cite this episode as an example of mistreatment of Italians in this country. Richard Gambino's book *Vendetta* recounts the incident.[21] He presents a most imaginative account, based on conspiracy theories, that has enjoyed popularity in recent years.

Gambino posits that the lynching was part of a strategy of New Orleans' elite to preserve their economic, social, and political privilege: "The campaign against the Italians was part of a struggle involving four factions of New Orleans' population. The first was made up of the old pre-Civil War commercial and professional elite, predominantly of Anglo-Saxon background, also including people of French and Spanish stock, and joined since the Civil War by increasing numbers from the Irish and German populations."[22]

According to Gambino, this faction organized the Reform Democrats in the 1880s and 1890s. The second faction, the Ring Democrats, was composed of the larger labor segments of these same ethnic groups—mostly Irish but also some blacks. The third faction was the Italians and the fourth was the blacks. "The first faction, the anti-labor, anti-Black, anti-Italian elite of New Orleans, having succeeded in enlisting the white unions and many Blacks in the repression of Italians, immediately turned on them to crush them also, the final phase of its divide-and-conquer policy."[23]

While Gambino's analysis is not without merit and can be substantiated in part, it also is a bit of a stretch. Some of his claims are overdone: the incident helped erase all the rights and power achieved by Louisiana's black people after the Civil War; it set back the labor movement in New Orleans; it contributed to America's closing the gates on immigration. The declaration most difficult to accept, however, is that the events helped launch the "New Navy" of the United States and led to the Spanish-American War.[24]

The lynchings generated by Hennessey's assassination, and

the assassination itself, were tragic acts of inhumanity, but they were not without precedent. The history of blacks in America is filled with comparable examples of mistreatment. Unfortunately for them, there was no country protesting on their behalf.

The assassination of Hennessey and subsequent lynchings took place during troubled times in the South. In the aftermath of the Civil War, deep, lingering animosities existed in Louisiana (and the rest of the South) toward the North and blacks over Southern Reconstruction. White supremacist sentiment was soon to take on a legal form, in the Jim Crow laws enacted by state legislatures all over the South. Furthermore, hatred of foreigners was on the rise, as immigration from southern and eastern Europe increased. Competition with immigrants for jobs and business opportunities was becoming more frequent. Compounding these fears, hatreds, and jealousies was the acceptance of violence that characterized the 1890s. It was rather common for men to carry loaded pistols. Disagreements were often settled by dueling if one were a gentleman or by ambush if one was not. There was so much unlawful killing in Tangipahoa Parish at this time that it became known as "Bloody Tangipahoa." Samuel J. Hyde's study of this reign of terror, including hangings, bushwhackings, duels, and family shootouts, makes it perfectly clear that there was no more dangerous place in the United States at that time.[25] In short, the Gay Nineties were not only gay but quite violent. The highest homicide rates this country has ever experienced occurred during this period.

New Orleans experienced the turbulence of the times.

> A general atmosphere of crime plagued [the city] in the last twenty years of the twentieth century. . . . There was a coarsening of the moral fiber of the Crescent City that had resulted from military occupation during the Civil War and the struggle to overthrow Reconstruction carpetbaggers in the 1870's. . . . Extraordinary violence included race riots. . . . Ladies made it fashionable to defy authority by taunts, jeers, and other minor

infractions of the peace. . . . Reconstruction added the defiance
of law by persons from all walks of life, with their leaders being
members of the upper classes. . . . The hated Metropolitan
police of Reconstruction, under carpetbag control, had ruled
with the brutal might of an army. . . . As a port [New Orleans]
had received the flotsam and jetsam of European society to
swell the ranks of native criminals. . . . As the entrepot for western produce [the city] was in touch with the frontier and its
brawling culture.[26]

Added to the miseries enumerated by Joy Jackson was the
fact that the city was bankrupt. Its treasury was unable to sustain
a sufficient police force. Moreover, residents were fearful and
distrustful of the police, who were widely considered to be corrupt. As a result, the general feeling among the citizens was that
they must rely upon themselves for their own protection.
Vigilanteism was always threatening to erupt. This was the mental and moral climate in New Orleans on that fateful night on
October 15, 1890, when David Hennessey was assassinated.
Things would not get better soon. Indeed, they would get much
worse, resulting in the March 14, 1891, lynching of the eleven
Italians. Only when we fully appreciate the times during which
these events took place can we maintain balance. We should
not excuse these crimes, nor should we continue the vendetta.

The Hennessey Affair was an incredible event. The story
deserves repeating not only because it reflects criminal activity
among a minority of Italian immigrants but also because it lays
bare the animosities and prejudices the native white
Americans felt toward Italian immigrants. For many years afterward, Italian-Americans had to countenance the mean-spir-
ited, derogatory query, "Who killa da chief?" Before describing
and assessing the various accounts of the Hennessey murder
and subsequent mass lynching, we will examine the effects the
sordid affair had on the Gennaro family in New Orleans.

Don Gennaro, president of the East Jefferson Italian-
American Society (1996), gave the following history of his family

to the *Italian-American Digest.* Leaving their home in Sciacca, Sicily, Nicolo Gennaro, Celia Marino, and their nine-year-old son, Michael, arrived in New Orleans in 1884. In his youth, Michael peddled fruit in the city. Sometime later he married Vita Rodosti. The couple had two children, Calogero and Cecile. In 1930, Calogero journeyed to Sciacca to marry. The following year, he and his bride, Ignazia, settled in New Orleans. Calogero and Ignazia owned and operated a restaurant and bar at 1932 Felicity Street. The couple reared five children, including Don.

Ignazia's mother, Filippa, once lived in New Orleans with her parents, Giuseppe Antonio Gennaro and Ignazia Chiarello Gennaro, on Girod Street, near the Hennessey family, with whom they were friends. But when Chief of Police David Hennessey was murdered, Italians were accused of the crime. Fearful of retaliation by non-Italians in the community, Giuseppe, Ignazia, and their daughter, Filippa, returned to Sciacca in 1891. Their haste to leave is reflected in the fact that in the middle of the day they took Filippa out of John McDonough School.[27]

The Hennessey Affair received worldwide attention, resulting in hundreds of separate stories of the events in books, newspapers, magazines, and investigative reports by governmental authorities in the United States and Italy. The two most comprehensive and enduring recapitulations of the Hennessey murder and subsequent lynching are to be found in the works of Richard Gambino and John S. Kendall.[28] The latter's work is used as the basic source in what follows because Kendall included a wealth of detail on the local scene owing to his newspaper experience. Despite his obvious prejudice in the matter, he was thorough.

According to Kendall, the story begins some ten years before the assassination. Kendall's thesis rests on the premise that the *Mafia* existed in New Orleans in the 1880s. On July 5, 1881, four New Orleans policemen made an extremely important arrest of a criminal who had fled Italy. The criminal was named Randazzo, which was an alias for Esposito. Two of the arresting policemen were brothers, Mike and David Hennessey; the other two were New York detectives retained by the Italian government. The arrest was effected with very little fanfare. In fact, it was secret, as the four feared that the Italian criminal element would come to Giuseppe Esposito's aid. Esposito was not even "booked." As Kendall describes:

> Even when Randazzo, or Esposito, was eventually smuggled on board a steamer sailing to New York, he was taken from the police station with the utmost caution; put into a skiff at the foot of Canal Street and rowed to the ship under the shadow of the wharves, where no one could spy upon the operation. Safe in a stateroom, heavily ironed, and closely watched by the four detectives, the desperado was taken north by sea. In New York an Italian warship was waiting to convey him to Italy.[29]

What did Giuseppe Esposito do to merit such travel arrangements? He did no more than other Sicilian *Mafiosi* had done; he robbed, extorted money, bribed policemen, and kidnapped. These acts were part of a criminal subculture that had plagued Sicily for at least 200 years. It was not what he did but to whom he did it that got Esposito this extraordinary trip home.

As a lieutenant to a brigand by the name of Leone, Esposito and some sixty others kidnapped an English clergyman in Italy, cut off his ear, and sent it to his wife with a ransom note. She went to the English authorities for help. The delay prompted a second note from the bandits, containing the cleric's other ear and a promise that if the ransom money was not sent his severed nose would soon follow.

Officials in Italy, pressed for action by Great Britain, were relentless in their search for the kidnappers. A bloody arrest soon followed. Esposito was the only bandit not killed or seriously wounded. Miraculously, he managed to escape after being captured, eventually making his way to New York and thence to New Orleans, where he established himself in a fruit and vegetable business.

Esposito also married, or rather remarried, for he already had a wife in Italy. His wife in the United States would later say what a good husband and father he was (they had two children). His wife in Italy, however, continued to press the Italian government to search for this deserter.

The Italian government knew that Esposito had escaped to America and suspected he had gone to New Orleans via New York. The Italian consulate in New York requested that the New Orleans police look into the matter. The chief of police assigned two of his toughest cops to the job, David and Mike Hennessey. Their most difficult problem was proving that Randazzo, their suspect, was the infamous Esposito. Ingeniously, they got an artist to sketch Randazzo in a restaurant that he frequented. As incredible as it sounds, Esposito was sketched once before.

While attempting to kidnap an Italian prince, Esposito and his men had mistakenly seized a visiting American artist. To prove he was an artist, he was commanded to sketch Esposito. His captors also compelled the artist to write a ransom note. This he did on the back of the sketch. Having discovered his mistake, he attempted to rewrite the letter. Esposito's vanity intervened. Esposito desired to have this sketch "correct" the false impressions the general population had of his personal appearance, so both the sketch and ransom note were sent. Thus by a series of very improbable accidents, Esposito got caught in New Orleans by two local detectives. Esposito was eventually tried in Palermo and found guilty. King Humbert I commuted his death sentence to life imprisonment. According to Kendall, Esposito's friends were outraged that his capture was caused by his abandoned wife.[30] Subsequently, a *Mafia*-styled slaying of this suspected turncoat—the wife—took place.

By telling of the Esposito affair, Kendall makes an unsubstantiated case for *Mafia* activity in the city and a vendetta against Hennessey.

The more relevant events leading to the assassination involve two immigrant families who competed for the handling of fruit cargo at the Port of New Orleans. A bitter rivalry developed between Tony and Charley Matranga and the Provenzano brothers, which eventually led to a shootout. Tony Matranga was wounded in the leg. Members of the Provenzano party were arrested, tried, and found guilty. Many believed that the police were unduly protecting the Provenzano brothers. The Matranga family claimed that the prisoners were given better than usual treatment.

According to Kendall's theory, Chief Hennessey was shot because he took sides in the rivalry or appeared to do so. In any event, it was no surprise to anyone when Charley Matranga, some of his associates, and some other enemies of the Provenzano brothers were arrested for the assassination of Hennessey.

On November 20, 1890, indictments were returned against twenty-one men. A motion to quash those indictments was sustained, because people other than grand jury members were present when they were handed down. Subsequently, a new grand jury returned identical indictments on nineteen of the accused. Ten were never brought to trial, six were found not guilty, and no verdict was reached on the remaining three. All of them were imprisoned in the Orleans Parish jail on the day the lynching occurred.

The tragedy that followed is better known than the events that led up to it. On March 13, 1891, the afternoon following the trial, a number of New Orleans citizens elected W. S. Parkerson to lead them in their fight for justice. The next morning, at the Henry Clay Monument on Canal Street,[31] Parkerson met with the Committee of Fifty, a citizen's group appointed by New Orleans' mayor and city council to investigate the existence of organized-crime societies in the city. After the crowd was excited to the point of frenzy, Parkerson and the committee went to get their guns, which had previously been conveniently cached on Bienville Street. As they proceeded toward the Parish Prison, armed and eager to see justice done, they were joined by angry citizens from every street they crossed.

When the mob of about six thousand reached the jail, some of them forced their way in and rounded up eleven of the prisoners. Nine of these were shot on the spot. The other two were taken outside so that the larger crowd there might also participate in this vigilante justice. Kendall sums it up as follows:

> There was no particular reason why the task of exterminating the Mafiosi should not have been completed within the confines of the prison. But this obviously, would have concentrated responsibility upon the little group which had charged itself with the unpleasant duty. It was necessary, in order that the uprising should retain its special character, as a resumption by the people of its previously delegated authority, that the thousands milling around in Congo Square and the adjacent streets should participate in the slaughter.[32]

Kendall adds that this procedure was suggested by lawyers in the mob, which comprised some of the ablest legal talents in the community.

The two who were "thrown to the crowd" were hanged and then shot to death. Parkerson and the crowd assembled at the Clay Monument for a victory speech.

Eventually, the United States government paid Italy the sum of 125,000 lire in damages, but only after long and delicate negotiations.

A TWENTIETH-CENTURY HANGING

Beginning at noon on May 9, 1924, in Amite, Louisiana, six Italians were legally hung in pairs—two by two by two—for the murder of Dallas Calmes on May 6, 1921. Never in the history of this country were so many hanged for the killing of so few. It was all legal and above board, but it was the sternest justice ever meted out by the courts of this nation. Natale Deamone, Joseph Bocchio, Rosario ("Roy") Leona, Joseph Giglio, Andrea Lamantia, and Joseph Rini were involved in a botched bank robbery attempt that resulted in the murder of Calmes. Calmes owned a restaurant and lived above it next door to the bank. He was awakened by his wife, who had heard a sound like a plank being pulled from the alley fence, then saw an intruder. With a pistol in hand, Calmes went into the alleyway and hollered toward the darkness, "Halt there! Halt there!" His shouts were met with a deadly volley of gunfire.

Following the suspects' arrest, fear of their lynching by the townspeople was so great that they were transported to New Orleans. The Italians remained incarcerated there until the trial date, when they were returned by train to Amite. The trial, officially known as *State of Louisiana v. Joseph Rini et al.,* was a spectacle. One observer dramatically claimed that the court-house resembled a heavily guarded fortress. Fourteen fully armed deputies were strategically placed in the courtroom and around the grounds by Sheriff Lem Bowden to ensure peace in the community and safety for the defendants. Judge Robert Ellis, a publically declared dues-paying member of the Tangipahoa Ku Klux Klan, presided over a trial whose opening session was witnessed by approximately 1,000 overwhelmingly prejudiced spectators congregated in and about the court-room. They applauded arguments made by the prosecution and hissed those offered by the defense. Amid charges of bribery, jury tampering, intimidation, and clandestine *Mafia* activities, it took the jury twenty-two minutes to return six guilty verdicts on the charge of first-degree murder. The verdict appealed to the crowd of 2,000 onlookers, who were there to witness and applaud this historic moment. Three National Guard units were on alert should the "wrong verdict" have come down from the jury. The Italians were condemned by Judge Ellis on July 30, 1921, to be "hanged by the neck until dead."

Five months later, on January 2, 1922, the Louisiana Supreme Court announced a reversal of *State of Louisiana v. Joseph Rini et al.,* which, in effect, set the stage for a second trial. The case was scheduled to be heard by the same Judge Ellis.

The defense petitioned for but was denied a change of venue. The second trial was virtually identical to the first one. In short order, over protests by the Italian Embassy of judicial impropriety, the defendants were found guilty and subsequently condemned to death by hanging. After repeated attempts for a new trial failed, and after Rosario ("Roy") Leona confessed that he and he alone shot and killed Dallas Calmes, the decision to hang all six defendants was final. They were finally hung on May 9, 1924, thus satisfying the spirit of vengeance in Louisiana.[33]

ITALIAN CRIMINALS AND THE *MAFIA*

Charges about the presence of organized crime in New Orleans and Louisiana go back to the nineteenth century. They have never gone away completely. These claims have come from political officials, including the mayor and city council of New Orleans, the Metropolitan Crime Commission of Greater New Orleans (a privately funded, "good government" body), and the FBI and congressional committees. Journalists and other writers also joined the chorus, calling New Orleans the home of an Italian and Sicilian organized criminal syndicate modeled after the Sicilian *Mafia*. After reviewing all the police investigations, judicial records, books, magazine articles, newspaper accounts, commission reports, and agency documents on the subject, Michael Kurtz, a respected historian, concludes that organized crime in Louisiana is a myth. He says the supposed evidence brought forth, by whoever makes these allegations, simply does not support them. This is especially true of the claims made immediately following the Hennessey murder. Though there is considerably more evidence about organized crime in Louisiana in the twentieth century, mostly centering on Carlos Marcello, the issue remains unresolved. According to Kurtz, this is because of the vast amount of sensationalism surrounding Marcello and the scarcity of evidence connecting him to a *mafia*-structured crime family. Granted, lack of proof of organized crime does not mean organized crime is nonexistent. Neither do unsubstantiated claims, no matter how often or by whom proclaimed, qualify as truth. The absence of proof necessarily leaves the question unresolved.[34]

Claims of *Mafia* activities in New Orleans first surfaced in 1855, following the stiletto knifing that killed Francisco Domingo. This Sicilian had received a threatening note containing a depiction of a black hand. In the next five years, six similar murders were recorded in the city, prompting the *New Orleans True Delta* to call upon authorities to clean up a gang of Spanish and Sicilian criminals. Since none of these murders was ever solved, no conclusion could be made one way or the other concerning the existence of the *Mafia* in New Orleans.

Joseph Macheca, born in New Orleans in 1834 of Sicilian parents, was a successful businessman with interests in real estate. He founded a steamship company, which later became the United Fruit Company. He was active in city politics during Reconstruction, when violence, rioting, and killings were often associated with political campaigns. In 1868, to protect his political and economic interests, Macheca founded the Innocents, an organization of Sicilians who served as his personal bodyguards and as a security force for his business and political activities. According to Kurtz, David Chandler in *Brothers in Blood,* without any proof, says the Innocents represent the origins of the Louisiana *Mafia.*

Other allegations of *Mafia* activity center on the Hennessey Affair. John Kendall, as we have already noted, claims Giuseppe Esposito founded organized crime in Louisiana. This baseless assertion is refuted by the simple fact that Esposito's record reveals him to be a petty criminal who acted alone. In fact, he was largely alienated from the Sicilian community in New Orleans, which was responsible for betraying him to the authorities.[35] *Mafia* theorists counter with the observation that Esposito was arrested by Hennessey, who later was murdered in retaliation by *Mafia* associates of Esposito.

The best-known reputed *Mafia* figure in the history of New

Orleans was Carlos Marcello. As every native New Orleanian knows, Marcello was singled out as being the kingpin of crime in Louisiana and the Gulf Coast. He came to be known as the head of the Dixie *Mafia*. Before his death, Marcello was accused by federal authorities of an unending list of crimes, including conspiracy to assassinate the president of the United States and the U.S. attorney general.

The U.S. House Committee on Assassinations, which published its findings in the spring of 1979, looked into the role organized crime played in the assassination of Pres. John F. Kennedy.[36] Carlos Marcello was the primary target of the investigation because he had been singled out in Robert Kennedy's crackdown on organized crime. The committee's brief review of Marcello's "career" as a criminal is worth recounting here.

According to the committee, Calogero Minacore (Carlos Marcello) was born on February 5, 1910, in all probability in Tunis.[37] He was arrested in New Orleans in 1929 as an accessory before and after the robbery of a local bank. A few months later, he was convicted of assault and robbery and sentenced to the state penitentiary for nine to fourteen years. His stay in prison lasted just short of five years. He was pardoned by the governor in 1935. Shortly afterward, Marcello was charged with a number of crimes, including two assaults, two robberies, violation of federal internal revenue laws, and assault with intent to kill a New Orleans police officer. He was not prosecuted. In 1938, he was arrested for the sale of twenty-three pounds of marijuana. He got the sentence reduced to ten months in jail and the fine reduced from $76,830 to $400.

Other charges were brought against Marcello in the ensuing years, but he was never prosecuted. By the 1940s, he had earned the reputation of being the biggest gambling figure in the area and was said to dominate the slot machine, pinball, and jukebox trade in the New Orleans area. By the 1950s Marcello had expanded his gambling operations to include the largest racing wire service and two of the largest casinos in the state. The Beverly and New Southport clubs were located just over the Orleans Parish line in Jefferson Parish. Big losers as well as big winners could expect limousine service home, "on the house."

During the Kefauver Hearings,[38] Marcello invoked the Fifth Amendment and refused to respond to questioning. Although convicted of contempt of Congress, he was successful in having the conviction overturned. The Kefauver Committee concluded that Marcello's domination of organized crime stemmed from massive payoffs to corrupt local politicians and policemen.

It was during these hearings that the question of Marcello's deportation was first raised. Then, in 1953, the United States government began unsuccessful attempts to exile Marcello. It was not until the Kennedy administration focused on organized crime figures and corrupt labor leaders that any real attempt to deport Marcello would take place.

On April 4, 1961, Marcello was spirited away by IRS officials to the New Orleans airport and thence to Guatemala. Two months later, he was back in the United States and successfully fought off subsequent attempts to deport him.

The House Committee on Assassinations recounted these events to build their case that Marcello conspired to kill President Kennedy. With this "evidence," they established motive. Additional evidence was mustered to establish means and opportunity.

The plot was reputed to have been hatched in a farmhouse at Churchill Farms, Marcello's fishing camp back of Westwego, just outside of New Orleans. According to the government's informant, Edward Becker, Marcello and Carl Ropolo met several times in 1962 to work out a business deal. It was at the first of these meetings, according to Becker, that Marcello made remarks about assassinating the president. One of the more quotable remarks by Marcello was, "The dog will keep biting you if you only cut off its tail."[39] On another occasion, Marcello was heard saying, "If you want to kill a rooster, you cut off its head not its tail." The FBI believed that this meant Marcello intended to kill President Kennedy or his brother, Robert, who was then the attorney general of the United States.

The committee concluded that Carlos Marcello, Santo Trafficante, and James Hoffa each had the motive, means, and opportunity to plan and execute a conspiracy to assassinate President Kennedy. It further concluded that it was unlikely any one of them was involved, but their involvement could not be precluded. With that last remark, the committee added a certain respectability to conspiracy theories, particularly those involving organized crime figures.

One final point warrants mentioning. The FBI agent in charge of the Marcello case at New Orleans, Regis Kennedy (no relation to the president), during the 1950s and early 1960s repeatedly reported that evidence linking Marcello to organized crime was lacking. The committee saw this as ineptitude on the part of Regis Kennedy, even though a number of people attested to this agent's ability and thoroughness in other investigations.

While the evidence linking Marcello with the assassination of President Kennedy was lacking, federal authorities continued to investigate him for other alleged crimes. In March 1981, Marcello was tried under the RICO statutes. After months of wiretapping in what came to be known as the BRILAB case (short for bribery and labor), the authorities had the evidence to connect Charles Roemer, Louisiana commissioner of administration, and Marcello with a Californian named Joseph Hauser, an insurance company owner, in a scheme involving kickbacks from Louisiana insurance contracts. Indicted, tried, and convicted in this BRILAB scheme, Marcello received a seven-year sentence. From a California court he also received a ten-year sentence. The sentences were to run consecutively, and Marcello began serving seventeen years at the federal prison in Texarkana, Texas.

During his stay in prison, Marcello suffered a series of

strokes and was moved to the Federal Medical Center in Minnesota in March 1989. At seventy-nine years old and in ill health, he seemed unlikely to serve his entire sentence. It wasn't death that would free him. In June 1989, his freedom was granted by the U.S. Court of Appeals, which reversed the 1981 BRILAB conviction. The mail-fraud statues on which his and Roemer's convictions were based were invalidated by the U.S. Supreme Court. In the fall of 1989, Marcello walked out of prison a free man. But the Marcello name surfaced again, at least locally, when Carlos's nephew, Peter Marcello, was arrested for drug trafficking and his brother, Salvadore, pleaded guilty to a charge related to money laundering.

Despite the avalanche of words on Carlos Marcello and the *Mafia*, it is risky to disagree with Kurtz's assessment of the situation. He says:

> With little difficulty, the historian can discover innumerable statements about Carlos Marcello as a mobster, a "godfather," etc. While it is not possible to disprove these claims, the absence of proof leaves the historian with no alternative than to question their reliability. For example, the "*Mafia* family," of which Carlos Marcello is the "boss," appears to exist only in fantasy. The FBI managed to infiltrate and expose virtually all other organized criminal syndicates in the United States, but it failed to do so with the Marcello organization. In a 1961 report on Marcello, for example, the FBI admitted that it knew nothing whatsoever about the structure of the Marcello empire, nor did it possess any knowledge of the identity of the individual members of that empire. None of the characteristics of the *Mafia* have ever been reliably attributed to Marcello, and the State of Louisiana has escaped the turmoil of the gangland-style executions associated with organized crime in such places as Chicago, Miami, and New York. . . . The rise of Carlos Marcello and the publicity about him does not corroborate the allegations of his *Mafia* connections, and the existence of his organized criminal empire remains the subject of speculation rather than fact.[40]

Marcello is an example of the arch-criminal type hunted by the FBI yet idolized by a segment of the respectable public. He did not get the cheers Al Capone got, but some local people, unconnected to crime, still boast they knew him or his family. At one funeral conducted by Mothe's Funeral Home on Vallette Street in Algiers where Marcello was in attendance, the son of the dead woman avoided a group of men who were disparaging Marcello. Later the son said he grew up with Marcello, and although he never associated with Marcello in their adult years, he refused to believe that Marcello was the criminal the authorities made him out to be.[41]

Carlos Marcello achieved a certain celebrity status. In this regard, he is as American as Kennedy or Washington. He embodies the American dream and echoes its most sacred values. He was a self-made man, materially successful and powerful. He was sufficiently irreverent toward the establishment to please some ordinary Americans. In short, he had all the requisite traits of an American hero. When he is honored, it is because he was a self-made man, an American success. When he is damned, it is because he was an Italian gangster.

All the publicity that accompanied his trials, imprisonment, and release reinforced the Italian gangster stereotype. Whatever social, economic, and political gains Italian-Americans have made over the generations are destined to be at least partially eclipsed by the persistence of this stereotype. Who remembers Italian-American scientists, congressmen, governors, and bishops? The arithmetic of prejudice is very strange. A thousand honest citizens contributing their time, talents, and energies to their community count less than one reputed organized crime figure. And so the third and fourth generations, the grandchildren and great-grandchildren of the immigrants, like their ancestors before them, must continue to search for justice.

CHAPTER EIGHT

Religion:
The Quest for Beauty

ST. FRANCIS IS SCOLDED

When she disembarked from the British steamer at the Press Street Wharf in 1901, Anna was eager to rejoin her husband. A year had come and gone since last she had seen Chico. Her first thoughts were of him and the life they were to live so far from their home village. As she clutched the tiny hand of her four-year-old daughter, she could not have imagined how the story of little Mary's life was to unfold.

Three years on a sugar plantation in Jefferson Parish passed quickly for Mary, but they were long difficult years of sacrifice for Chico and Anna. The family was able to save enough to lease some uncleared land. Eventually, they could retail fresh vegetables in their own grocery store. Mary would remember all those years as happy ones. Later in life, she would delight in reminding her brothers, Joseph and Frank, and her sisters, Lucy and Grace, about their childhood days and how much fun it was to work and play in the grocery store.

But there were other memories of difficult times, like when Mamma was sick and had to leave the little ones in Mary's care. It was Mamma who taught Mary to place her trust in St. Francis. Mary believed that she owed everything—prosperity, healthy children, and her own health—to the intercession of St. Francis. As a testament to her faith, Mary had an almost life-sized statue of her favorite saint in front of her Metairie home.

Now in her seventies, Mary enjoyed the protection that St. Francis could procure from heaven. St. Francis stared down at the boulevard from the special nook that Mary had carefully prepared for him. Surrounded by the sweet perfume of flowers, the statue reflected the tranquillity of a soul at peace.

Often, the head and outstretched arm of St. Francis served as perches for the birds. Today the peaceful scene outside Mary's house contrasted markedly with the agitation within.

Mary was beside herself. She searched every nook and cranny of her house, but nowhere could she find the diamond ring her beloved husband had given her. In her agitation she missed the irony of the scene. The child of peasants was upset because she had misplaced a ring that in Sicily only women of noble birth could own.

Her frustration and anger turned her into a crazy woman. "I looked everywhere," she said out loud. "St. Francis, please let me find it!" But her pleas for help went unanswered. St. Francis remained silent as stone.

For three days she poured her heart out to St. Francis and for three days her cries for help went unanswered. If Francis was battling the devil to sustain Mary's patience, he was about to lose.

Mary recalled the story her mother told her of how in her native village the angry villagers had thrown the statue of St. Angelo into the horse pond when the rain they had prayed for didn't come. Oh! What sweet revenge she could have if only there was dirty water around with which she could "baptize" St. Francis, she thought. Then she hatched a sweeter plot.

In a fit of calculated revenge, Mary grabbed the statue and ripped every flower from its bosom. Every blossom in and near its nook met a similar fate. She cursed the saint in the foulest of language. Her anger gave her the strength of a soldier in battle, to accompany her sailor's tongue. She turned the great statue around, as if it were a naughty child made to face the corner. Through it all, the great saint uttered not a word in his own defense. In stone as in life, Francis accepted ridicule with humility.

Mary returned to the house, still angry with the saint for abandoning her. But before long, she felt something under her right slipper. Pressing her fingers on the very spot where she had been standing, she

found nothing. The only things she could feel were the long piles of car-
pet. Still angry, she resumed her march toward the kitchen. Once again
she felt something under her foot. And again she reached down to feel
the carpet and found nothing. Two more steps and the pressure on her
foot broke her train of revengeful thought. It came from the slipper, she
surmised. Removing the old cloth slipper, she carefully fingered her way
along the bottom until she located a bump. And from between the inner
and outer soles, she retrieved her diamond ring!

The joyful and grateful mood that seized her was as intense as the
anger that had gripped her previously. With praises and gestures of grat-
itude, she made her way to St. Francis. She positioned the saint in his
usual place of honor and festooned his niche with freshly cut flowers.

St. Francis tranquilly stared down at the garden below; the hustle of
the avenue beyond the garden plot, he faced with serenity.

The story of Anna and St. Francis is more factual than fictional. These events not only happened; they frequently happened and still do. Stories like Anna's were commonplace in
the Old Country.

In Sicily, if the patron of fishing—Saint Francesco Di Paola—
did not produce a shoal of tuna fish at the proper time, his
statue was taken from its niche down to the beach. There the
fishermen gathered and threatened, '*Ah ca vi buddamu!*' (Ah,
we will duck you if . . .) During the eruption of Vesuvius, when
all prayers to the city's patron (Saint Gennaro) failed to stem
the stream of lava headed for Naples, his image was placed in
the path of the stream. 'You can either die, or save us,' the people shouted. The saint raised two more fingers (on his outstretched hand) and the flow of lava turned aside into the sea.[1]

Whether in Sicily or Louisiana, the Sicilian's devotion to a
saint depends on the perceived faithfulness of the saint. The
non-Sicilian's first response is apt to be: What blasphemy!
What lack of faith! But we do not curse friends because they do
not exist. In anger, perhaps we curse the saints because we are

certain they do exist. Sicilians may rightfully be accused of blasphemy, but it would be incorrect to charge them with lacking faith. To *Sicillani*, the saints are as real as stubborn husbands and spoiled children. The saints, in disbelief, must smile down from heaven on the faithful who, in a moment of temperamental exasperation, are not so devout. After all, most of us would rather be cursed than forgotten.

HUNGER FOR BEAUTY

The story of the Italians of Louisiana would be incomplete without an account of their religious transformation. From medieval Catholicism steeped in paganism and anticlericalism, to faithful sons and daughters of the organizational church, the Italians of Louisiana have experienced a profound religious transformation. In this chapter, we examine these changes and attribute them, in part, to the immigrant's hunger for beauty, which is frequently inseparable from his hunger for drama.

The hunger for beauty is expressed in a variety of ways: art in all its forms, architecture, handicrafts, and personal grooming. Italy has produced more than its share of musicians, artists, dramatists, and architects. The hunger for beauty can be seen on the streets of Italian cities as well as in their cathedrals. Italian statuary and architecture are especially remarkable in expressing religious themes. In Italian churches and monasteries we see the finest unveiling of beauty, with its incessant yearning to rise above the ordinary wedded to man's universal quest for God. In an Italian cathedral it is hard to miss the point that God is beauty. Compare this to church architecture in colonial North America. What a stark place was the church of the Puritan—no gold, no frescoes, not a single statue or painting adorned its walls! The Puritan saw God as a judge Who was repulsed by idolatry and vanity, and therefore he made his church as plain as a deacon's bench. By contrast, the Italian sees God as beauty Itself, and so beautifies Beauty's Home, taking refuge in Him to escape the ugly ordinariness of the world.

OLD WORLD CATHOLICISM

The Catholicism the Italian immigrants brought with them to Louisiana was molded in feudal Italy. As everywhere, religion served the purpose of integrating and making sense out of a sometimes chaotic and cruel world. It also legitimized the power and privilege of a few over the masses. In southern Italy, because the church was also a landlord, distrust and resentment of the hierarchical church were entrenched. Yet there was an uncomfortable mix of anticlericalism and popular Catholic piety. It gave meaning and purpose to a world full of malevolence from landowners, rulers, and nature. The crucified Christ, the Mater Dolorosa, the angels, and a pantheon of saints all supplied relevant models of courageous suffering with whom the peasants could identify.[2]

Neither their anticlericalism nor their Catholic piety was pure. In Italy, the laity's opposition to the clergy was mixed with a love for the parish priest much as contemporary Americans love (or like) their personal physicians but hate the medical profession. After all, the local priest was frequently one of their own, likely born and reared near the same village church he now administers. If he were not known personally to every parishioner, then certainly his family was known to them. Peasant piety was a mixture of pagan customs, magical beliefs, Mohammedan practices, Christian doctrines, and *contadino* pragmatism.[3] Above all else, they believed that the world was full of danger from nature and powerful evil forces, if not from a God Who was disappointed in the failures of His own sinful followers. For protection, they armed themselves with an arsenal of spiritual allies. Besides to God Almighty, they appealed to a host of other lesser, though powerful, supernatural beings, like Mary, the Mother of Jesus; Joseph, Jesus' foster father; the angels; and an army of saints. To ensure that these spiritual benefactors did not forget or ignore them, the old ones fervently commemorated them on special feast days, offered them unique devotionals (novenas, for example), and otherwise prayed to them for intervention with God on behalf of their distinctive requests. Festivals, devotionals, and prayers were typically combined with food, music, and parades to create a festive, though religious, celebration. Sometimes secular influences overpowered the sacredness of the event, as is the case with the famous (or infamous) Mardi Gras in New Orleans and Rio de Janeiro. Some critics make the same complaint about the overwhelming materialism associated with Advent and the Christmas season.

The observance of numerous holidays and feasts, as well as private devotions, brought the community together and gave the peasants a respite from the daily routine of work. Religious feasts, especially those associated with holy days,[4] helped to comfort the broken in spirit with the promise that everything in this world, so bereft of justice as it is, would be rectified in the next.

Religious fetes and pageantry transformed humdrum existence to collective experiences bigger and grander than life. The limited earthly life was escaped for an exciting moment as the statue of a patron saint or Madonna was carried through the streets. When nothing in life gave cause to rejoice, the Italian peasant could count on religion to supply such cause.

The Italian immigrants to Louisiana were culturally Catholic, but in their religious beliefs and practices, they were far from the models the church held up for emulation. Processions, superstitions, anticlericalism, and the cult of saints were all part of immigrant spiritual life.

One of the most conspicuous mixtures of Sicilian religion and magic can be found in the beliefs and practices associated with the *malocchio,* or Evil Eye. If linguists are correct in their assertion that the more importance attached to an idea, the more ways there are of expressing it, then the Evil Eye ranks high in significance among Sicilians, for they have many ways of expressing this thought: *il mal occhio*, the Evil Eye; *occhio cattivo*, bad eye; *occhio di morte*, eye of death; and *occhio triste*, wicked eye. The Evil Eye is an ancient Greek notion that considered pools of water to be the eyes of underground monsters (dragons). In some sections of southern Italy, even today, pools of water are called *occhio*. "The south Italian thought of the Evil Eye as a power inborn in certain men and women, who by a mere glance could cause physical injury, business reverses, sickness and even death."[5] An infant could be born "with the eyes," for example, if during the celebration of Mass a pregnant woman turned her back to the altar when the host was elevated during the transubstantiation. A telltale sign of *malocchio* is supposedly found among those whose eyebrows have grown together above the bridge of the nose. Obviously, this evil force, *malocchio*, is capable of great harm and is to be avoided at all costs. To guard against it and other dangers, like witches, wearing amulets and praying to special saints were widely practiced customs.

In some cases, anticlericalism and resentment toward the Italian church for preventing land reform combined with radical political ideologies. Certain peasants were acquainted not only with the work of Marx but Darwin as well. Some felt that Darwin complemented Marx because, by proposing a natural origin of man, he seemed to undermine the authority of the church. But by no measure can one say that significant numbers of peasants were atheistic Marxists.

The socialist philosophy with religious overtones seems to have caught on in late-nineteenth-century Sicily. The socialists' leadership began in the towns and spread to the countryside. However, peasant unrest was not entirely new in Sicily—the peasant leagues (*Fasci Siciliani*) or at least peasant organizations were around long before.[6] From 1891 to 1894, widespread rioting and strikes broke out. The *Fasci*, under predominately

socialist leadership, expanded rapidly. Their political thought
was miles away from the theorists of the day. E. J. Hobsbawn
says that the people attracted to the socialist movement were
medieval in outlook. Unaware of any inconsistency, they could
shout, "Down with taxes," and in another breath enthusiastically proclaim, "Long live the King and Queen." Oblivious to
the contradictions between their religious instincts and socialist ideas, they could reverently carry their crucifixes and saints'
images before them in political processions, even into *Fascio*
headquarters.[7]

The movement that came to Sicily was like a new religion.
Many peasants thought the traditional priests had betrayed
them and did not practice the true faith of Jesus Christ. "In
Bisacquino, Father Lorenzo, the chaplain of the Church of the
Madonna del Balzo, was called 'the Socialist' because, in the
intervals between giving the peasants tips on the lottery, he
openly said that joining the *Fascio* did not mean excommuni-
cation and that St. Francis had been one of the first and greatest of socialists who had, among other things, abolished
money."[8] Among the sulfur miners in Grotte, an ex-priest
founded an evangelical church and taught his parishioners
Christian Socialism.[9]

Scholars frequently point out that *Fasci* activity and mass
immigration were related, although they disagree as to how.
We do know that villages with strong *Fasci* organizations experienced heavy out-migration in the 1890s. Many of these immigrants came to Louisiana. For example, the village of Piana dei
Greci (now called Piana degli Albanesi) contributed many
immigrants. Near Palermo, it was populated by Albanians who
fled the Turkish conquest. The inhabitants had a reputation of
rebelliousness long before the *Fasci* movement. "When the
Fascio arrived, rather late, in April 1893, it recruited virtually
the entire adult population."[10]

And thus the immigrant's religious mentality was not only fashioned by pagan and Christian elements but by the popular
socialist philosophy of the late nineteenth century. Furthermore,

the Christian elements were not just from Roman Catholicism. Although most immigrants were reared as Roman Catholics, significant numbers were Byzantine Catholics whose ancestors had fled the Adriatic coast and Turkish rule in the late fifteenth century. They had settled the small villages of Sicily and southern Italy, including Piana degli Albanesi, Palazzo Adriano, Mezzojuso, and especially Contessa Entellina.[11] They were commonly referred to as Gheghi.

There is some confusion in the literature and in the public's mind about Eastern or Byzantine Catholics. These Catholics have been confused with Eastern Orthodox Christians, who are not in union with the See of Rome. Byzantine Catholics are, but their liturgy is somewhat different. The language used in worship is not Latin but Greek. For most of these Byzantine Sicilians, the Roman Catholic Church in Louisiana did not, and probably could not, immediately respond to their unique religious needs. They eventually worshiped in the Roman Catholic churches.[12] Given these religious traditions and complexities, it is no wonder that the immigrants were puzzled by the Irish-dominated Catholic Church in America.

THE CHURCH IN AMERICA

The Catholic Church in nineteenth-century America was an immigrant church. In pluralistic Protestant America she steered a course of accommodation to a secular democratic society. Sensitive to the charge of being an agent of a foreign power (popery) and forced to endure blatant discrimination, she assumed a defensive posture.[13] This soon translated into church policy that had one eye on the immigrants' material welfare and the other on their spiritual well-being. The national parish, which for the Italians appeared as early as the 1860s, helped to accomplish both. While providing the immigrant with a place to worship administered by priests who were fellow countrymen, it helped to hold the immigrants within the fold against the intense proselytizing of Protestant evangelicals. The parish also rendered all sorts of financial assistance and social services to immigrants. And it introduced the immigrant to American ways. Paradoxically, the national parish was a vehicle for the Americanization of the immigrant even though it reinforced Old World nationalistic loyalties. The church hierarchy felt that Americanization was necessary for the newcomers' benefit and for the church's acceptance in America.

This zeal for the soul and the material welfare of the immigrants at times took on a sense of urgency. New waves of anti-Catholicism were felt in the first two decades of the twentieth century. Until the Quota Laws were enacted in 1921 and 1924, millions of southern and eastern Europeans flooded the shores of America. The great majority were Catholics from Poland and Italy. Toward them, the church played her ancient role of mother. To protect them and to defend her precarious position in America, she charted a course toward Americanization. It was not a straight route.

The English-speaking Irish clergy became the church's main instrument of Americanization. Thus, Americanization was first accomplished by the Hibernianization of the immigrants. They were to become somewhat Irish before they could become characteristically American.[14]

The position the Irish clergy held within the church made it inevitable that English, outside of the official liturgy, would be its language. Reverence for and loyalty to the clergy, along with conservatism and liturgical reserve, were part of the legacy of the Irish. More expressive displays of piety were discouraged. This provoked no small amount of resentment in Polish, Italian, and other non-Irish Catholic immigrants.[15] They charged that the Irish clergy were insensitive to their cultures. However, succeeding generations of non-Irish Catholic immigrants gradually accommodated themselves to the norms set down by the Irish clergy. This has been documented for the Italians of New York.[16] In Mass attendance, reception of the sacraments, and financial support of the church, Italians have followed the Irish norms.

THE CHURCH IN SOUTH LOUISIANA

In South Louisiana, the Italian immigrant's relationship with the Catholic Church was somewhat different, although the result was similar. South Louisiana was unique in three ways: the Catholic Church was dominant, French and German clergymen predominated, and culturally the area was a New World transplant of Mediterranean traditions.

The Catholic Church played a major role in Louisiana life from the beginning of its French settlement. It established schools and hospitals, and the colony's social cycle was tuned to the religious calendar. Ash Wednesday, All Saints Day, and All Souls Day were, as they still are, actively observed. Since its founding, New Orleans has been a Catholic city in both meanings of the word. Catholics were a majority, and a number of ethnic groups contributed to its catholicity. While the French originally dominated the colony, French- and English-speaking blacks and Spanish, German, Irish, Italian, and other less numerous ethnics contributed to the shaping of the city's cultural life. Although the Irish were a significant immigrant group in nineteenth-century New Orleans, they constituted neither a majority of the faithful nor of the clergy. St. Patrick's Church, the second church built in the city, served the entire English-speaking Catholic population, not just the Irish. The French and German clergy, while more numerous than the Irish, had to accommodate themselves to the social and cultural melange of South Louisiana. Like it or not, the clergy had to work within the context of local beliefs and practices, which included a tolerance for vice, a flirtation with pagan religious elements originating in West Africa and the Caribbean, and genuine Catholic piety.

By virtue of the similarity of culture and the more tolerant attitude of the clergy, Italian immigrants found South Louisiana a hospitable place. The forms of Catholic piety the Italian immigrants practiced, their appreciation of the arts, and their love for pageantry and good food were not obstacles to community participation. Quite the contrary, they found themselves in a somewhat familiar world. They also found the church more responsive to their needs than they generally found in other areas of America.

By 1891, an Italian parish church was organized and located at the corner of North Rampart and Conti streets.[17] Fr. J. A. Manoritta was the first rector of St. Anthony of Padua. He and Father Demautize lived a short distance away in a rectory at 1114 Chartres Street. At that same location was a convent for sixteen Missionary Sisters of the Sacred Heart and a school with 300 pupils operated by the nuns. The archbishop's residence was on the same site. St. Anthony of Padua Church was eventually relocated to Canal and Olympia streets. The 1920 church directory listed three Dominican priests, Fathers Gonzales, Revilla, and Peratta, as serving the parish.

St. Anthony drew its parishioners from the entire New Orleans area. Many of the sons and daughters of immigrants who lived in the truck-farming areas of Carrollton or across the river made their first communion there.

In 1900, St. John the Baptist Church, at the corner of Dryades and Clio streets, served the Italian population, which was attracted to this area because of its farmers' market. Pastored by Father Laval, who was assisted by Fr. John La Rosa, it operated separate schools for boys and girls. The 124 boys were taught by lay teachers. The school for girls was associated with Dominican Academy and had 244 students.

The area around St. John the Baptist was invaded by businesses after 1900, and the residents, including the Italians, vacated the location. Father La Rosa continued to serve the Italian population at the Mission Chapel of the Sacred Heart, situated along with the convent and school at 817 St. Philip Street, near Bourbon Street. The Missionary Sisters of the Sacred Heart, a New York-based order of Italian nuns, also operated an orphanage for the Italians at this address. Operated by Mother M. Magdalen Martinelle in 1900, it had fifty orphans.

At that time, the orphanage had grown, and the thirty-three nuns were not only caring for the children at the original location but had also opened a larger orphanage at 3400 Esplanade Avenue.[18] Their St. Philip property remains as the convent of the Missionary Sisters of the Sacred Heart.

After 1900, St. Mary's the Italian, at 1114 Chartres Street, became the "Italian church" of New Orleans. The 1920 directory listed Fathers Gagliardoni, O.M.I., J. Laboure, O.M.I., and A. Gaudino as the priests of the parish.[19] The school was conducted by fourteen Missionary Sisters of the Sacred Heart. There were 392 boys and 438 girls registered. The church and school were so important to the Italian community that their formal dedication was a major event. The circumstances leading up to this were as follows.

In August 1914, the Archdiocese of New Orleans under the guidance of Archbishop Blenk finally realized the goal of Archbishop Francis Janssens to establish a church for the Italians in the French Quarter. St. Anthony's was too small for the growing number of communicants, and when the way was clear for the relocation of the archbishop's residence, St. Mary's was designated to serve the Italian population. As the church and convent were the oldest religious edifices in New Orleans, a newspaper headline read: "Italians to use New Orleans' oldest place of worship."[20]

Work on the convent and church was begun back in 1727 and finished in 1734. The Ursulines had used it for ninety years and it was the bishops' residence for the next ninety. When it was designated for the Italians, its French architecture was altered by removing the back of the church and erecting an Italian dome. The pastor for this newly created church was V. M. Scramuzza, who was assisted by Fathers R. Rossi and Louis Paroli, both belonging to the Order of St. Benedict. Father Paroli was one of the most active priests working among the Italians in Louisiana. He was present when the Italian community celebrated the dedication of the church.

The Italians celebrated the event in a big way. The night before the first Sunday that the property was to become St. Mary's the Italian, Chinese lanterns were hung in two strings from the church door to across the street in the shape of a V. In front of the church was a brass band composed of the parish faithful. At their sides hung large flags of Italy and the United States. The celebration was organized by the *Societa Madonna del Balzo,* composed mainly of parishioners from Bisacquino, Sicily, which, as noted earlier, was active in the political unrest of the 1890s. After the celebration and vespers, the members of the society and other parishioners went home to contemplate the parade through the French Quarter and the High Mass that would take place the next morning.

As important and as well attended as the dedication of St. Mary's the Italian was, it was not equal to the solemn ceremony mourning the death of King Humbert of Italy. In 1900, the Italians of New Orleans gathered at the St. Louis Cathedral for Mass celebrated by Bishop Rouxel, with a number of priests assisting, including Fathers Paroli, La Rosa, and Scotti. The Italian consul, Papini, a forty-five-piece orchestra led by Prof. George A. Paoletti, and fourteen Italian sodalities were in attendance.[21] "One hour before the service, the Italian societies assembled at Perfect Union Hall at the corner of Kerlerec and Rampart streets and formed into processional array to Canal to Chartres and thence to the St. Louis Cathedral."[22]

Among the fourteen organizations represented that day were the *Giuseppe Garibaldi* and *Loggia Garibaldi* societies. To a non-Italian it may seem unfathomable for the followers of Garibaldi to attend a Roman Catholic Mass. After all, Garibaldi opposed popes on two important occasions. Yet, this is the confusion or the genius, whichever one prefers, at which the Italians are adept. Inconsistency is not necessarily an impediment to action. At times, the immigrants could be intensely anticlerical and yet capable of both public and private piety. For many, the hatred they bore for the clergy waned as their lives were touched by responsive clerics in Louisiana.

The Missionary Sisters of the Sacred Heart and the priests who assisted them were the newly immigrated Sicilian's first exposure to the institutional church in Louisiana. The order's scope of influence and service continued to grow in the early twentieth century. Today the building at 817 St. Philip is the Cabrini Day Care Center and is still run by the nuns. The orphanage at 3400 Esplanade Avenue is now Cabrini High School. Both the day-care center and the high school serve the general population—black, Hispanic, and white children attend the day-care center. No longer are there a significant number of Italian children in the area.

The guiding force and the reason for the order's success in New Orleans, Chicago, New York, Seattle, Latin America, and numerous other places around the globe was Mother Cabrini. The stories of this remarkable woman have become part of the popular lore of New Orleans.

Some would say that from the very beginning of her life and work she was destined for greatness. On the morning of her birth in Italy, the thirteenth child of Agostino and Stella Cabrini, doves circled the Cabrini courtyard and settled there. Because the doves were never seen prior to Mother Cabrini's birth, her most ardent followers would later read this as a sign from God.[23]

When the biographers of saints stress the miraculous events, they perhaps do their readers a disservice. Would not the reader profit more from seeing a life-sized individual struggling with human limitations? Maybe we excuse our own mediocrity by convincing ourselves that people like Mother Cabrini are saints from birth and have special qualities and graces we ordinary Christians could never hope to have.

The serious biographers of Cabrini tell us she inherited not only her religious zeal from her parents but also her class's narrowness of vision. She could be shrewd in matters of business. Once while soliciting a valuable piece of property from a wealthy immigrant, she implored so eloquently that he burst into tears. Within a moment, Mother Cabrini capitalized on his compassion, convincing him to sign an ironclad contract on their agreement.

Mother Cabrini was canonized because she struggled with her limitations and failings and matured slowly into the saint that she is honored for being. She was canonized because she loved with a harsh and dreadful persistence. Harsh and dreadful to herself, for she spent herself on others. Harsh and dreadful sometimes to others, for she expected and demanded so much from them.

Her whole early religious life was directed by a burning desire to be a missionary to the Far East. That unfulfilled desire was reflected in the name she chose in the religious state. Francesca Xavier Cabrini dreamed of being like Francis Xavier, that truly remarkable Jesuit who worked so long under so many obstacles in the Orient. However, Bishop Scalabrini described to Cabrini the poor state of the Italian immigrants in America and repeatedly begged her to go there. He failed to persuade her; Pope Leo XIII himself finally directed her to go. Mother Cabrini and her sisters sailed for New York on the Feast of St. Joseph, 1889.

Within two years the order had opened orphanages and schools in New York and Nicaragua. It was from Nicaragua that Mother Cabrini first visited New Orleans on a return trip to the States. She met with Archbishop Francis Janssens, who was eager for the order to work among the Italians. She promised the archbishop and the Italians that she would send sisters to New Orleans. A couple of months later three sisters arrived. In August of 1892, Mother Cabrini and four other sisters joined them and set about expanding and renovating the property on St. Philip Street.

The Missionary Sisters performed their charitable works among the immigrants with few financial resources. They begged for what they got, making frequent visits to the shops and stores owned by immigrants. Today, many children of immigrants can tell how their fathers aided the good sisters, if not with monetary contributions, then with produce or clothes. Of course, the numerous Italian organizations in and around the city supported the order's efforts, presumably through an organization of their presidents.[24] Also there was the citywide support elicited through festivals, many of which were held at the Fair Grounds. The local newspaper would prod the citizens of New Orleans to attend these fairs and sometimes would have its own booth. One such occasion in 1896 featured six booths depicting different themes, like Franco-Italian, Italo-American, and American.[25] Horse races, chariot races, games of chance, and food helped to draw the crowds. Judging by the list of names of persons working the booths, the nuns had the support of the entire citizenry. There were more non-Italian names than Italian ones.

In the many commentaries on the history of Catholicism in New Orleans and Louisiana, rightful recognition is given to the enormous contributions of the Society of Jesus (Jesuits), the Ursuline Nuns, and the Missionary Sisters of the Sacred Heart in serving the educational, spiritual, and other needs of their constituents. They deserve all the credit accorded them and more. Other religious orders of men and women were also laboring diligently to reduce suffering and pain, to serve the needy, and to educate the Catholic children of the area. These sisters, brothers, and priests were already operating schools, orphanages, hospitals, and other charitable institutions for the indigent when the large influx of Italian immigrants came to Louisiana. The list of religious communities in such service to the people[26] of Louisiana in 1890 is both long and illustrious, including: the Sisters of Loreto, Sisters of Charity, Christian Brothers, Marianites of Holy Cross, Sisters of Mount Carmel, Congregation of the Most Holy Redeemer (Redemptorists), Sisters of the Holy Family, Congregation of Holy Cross, Marist Brothers, Sisters of Mercy, Dominican Sisters, Brothers of the Sacred Heart, Benedictine Sisters, Sisters of the Most Holy Sacrament, Sisters of Notre Dame, Sisters of the Immaculate

Conception, Society of the Holy Spirit, Sisters of St. Joseph, Sisters of Christ Charity, Sisters of the Blessed Sacrament, Sisters of Divine Providence, Franciscan Sisters, Sisters of the Incarnate Word, and Sisters of the Holy Ghost.[27]

The immigrants saw for themselves the selfless dedication of nuns who cared for orphans, the sick, the elderly, and the poor. Above all it was in the classroom under the guidance of teaching nuns that the immigrants, or more accurately their children and grandchildren, had a new religious consciousness fashioned. When there were no classrooms, as was the case on the plantations, the nuns went to the immigrants. While the immigrants may have harbored some suspicions about their priests, no such misgivings could be noted toward the nuns. They were universally loved by all Catholics, even the Sicilians! It did not matter whether or not the immigrants sent their children to Catholic schools; they still admired the nuns. Thus the nuns were uniquely and strategically in position to be the ambassadors of the faith to the immigrants and to teach the faith to their descendants.[28]

RELIGIOUS CELEBRATIONS

The most visible and enduring religious practices of Italian-Americans in Louisiana are the St. Joseph altars and the St. Rosalie processions. Both are expressions of popular Catholic culture, with its emphasis on praying to saints and giving thanks when prayers are answered. Although the precise forms taken in Louisiana are somewhat unique, similar practices are very common in "Catholic" countries. Their theological roots can be traced to the basic Christian belief that death is conquered by Christ's death and resurrection. Just as a living friend may be asked to pray with and for someone, the dead who lived heroic Christian lives can be petitioned to intercede on behalf of living Christians and others. For the believers, the saints constitute a community and are therefore part of the church, paralleling the community of living Christians.

These are not, as some believe, medieval assertions surviving into modern times. Rather, they date back to nascent Christianity. In the Acts of the Apostles (5:15), St. Luke points out that Christians so revered St. Peter that they would place their sick in the path of his shadow to heal them. James (5:16-17) tells us, "The fervent petition of a holy man is powerful indeed," and cites Elijah as an example.

Although praying to saints has both historical and theological justification, it has at times bordered on idolatry among the populace. In some cases it has assumed the form of ancient pagan rites to gods and demigods with only a thin Christian veneer. The official church has been critical of this but lenient. Often it was impotent to control the uneducated classes. It should not be assumed that the Roman Catholic Church has placed its imprimatur on all aspects of the veneration of the saints.

The St. Joseph altar, St. Rosalie procession, the lesser-known St. Anthony of Padua procession, and similar homage paid to other saints grew out of the religious experiences of immigrants. The origin of these observances followed a rather common pattern, with each of them drawing upon local traditions. First the supplicant is faced with some difficulty, either a personal problem like sickness, or collective adversity such as drought, famine, pestilence, or war. Prayers of intercession are offered to a special saint known as a patron.[29] As a sacred vow, the supplicant promises something in return for prayers that are answered favorably.

ST. JOSEPH ALTARS

St. Joseph, husband of Mary and foster father of Jesus Christ, enjoys an exalted position in Roman Catholicism. He was proclaimed by Pope Pius IX to be the patron saint of the universal church. Joseph is also the patron saint of Mexico, Canada, Bohemia, Belgium, Peru, Russia, and Vietnam. Owing to his trade, Joseph is also the patron of carpenters, cabinetmakers, joiners, and all workers. Pope Pius XI designated him in 1937 as patron (protector) against atheistic communism. Joseph is also the patron of (a happy) death, fathers, Chinese missions, prisoners, social justice, and house hunting. A custom has developed in South Louisiana around his role as patron of house hunting. Believers who want to sell their homes will bury a small statue of St. Joseph upside down in the backyard until the house is sold. Presumably, St. Joseph will tire of the inconvenience of standing on his head and cause the house to be bought. Stories abound in South Louisiana of houses that would not sell until St. Joseph was temporarily buried in the backyard! Obviously, he is busily occupied with the petitions and prayers of his contemporary, worldwide supplicants.

However, St. Joseph was largely passed over in the first 1,600 years of the Roman church's existence, although interest in Joseph was apparent in the Eastern church during that time. The first printed Roman missal (1474) does not commemorate him, nor does the designated church calendar in the fifteenth century. The Roman Ritual officially issued in 1614, while making mention of Mary, Peter, Paul, Michael, and many Old Testament prophets, is silent on Joseph. Because of the unsanctioned attention given to St. Joseph by the Carmelite nuns as far back as 1498, and in response to the growth of local devotionals to Joseph, the Vatican under Pope Gregory XV designated St. Joseph's feast a holiday (holy day) of obligation. The obligatory nature of the feast has since been rescinded, though the popularity of the Feast of St. Joseph has not diminished down to this day.[30]

In our time, not only is St. Joseph a popular religious figure in Catholic liturgical and theological matters, but he is held as enormously powerful in the public mind. He and Mary stand apart (and above) the saints, located somewhere between the Trinity and the saints and angels. This undoubtedly is due to the fact that Joseph is a member of the Holy Family, as close as humanly possible to the divine Christ Child. Consequently, his mediation with God on a petitioner's behalf is thought to carry enormous spiritual force. "The Legend of the Devotees of St. Joseph," in a whimsical fashion, illustrates the Carpenter's heavenly power.

> Once there was a man, the famous bandit, Mastrilli, who was devoted to St. Joseph. He addressed all his prayers to St. Joseph, lit candles to St. Joseph, gave alms in the name of St. Joseph: in short, he recognized no one but St. Joseph. His dying day came, and he went before St. Peter. St. Peter refused to let him in, since the only thing to his credit was all those prayers he had said during his lifetime to St. Joseph. He had performed no good works to speak of, and had behaved as if the Lord, our Lady, and all the other saints simply did not exist.
>
> "Since I've come all the way here," said the devotee of St. Joseph, "let me at least see him."
>
> So St. Peter sent for St. Joseph. St. Joseph came and finding his devotee there, said, "Bravo! I'm really pleased to have you with us. Come on in right now."
>
> "I can't. He won't let me."
>
> "Why not?"
>
> "Because he said I prayed only to you and none of the other saints."
>
> "Well, I'll be! What difference does that make? Come on in all the same."
>
> But St. Peter continued to bar the way. A mighty squabble ensued, and St. Joseph ended up saying to St. Peter, "Either you let him in, or I'm taking my wife and my boy and moving Paradise somewhere else."
>
> Since his wife was our Lady, and his boy was our Lord, St. Peter thought it wiser to give in and admit the devotee of St. Joseph.[31]

St. Joseph altars[32] closely follow the pattern previously described. People usually pray to St. Joseph to intercede on their behalf and promise to erect an altar in his honor annually for a certain number of years if their prayers are answered. Some writers claimed in the late twentieth century that the custom was dying out with the immigrant generation,[33] but in

New Orleans, Baton Rouge, Hammond, Tickfaw, Independence, and Amite (in Tangipahoa Parish), it has actually gained strength in recent times. Although almost all altars are erected by people of Sicilian extraction, many more non-Sicilians assist in making them, help prepare the food for them, and visit them.

Usually, where the custom is practiced, there are more altars than can be accommodated on the designated feast day, which is March 19. The celebrations are then staggered around the feast day. Invitations announcing St. Joseph altars to the public are published in church bulletins, circulars, and newspapers and broadcast over local radio stations. In 2001, the *Italian-American Digest*[34] carried notices of St. Joseph altars in New Orleans, Gretna, Belle Chasse, Metairie, Covington, Madisonville, Folsom, Ponchatoula, Hammond, and Lafayette. These altars were sponsored by institutions, such as churches, societies, religious sodalities, and restaurants and other business establishments. For example, the Hammond altar was presented by Holy Ghost Catholic Church in return for St. Joseph's protection and oversight of the construction of a new church building. The congregation adopted St. Joseph as their patron saint to watch over the fund-raising drive and actual construction. Members of the parish made an altar each year after the pledge was made, until the project was completed in 2002.

God must have wondered if He should answer the prayers of the ladies preparing the St. Joseph altar for Holy Ghost Catholic Church in the spring of 2001. His confusion is perhaps understandable in view of the prayers He received from them. It was the middle of February, more than a month away from the celebration of the Feast of St. Joseph. The ladies, largely of Sicilian ancestry, were baking breads and assorted Italian cookies, which were to be frozen in advance of the actual day of celebration. They would be cooking six weeks altogether. The closer the day, the more likely they were to prepare the fish, vegetables, and other meatless foodstuff that would adorn the table. Out of the generosity of his heart, a parishioner who is a successful businessman with many real-estate properties in Hammond loaned the ladies a large restaurant he owned. The restaurant was unoccupied at the time, but it was for rent. It was a great place for the ladies to do their work, and the large walk-in freezer could easily accommodate the results of their culinary labors. This man's generosity was rewarded by the ladies praying to God that this charitable man would not find a tenant for his restaurant until after St. Joseph's Feast.

The altar tradition in Sicily is confined to a small number of towns, particularly, but not exclusively, those populated by descendants of fifteenth-century Albanian immigrants, like Contessa Entellina.[35] Elsewhere in the United States, Italian immigrants have perpetuated St. Joseph altars, but not with the fervor that is found in Louisiana. This is not surprising since the great majority of the Italians in Louisiana originated from Sicily. Furthermore, the practice is probably more acceptable in the Mediterranean culture of South Louisiana.

Accounts given by immigrants of how the custom originated vary, although the famine story is the most frequently given. Times and places given differ considerably. Some accounts put the event in Sicily in the late nineteenth century.[36] In other accounts, the time is the flight of the Holy Family at Christ's birth. Both Nazareth and Jerusalem have been given as the place of origin. Mary Ann Tusa McColloster has recorded three variations of the story reported to her by Sicilian immigrants. In one account, the Holy Family while traveling through Sicily was refused shelter and food by two families. Finally a third poor family offered help. When the Holy Family left, an enormous amount of food miraculously appeared. The poor family then invited the neighbors to partake of the food. A second version places the event at Nazareth, with the villagers celebrating the Holy Family's visit to their village and successful escape from Herod.

A third account puts the event at Jerusalem before Jesus'

birth. Joseph and Mary's request for food and shelter was turned down by a household in which a lady was combing her hair. A second household, in which an occupant was making bread, refused. The third household was no more than a poor family in a simple barn, but they supplied the help requested. This took place on Good Friday. The prohibitions against combing your hair or making bread on Good Friday derive from this story, McColloster was told. This unsophisticated account glosses over the obvious problem of placing Good Friday prior to Jesus' life, let alone death. Its real merit, however, is that it underscores the charity of the poor. In this regard the story reflects the *contadini*'s disdain for the rich. Thus, it echoes the core symbolism of St. Joseph altar celebrations.

These fanciful tales are given by only a small number of people. Most immigrants admit that they do not know exactly how the altars got started. Because the event is clearly a thanksgiving celebration and food is central, it seems probable that some kind of survival of famine, worked through the intercession of St. Joseph, occurred. McColloster puts the origin in the fifteenth or sixteenth centuries when Albanians were forced out of their homeland. It is probable that refugees would have experienced difficulties resettling in a poor region of Europe. Is it not also characteristic of the poor to give what little they have? The generosity of the poor is not only a recurring theme in Sicilian culture but also in both the Old and New Testaments.

Whatever the origin of the altars, the additions and modifications of St. Joseph Day celebrations over the centuries have made them a unique respite from the penitential mood of Lent. A great deal of time and money, often begged from neighbors and relatives, is expended in preparing for the feast. On the eve of the feast, the priest is invited to bless the food. There is great variety in the amount and types of food. Because it is Lent, fish is served. This might be either the *sarde* (sardine), as in Contessa Entellina, or the redfish, as in New Orleans. Pastas with or without meatless gravies (*Milanese*) are displayed. Breads are essential and sweet pastries of every type are found. One of the more characteristic pastries is the *pignolata* (pine cone), made from a dough of eggs and flour that is rolled and stretched like taffy and then cut into half-inch pieces. When dry these pieces are fried in deep fat. Melted sugar is poured over the drained pastry pieces and they are molded together into a pyramid shape before they dry. Some of the St. Joseph's faithful believe that the hot sugar, which blisters the fingers, is intended to be a penance.

Some of the more quaint items distributed are the "lucky beans" or large *favas*. The dried beans are given to visitors, who usually save them as one keeps four-leaf clovers or rabbits' feet. The more religiously orthodox insist they are "blessed beans"; the less orthodox believe they are "lucky beans." Mary Lawson was a devout believer in the protective power of the *fava* bean. She kept a blessed, dried fava bean in every one of her approximately thirty purses, except the pocketbook she had with her the last time she was hospitalized immediately preceding her death. Her oldest nephew, Jerome, discovered this vexing fact when, after Mary's death, as executor of her estate, he inspected all her purses in the process of disbursing her possessions. Was that merely a coincidence, or is there something more to the legend of the bean than simple superstition?

The *fava* bean has been a symbol of fertility and a protection against famine. It requires less moisture than other varieties of beans, making it more resistant to drought. As a result, it was available for consumption when little or nothing else would grow. It is said that in Sicily when rainfall was plentiful, *favas* were used for animal fodder, but when drought began to occur annually, the people turned to the *fava* for their own tables. In this fashion, according to some Sicilians, the bean represented good fortune (luck) or a blessing or perhaps both! Those who respect the custom of the *fava* bean but have a more secular view of its merits believe *favas* are to St. Joseph Day what eggs and rabbits are to Easter.

The actual distribution of food at a St. Joseph altar must await the completion of a short skit or reenactment of the Holy Family's flight and search for shelter. Small children, dressed in biblical costumes, represent Jesus, Mary, and Joseph. Sometimes an old, gray-haired man is chosen to represent Joseph. Historically, the children were chosen from the poor families in the neighborhood or from orphanages. Sometimes all three characters are children with additional children serving as other saints or angels. In one of the many versions of the story, three children knock at three different houses. At two of the houses no responses are given. Three knocks are pounded out at the third house, and the greeting *"Viva Gesù, Maria, e Giuseppe"* is the signal for the children to enter.[37] After each child is allowed to sample everything, the public is invited to eat.

A similar celebration is found in Contessa Entellina.[38] Vegetables and nuts are gathered from the mountains. There the *favas* are "blessed" beans and have no magical powers. A procession follows the feasting, and a statue of St. Joseph is placed on a platform and carried to the church. Fireworks punctuate the procession at the halfway point and again at the church. These elements are missing from the practice in New Orleans. However, they are found in St. Rosalie processions.[39]

Apparently, for a long time, St. Joseph Day has provided the general population of New Orleans with a mid-Lenten release in the form of parties, dances, and balls. In 1858, the *Daily Picayune* carried an announcement of a masquerade ball to be held on St. Joseph Day at the Orleans Theater.[40] Balls and parties on St. Joseph Day even when it occurs during Lent have been common practice.[41]

By the 1940s the celebration of St. Joseph Day spread to the black community. Rev. Maude Shannon was the first black to build a St. Joseph altar. According to one account, she responded to a voice urging her to do so.[42] The altars built by her and her congregation had all the Italian foods along with stuffed eggs and potato salad.

By coincidence or divine plan, depending on your beliefs, St. Joseph Day in Louisiana is associated with the Franciscan San Juan Capistrano Mission in California. Since 1776, the swallows of Capistrano have departed on October 23, St. John Day, and have returned on March 19, St. Joseph Day. A New Orleanian, Leon Rene, immortalized the annual event with his popular composition, "When the Swallows Come Back to Capistrano."[43]

ST. ROSALIE (ST. ROSALIA)

A significant, though lesser-known, observance is the annual celebration and procession in honor of St. Rosalie held by Italians of Harvey and Kenner. The commemoration in Kenner is older and dates back to 1900.

St. Rosalie (1160-?), a Sicilian saint born of noble parents, lived a life of prayer, solitude, and austerity in a cave on Monte Pellegrino just outside Palermo. She died in that cave unattended and unnoticed, and was eventually completely buried by stalactitic deposits. In 1624 a plague epidemic broke out in Palermo. According to the legend, one of the victims had a vision of St. Rosalia in which instructions were given to search the cave at Monte Pellegrino. The bones of the maiden were discovered, then carried in procession through the streets of Palermo, and the pestilence abated. In gratitude, St. Rosalia was made the patroness of Palermo, since renamed patroness of all Sicily, and a church was constructed at the site where her remains were discovered.[44] St. Rosalia's importance for Italian immigrants in Louisiana stems obviously from the fact that they brought their devotion to her with them to the United States: a devotion enormously intensified by the frequency of epidemic diseases in the New Orleans area.

In Kenner in 1899, anthrax posed a threat. The farmers believed that through the intercession of St. Rosalie the pestilence disappeared. The following year, the parishioners of St. Mary Church, pastored by Father Roth, secured permission to erect a statue in the saint's honor. In Harvey in 1918, an influenza epidemic prompted the immigrants to pray to St. Rosalie. They firmly believed that it was through her aid that the epidemic ceased.

Both in Kenner and Harvey, the Italian immigrants prayed to St. Rosalie to be spared and in both cases they believed she had answered them. It was then their responsibility to show their gratitude to the saint and ensure their continuing protection by honoring the Feast of St. Rosalie in a special way.

The official Feast of St. Rosalie is September 4, but the Italians of Kenner and Harvey negotiated the actual day of observance. Neither Kenner nor Harvey was large enough to have separate celebrations without support from the other. The various sponsoring organizations agreed to celebrate on different Sundays in September. When Harvey celebrated on the first Sunday, Kenner would follow with its celebration on the next Sunday. The following year the communities would alternate, and so peace and good attendance were assured.

One of the most detailed accounts of the St. Rosalie processions can be found in Lyle Saxon's *Gumbo Ya-Ya*. The account that follows is based on that able writer's vivid and well-written description of a 1941 procession. The celebration in Harvey began with a festival and bazaar on Saturday night. Sunday afternoon following morning High Mass, the participants gathered at St. Joseph's Church in Gretna and prepared to walk the two miles to St. Rosalie's Church in Harvey. The celebration incorporated a fireworks display and a cannonade. Bells signaled the appearance of the life-sized statue of the saint, robed in blue and white. The statue carried a skull and prayer book in one hand and a crucifix and lily in the other. For the celebration the statue was crowned with real flowers, which partially covered the plaster of Paris wreath. Bouquets were placed at the foot of the statue. Red, green, and gold satin streamers were also attached to the statue. Prior to the procession, Frank De Salvo, president of the Victor Emmanuel III

Society, unpinned the money attached to the streamers and recorded the amount. "While he was engaged in this, women crowded around, many with tears striping their cheeks, mumbled prayers, and laid gnarled, work-worn fingers on the hem of the image's plaster robes, and on her feet."[45]

The procession was headed by Boy Scout Troop 200, then followed Father Wester, pastor of St. Joseph's Church, who was flanked by a half-dozen altar boys. Following the priest were numerous societies: the Victor Emmanuel III Society of Harvey, *Organizzazione Italiana San Giuseppe di Amesville* (Marrero), and, last in line, the Italian Fraternity of St. Rosalie of Kenner. (The Italian Fraternity of St. Rosalie would sponsor the celebrations the following Sunday in Kenner.) The thirteen-piece Roma Band was behind the organizations, and the statue of St. Rosalie and her bearers were directly behind the band.

Two hundred little girls under five years of age followed the statue of St. Rosalie. The girls were dressed in white with stiff little wings attached to the shoulders of their dresses. They wore crowns on their heads and recited prayers aloud. About a hundred acolytes followed, dressed in white robes, blue capes, and white skullcaps.

Next in the procession were the Children of Mary, adolescent girls dressed in white with blue veils. They recited the "Hail Mary." The men, mostly dressed in white, followed the children. At the rear of the procession were women, either barefooted or in stockings, some tearfully reflecting a more penitential mood.

When the procession reached St. Rosalie's Church, the festival and bazaar were already in full swing. Plates of meatballs and hot gumbo were for sale. Games of chance and dancing rounded out the festivities.

After the statue was placed in the niche it occupies all year and after due reverence was given to the saint, the worshipers joined the merrymaking in the schoolyard. At midnight the celebration climaxed in a fireworks display, which ended with a representation of the saint filling the night sky.

In Kenner, the procession begins and ends at St. Mary's; however, a number of stops are routinely made along the way. In his description, Saxon reported that the procession stopped at commercial establishments such as grocery stores and bars.[46]

One of the most striking features of the Kenner celebration is the collection of jewelry pinned to a red velvet heart on the statue. The watches, bracelets, rings, and stick-pins are referred to as the "jewels of St. Rosalia." This practice has been somewhat displeasing to the clergy. We are not sure of its origin.

Kenner typically concluded its celebration the way Harvey did, with a schoolyard bazaar, keno game, games for children, beer, soft drinks, and food. "Later there [was] a great fireworks display, when, as in Harvey, a brilliant *Santa Rosalia* [was] sent up in flaming fire work magic."[47]

OTHER RELIGIOUS SHRINES AND CELEBRATIONS

Besides Saints Joseph and Rosalie, St. Anthony of Padua has also been honored by the Italian community of New Orleans. In 1919, the *Times-Picayune* reported a procession through the business district and the celebration of religious services at Poor Claire Monastery.[48] However, the celebration of the Feast of St. Anthony of Padua (June 13) never had the popular support enjoyed by the Feasts of Saints Joseph and Rosalie.

A shrine built by an Italian in thanksgiving for a favor received is located near Donaldsonville in the sugar belt on the west bank of the Mississippi River, about fifteen miles downriver from Baton Rouge. The annual pilgrimage held on the Sunday after Easter is focused on a tiny white chapel with a steeple and tin roof. According to an account in the *Clarion Herald*, the story began in 1906.[49] Tony Musso's son, Lucien, had been very ill and the doctor had given him up for dead. The last rites having been administered to his son, Tony went outside to walk and pray. As he walked, he met a stranger on the road who offered to heal the boy. The stranger's ministrations were no more than nineteenth-century Sicilian folk medicine. He rubbed a mixture of gunpowder and oil over the boy's body and then held him over a kettle of boiling water that contained nine sprigs of parsley. The parsley was subsequently placed on Lucien's stomach, and he fell asleep. When Lucien awoke, he asked for food. The stranger, realizing the importance of this positive sign, approved that food be given to Lucien and took his leave.

The next day, Tony recognized the features of the stranger in a faded picture of St. Amico (Amicus), an eleventh-century secular priest and hermit. St. Amico was from Camerino, in the Marche region, although he eventually settled in Abruzzi. His feast day is November 3. Tony Musso saw the whole thing as a miraculous answer to his prayers. Some of his neighbors imported from Italy a statue of the holy man to be placed in a shrine. The family and hundreds of believers still celebrate the miraculous cure. With the black-robed statue in the lead, the believers, some barefoot, walk in a three-mile procession to Ascension Catholic Church in Donaldsonville, and there celebrate Mass. After the return trip to the shrine, the festivities commence.

Another version of the story has the saint seeking shelter in Donaldsonville. As the tale goes, he was refused a welcome by the more prosperous citizens and finally was sheltered and fed by a poor family who had a child near death. In gratitude, the saint cured the child, but this was discovered by the family only after the "stranger" left the home. It was sometime later that the family recognized the similarities between the "stranger" and the picture of St. Amico.

Not far from Donaldsonville and only six miles from White Castle near Bayou Goula, a very small chapel commemorates yet another miraculous cure. In 1903, Anthony Gullo, a sugarcane farmer, prayed on behalf of his oldest son, who was very ill. He promised God that if his son were spared he would erect a chapel to the Madonna. His prayer was answered and, with the aid of friends and neighbors, he built the nine-foot-square chapel.

Commemorative Italian religious sites are not in short supply in Louisiana. Congregants of Our Lady of Pompeii Catholic Church in Tickfaw support Our Lady of Grace Chapel,[50] located about one mile from the church. In the days, perhaps weeks, prior to their annual processional, the faithful offer rosaries and novenas. On the day of commemoration, the first Saturday in July, participants parade from the chapel to the church with song and prayer to honor their patroness, the Blessed Mother of Christ. Along the route, well-wishers and petitioners pin donations of money to a special ribbon that adorns the statue of Mary. In the early days of this celebration, inaugurated in 1927, gifts of jewelry and spiritual bouquets (special prayer cards) were also quite common. At the church, a Mass is celebrated, followed by a festival of food, drink, music, dancing, and other entertainments like games, including games of chance (cards, dice, roulette, bingo, and others). The next day, after Sunday Mass, the statue is returned to the chapel in another processional, which stops at the cemetery to bless the graves. Unlike the march the previous day, the return trip is entirely devoted to spiritual concerns.

Just to the north of Tickfaw along U.S. Highway 51 is the town of Independence, which was largely populated by Sicilian immigrants in 1920. Italian-Americans remain the most influential ethnic group in that community. Because of Sicilian religious custom, by World War II the town was literally surrounded by chapels built for one reason or another by Catholic Sicilian families. One of the chapels, still in use, is dedicated to St. Joseph.

On the day designated, usually the Sunday before March 19, when the church calendar recognizes the Feast of St. Joseph, a statue of St. Joseph is removed from the Mater Dolorosa Catholic Church in Independence, paraded through town, then returned to the church. During the processional, prayers are offered to St. Joseph, the rosary may be recited, and private prayers are said by the participants. Following the parade, the assembly and everyone else in the community is invited to enjoy the food and festivities associated with a St. Joseph altar. The devotion to St. Joseph is so deeply felt and widely embraced in this community that the mayor and city council, using municipal funds, purchased and installed a statue of St. Joseph on public land in the center of town. When asked if he thought the purchase of this religious statue with public money violated the separation of church and state, Mayor Phillip Domiano replied, "There ain't but one good Lord."[51]

Another chapel still available upon request, but no longer in general use, is located just off U.S. Highway 51 between Independence and Amite. It is dedicated to St. Expedito and owes its existence to Josephine Taoromina, a Sicilian immigrant who brought her devotion to St. Expedito with her when she came to Independence in the early 1900s. After she was married and living in her own home, Josephine, like so many others of her generation, set up a private devotional to St. Expedito in one room of her home. There, she and members of her immediate family would make petitions, offer prayers, and give thanks for the intercession of St. Spedite (phonetic spelling), as the saint is called by Janet Marciano, Josephine's granddaughter. As the popularity of the devotion increased to include extended kinsmen and neighbors, it was decided to construct a separate facility for devotionals to St. Expedito. Eventually, with assistance from the community, the Taorominas built a chapel detached from the house but still on the family's property. It contained a framed picture of St. Expedito, the Stations of the Cross, and votive candles. The chapel was used for private prayer, for recitation of the rosary by religious groups, for novenas, and for receptions following baptisms, confirmations, and weddings. But the biggest event associated with the chapel was the remembrance of the Feast of St. Expedito, celebrated the second Sunday in June. A statue commissioned in Italy eventually arrived and replaced the picture of the saint. Rosaries and novenas were conducted daily for two weeks prior to the feast. On the day of the feast, there was a procession with an Italian band and the statue of St. Expedito in the lead. The procession was followed by Mass and then a celebration on the chapel grounds. The festivities included, but were not limited to, a picnic, bingo, a raffle, and *boccia-ball.*

To this day, the chapel is adorned with the symbols of gratitude from those whose prayers were believed to have been answered by St. Expedito. Plaster, plastic, and wooden representations of parts of the human body are displayed in the chapel in thanks for favors granted. One woman whose husband lost the use of his hands due to strokes prayed to St. Expedito for improvement in her husband's condition. Physicians had assured the woman no improvement was possible. When her husband recovered sufficiently enough to drive and do some minimal hand work, the woman had plaster hands molded and placed in the chapel in remembrance of "the miracle." Others have contributed plaster casts from broken arms and legs, which hang from the chapel rafters as symbolic remembrances of prayers answered to mend broken limbs. There are also reproductions of eyes signifying favors granted to people who were losing their eyesight or required eye surgery. There is no question regarding the authenticity of the piety of these devotees. The real question is whether or not St. Expedito ever existed.

Butler's Lives of the Saints lists a St. Expeditus (no date) with the strangest commentary. It seems people invoked him when they were in haste. He became the patron of those who wanted to guard against procrastination.[52] No evidence supports the notion that there ever was a real person by the name of Expeditus. There is a story about an incident alleged to have taken place in France sometime in the 1600s. According to the tale, a packing case containing the exhumed remains of a saint originally entombed in the ancient Roman catacombs was sent to a community of nuns in Paris. The case was dispatched with the inscription *Spedito* on its exterior. The nuns mistakenly thought *Spedito,* meaning rapid, was the name of the saintly martyr and energetically set to work to propagate his cult. The account in *Butler's Lives of the Saints* goes on to say that from these simple beginnings, the devotion to St. Expeditus spread rapidly throughout sections of the Catholic countries of Europe. St. Expeditus was especially popular in Sicily, where he became the patron of the town of Acireale. From Sicily, *St.* Expeditus (*Spedito*) undoubtedly made his way to Independence in the twentieth century.

These examples of Catholic piety were cultivated in Italy, then transplanted to Louisiana by the immigrants. They express religious attitudes and practices related to favors requested and granted. But what did immigrants think, say, and do when God or their saints did not respond to their petitions? On this point, the historical record is unambiguous. When favors were not granted or not granted promptly enough, the ears of the saints may well have been burned by a volley of verbal abuse. Gossip about the saint's failure, even cursing, might be part of the rhetoric expressed by the abandoned devotee. Sometimes words of disapproval were followed by deeds of discontent, as illustrated in the story of St. Francis at the beginning of this chapter!

RELIGIOUS TRANSFORMATIONS

When the Italians came to the New World, the only possession they had to bring with them other than their family was their uncompromising faith. These two institutional resources, more than anything else, made it possible for them to survive in their new homeland. Over the course of approximately five generations, about 125 years, what remains of the immigrants' old expression of religion is greatly modified. How to describe what remains intact, what is changed, and what is new is no easy task.

For the old ones, religion was at once an intimate and a remote experience. Nothing was so close to the Italian peasants' conception of themselves as their traditions, and their traditions were all shaded by the sacred canopy of Roman Catholicism. Like Tevye and the other villagers in Anatevka,[53] Italians in the Old Country knew exactly who they were, because as far back as could be remembered, they were defined by the traditions surrounding them and their ancestors.

Like Tevye, they had no idea why or how these traditions came about, but they believed the authority of the past. This was true of devout and irreligious Catholics alike. Moreover, atheists were equally influenced by traditional Catholic culture. A religiously inspired sense of right and wrong was taken for granted in nineteenth-century peasant society. It was seldom, if ever, questioned.

While religion was deeply ingrained in the moral conscience of the peasant, the same cannot be said for the church, which was symbolically and sociologically removed from their daily lives. In 1900, the Catholic Church represented itself as an institution that stood between God and the laity. Priests were projected as the keepers of the keys to the kingdom due to their control over the sacraments, which were seen as essential to salvation. The priests and the church tangibly touched the lives of the parishioners for marriages, baptisms, confirmations, funerals, and perhaps little else. Except for a small cadre of devotees, Sunday worship service was not a part of people's routines. Some parents and their children, together with old women and a lesser number of old men, typically made up the complement of Sunday worshipers.

The church has undergone a revolutionary transformation since Vatican II in 1965. Religious tradition has no monopolistic claim on Italian-Americans the way it claimed the attention of the immigrants. One consequence of this has been a decline in spiritual adoration associated with religious festivals. Many of the festivals have faded away with the death of the immigrants.

Even when the festivals continue or intensify as some have, except for some small groups of devotees, the participants are there for fun and frivolity, not spiritual benefits.

When the Italians came to Louisiana, they were Catholic—perhaps in name only, but Catholic nevertheless. Their descendants remain largely, though not exclusively, Catholic. With Americanization over the generations, there has been an increase in marriages across ethnic lines, some of which have crossed religious lines as well. As a result, people of Italian descent are represented in a great many other Christian denominations. Like so many other Americans, they have been attracted especially to newer congregations of evangelical fundamentalists.

Another challenge to the traditional spirituality embraced by the immigrants has been the rapid encroachment of materialism and its companion, secularism, in the lives of contemporary Italian-Americans. As partners with most other Americans in the temporal abundance available in the United States, Italian-Americans have felt the full force of their degenerative effect on spiritual life. These twin forces of postmodern society have produced religious experiences in modern Italian-Americans that are very different from those of the immigrants who made it all possible.

The story of the Italians and their religion in Louisiana is one of gradual transformations, not abrupt, dramatic changes. Notwithstanding the decline in traditionalism, the inroads of other Christian denominations, the growth of materialism, and the rush toward secularization over more than a century of residence in the Pelican State, Italian-Americans have become more orthodox in their beliefs and practices. Their loyalty to the organizational church is now apparent in their greater acceptance of the clergy. This occurred primarily because the organized church extended into immigrant neighborhoods, cultivated a local clergy, and developed parochial schools. The Italian immigrants' arrival coincided with the rapid growth of ecclesiastical parishes throughout Louisiana, the founding of local seminaries, the founding of the Diocese of Alexandria (1910), and the establishment of a statewide system of parochial education largely operated by nuns.

In 1832 there were only 6 Catholic churches in all of Louisiana, but by 1890, about the beginning of the Italian influx, the number soared to 184. Moreover, Francis Janssens, archbishop of New Orleans from 1888 to 1897, sought to overhaul Catholic education in the state by establishing a parochial school in every ecclesiastical parish. Though the policy was never fully implemented, it resulted in the formation of many Catholic schools supported by all the local parishioners. Previously, Catholic schools existed, but they were entirely supported by personal contributions (tuition) from those parents. Thus, Catholic education was largely confined to the sons and daughters of a Catholic elite who could afford the expenses of such instruction.[54]

CHAPTER NINE

Becoming American
and the Hunger of Memory

Theodore Roosevelt once proclaimed, "We will have no hyphenated Americans." Contrary to presidential rhetoric, we have always had hyphenated Americans and will continue to have them into the foreseeable future. Hyphenated Americans are in the process of becoming Americanized. They are the products of mixed cultures, with their foreign ancestry pulling in one direction and their United States experiences pulling in another. Their forebears came from somewhere else, while they were born and reared in America. During the course of their cultural hyphenation, they run the risk of becoming marginal to both societies, the one they have not yet completely left behind mentally and the one to which they have not yet given their full cultural allegiance.

Some previously hyphenated Americans are no longer distinguishable from the general white American melting pot. With very few exceptions, their ancestors came from northern and western European countries like Ireland, France, Germany, and the Netherlands. Americans whose ancestors originated in southern and eastern Europe, including Italian-Americans, are not yet completely culturally invisible. Though they are close to completing the journey from hyphenated to unhyphenated, they continue to cast an ethnic shadow in

America's cultural landscape. Millions of others, like African-Americans, Chinese-Americans, Vietnamese-Americans, and Hispanic-Americans, also continue to struggle for complete acceptance. Whether or not their history will unfold as did the history of European ethnics in America remains to be seen.

Generational analysis is useful in assessing the Italians' journey into mainstream America. We take "generation" to mean persons born at about the same time who have had roughly similar experiences. For example, members of the post-World War II generation known as the "baby boomers" share, among other experiences, affluence.

The immigrant generation, the first to arrive, is the first generation. Accordingly, the second generation is the sons and daughters of immigrants. The third generation includes the grandsons and granddaughters of the immigrants. The Italians have been in America long enough to have a fourth generation of great-grandsons and great-granddaughters. In a sense, the fourth generation is comparable to Generation X Americans; their lives are yet to be lived. Very few have reached old age. They remain, to some extent, an unknown entity. However, inspired by the autobiography of Richard Rodriguez,[1] we see the third and fourth generations as largely Americanized individuals who have a longing for their roots.

Ethnicity was revived in the 1970s partly as a result of the new political reality created by the Civil Rights movement in the 1960s. Critics argued that the reemergence of ethnicity at that time was largely symbolic, for throughout the period, ethnicity was waning.[2] In Herbert J. Gans's view, this weak copy focused on style not substance, on leisure activities not everyday life. Richard D. Alba[3] states that in the 1960s and 1970s, third- and fourth-generation Italian-Americans entered American universities in substantial numbers. Many of them wrote about ethnicity to raise awareness among their peers. But the result was a minor lifestyle variation. There was no communal life, language, or culture.

The debate over symbolic ethnicity revolves around the meaning of events in the chronology of European assimilation. Perhaps Marcus Lee Hansen best describes this chronology: "What the son tried to forget, the grandson tries to remember."[4] Hansen meant that the children of European immigrants discovered that their Old Country skin was a barrier to acceptance in America and longed to cast it off. The grandchildren came to appreciate the heritage that was nearly lost.

CULTURAL, SOCIAL, AND PSYCHOLOGICAL TRANSFORMATIONS

The language scholars use in describing the process of Americanization need not be opaque. There are three dimensions to the process: cultural, relational, and personal. The cultural dimension is concerned with the extent to which American values, beliefs, and practices have replaced their Old World counterparts. The relational dimension examines relationships between the immigrant group and other Americans. It seeks to describe the extent to which immigrants and subsequent generations of Italian-Americans are neighbors, co-workers, friends, and kin with Americans who have no Italian ancestry. Finally, at the personal or psychological level, scholars have focused on the shift in identity that is part of the process of becoming American. Does the person see himself or herself as an Italian, a Sicilian, or an American?

"Making it" in America refers unambiguously to getting ahead economically and socially. The three most useful measures of this kind of success are education, occupation, and income. Income levels of Italian-Americans are comparable to or higher than those of other Americans of European Catholic ancestry. Italian-American Catholics are second only to Irish Catholics in earnings. By this measure, the third and fourth generations of Italians have "made it" in America. Moreover, the educational gap between first- and second-generation

Italian-Americans and Anglo-Americans has been largely closed by the third and fourth generations, and the occupational gap, as measured by prestige and percentage in the professions, has narrowed considerably yet persists.[5]

With regard to cultural traits, the use of the Italian language among third- and fourth-generation Italians has fallen off. James A. Crispino[6] reported that in Bridgeport, Connecticut, 72 percent of the second generation but only 10 percent of the fourth generation can speak Italian. Alba's analysis of national surveys reported very little evidence that uniquely Italian domestic values have survived. He summarizes:

> What remains of the family ethos is a mild version of family solidarity. Conservative attitudes with respect to the family have all but withered away; on questions of divorce, homosexuality, premarital sex, abortion, and non-traditional roles for women, Italian-Americans are now as liberal—or conservative, if one likes—as WASPs and other Americans. What remains is a slightly greater tendency to remain in the same place . . . and a moderately greater willingness to live with and keep company with relatives.[7]

Although less significant than language usage or family values, some immigrants' inclination to anglicize their names indicates assimilation. Many Italian immigrants had never seen their names in writing. They had no idea how to spell their names, and they depended upon immigration officials and customs agents to record them, perhaps for the very first time. As a result, brothers and sisters had different spellings of the same family name. For example, Salomone also became Solomone and Salamoni. Other immigrants deliberately changed their names. Castro Giovanni became Castle John, Perrino became Perrin, Canale became Canal, and in one case Di Agistino became Iverstine.[8] Given names were routinely Americanized. *Antonio* became Tony, *Giuseppe* became Joe, *Salvadore* became Sal, and so on. It almost never happened that other Americans Italianized their names, but it has happened.

A well-known Italian restaurant named Vinnelli's, which is famous for its pizzas, is located in Tupelo, Mississippi. The restaurant was founded in 1975 by Demetrois Kapenekas, who did not believe that patrons in Tupelo would buy pizza from someone by his name, so he changed it to Vinnelli.[9] The strategy must have worked because Vinnelli's Restaurant does a thriving business.

What is the nature of the relations between Italian-Americans and other Americans? Are Italian-Americans turning inward toward greater ethnic solidarity, or are they more open than previous generations? Marriage patterns are both clear and striking. Each successive generation increasingly married non-Italians. Seventy percent of the third and fourth generation married someone with no Italian ancestry. This means that Italians are increasingly entering the family networks of other Americans, and the ancestry of Italians in America is dramatically changing. In 1979, nearly 90 percent of older Italians reported unmixed ancestry, but only 20 percent of the youngest Italian-Americans had unmixed ancestry.[10]

The exit of Italian-Americans from their ethnic colonies indicates neighbor and friendship relationships with non-Italian-Americans. This occurred largely between 1930 and 1970. Partly because the largest concentration of Italian-Americans was in Northern cities and partly because Italians preferred to live with their co-ethnics, Italian-American segregation historically has been high. Chiefly after World War II, residential segregation decreased due to a variety of factors, not the least of which was suburbanization. However, residential segregation persists in some geographical pockets in cities like New York, Boston, St. Louis, Chicago, and San Francisco. It should be noted that segregation varies greatly from city to city and across regions. The fact that Italian-Americans are concentrated in the North, a region with high levels of residential segregation, suggests caution in drawing conclusions about the persistence of Italian-American settlement patterns.

Italian-American residential enclaves, wherever they persist, have become more diverse, with a greater presence of people of mixed or altogether different ancestry. This is true also of Louisiana's Italian-American population. The New Orleans French Quarter is not as Italian as it was before the mid-twentieth century, nor is Kenner, or the sugar parishes, or Tangipahoa Parish. The Italians have scattered residentially, making them less visible as a definable ethnic group. Where once one could identify schools, churches, community centers, neighborhoods, and other institutional settings as Italian, today it is more difficult, if not impossible, to do so.

The Italians' Americanization was reflected in political behavior. The more American they became, the more willing they were to practice their citizenship. Other Americans were also more willing to have them do so. Consequently, Italian-Americans began to offer themselves for elected and appointed positions in local, state, and national government.

Fiorello La Guardia was elected to the United States House of Representatives in 1916. John Pastore of Rhode Island was the first Italian-American governor of a state and in 1950 he became the first U.S. senator. Since then, other Italian-Americans have served in Congress and the Cabinet. In the 1990s, their participation in national politics continued to increase. However, like most Catholic ethnics, Italian-Americans historically have been underrepresented in national politics in both elected and appointed positions. Exceptions can be found. For example, at the state and local levels in New York, New Jersey, Massachusetts, Connecticut, and Rhode Island, where they comprise a significant proportion of the electorate, they have attained substantial power.

In Louisiana there has been, almost from the beginning, some representation of Italians in political affairs, but this activity has not been so strong as to contradict the national experience. *The Membership Roster in the Louisiana Senate from 1880-2004* reveals the following listing of senators serving in the Louisiana Senate prior to 1950 whose ancestry is Italian:[11]

Samuel S. Carlisle, West Carroll Parish, 1884-88
Anthony Sambola, Orleans Parish, 1892-94
L. Caspari, Desoto and Natchitoches parishes, 1900-1904
Dr. L. Lazardo, Acadia and St. Landry parishes, 1908-12 and
1912-16
Ralph Cuculla, Orleans Parish, 1924-28
Leo F. Terzia, Lincoln, Morehouse, Union parishes, 1932-36
and 1936-40
Clarence A. Lorio, East Baton Rouge Parish, 1936-40
Chester J. Coco, Avoyelles and Evangeline parishes, 1944-48
and 1948-52
Guy J. D'Antonio, Orleans Parish, 1948-52

How can this slow and partial progress be explained? Some consideration should be given to the working-class origins of most Italian-Americans. Following upward mobility, an ethnic group has to consolidate its position and accept lesser appointments within a political party before its members can reasonably expect bigger things. To what extent have Old World values critical of government held back Italian-American political participation? It's hard to say, but it must not have had much of a deleterious effect given the extent of Italian-American mobility and assimilation.

The Italian-American vote, until comparatively recently, had been solidly in the camp of the Democratic party. The immigrants and their largely working class children subscribed to Catholic conceptions of social justice. Unionism; government support for the unemployed, widowed, handicapped, and orphaned; liberal immigration laws; public education; and taxation that put a ceiling on income for the rich and a floor under the income of the poor were appealing ideas to them. This kind of political orientation was to be expected from immigrants and their children who brought with them rather well developed socialistic notions.

The general economic prosperity that followed World War II and the social mobility enjoyed by the third generation moved Italian-Americans as a group toward the political center, if not somewhat right of center. As a consequence, contemporary Italian-Americans are divided in their political loyalties. Collectively they are a nebulous mixture of Democrats, Republicans, and Independents. Many immigrants would be appalled at the political philosophies and the voting records of their progeny.

Some say Italian-American voting strength has been diluted by party switching. This argument suggests that in the Democratic "machines" in Northern cities, Italian-American politicians were blocked by Irish politicians in control of patronage. It has been suggested that the gangster label continues to work against aspiring Italian-American politicos. The Watergate tapes have Pres. Richard Nixon, a proven crook, in consultation with party confidants, considering appointing an Italian-American to a top federal post. At one point in the discussion, Nixon asks, "But where would we find an honest Italian-American?"[12] Although Italian-Americans no longer vote as an "ethnic bloc," there is little doubt that, similar to other European ethnics, they are full partners in the American political process.

If Italian-Americans were well on their way toward being thoroughly Americanized by 1970 and this trend continues, then how does one explain the resurgence of ethnicity in the 1970s? In that decade, the Civil Rights movement drew attention to the historical barriers erected against African-American aspirations. Once the root causes of discrimination were attacked and the movement found substantial support among whites, some rather remarkable changes in the politics of race and ethnicity took place. The political landscape changed in a way that favored ethnic revival. Many white ethnics seized the opportunity to remove whatever residual barriers to mobility existed. It became politically advantageous to be a "victim." In 1971, Italian-Americans gathered by the thousands in New York to contest the usage of words and phrases such as *Mafia* and *Cosa Nostra,* frequently used in the mass media and in government circles. This Unity Day Rally orchestrated by Italian-Americans illustrates how protests were politically legitimized during the Civil Rights movement. Thus, a dying ethnicity was revived by the new racial politics.

The newborn ethnic consciousness was and is symbolic; it demands no more commitment than attending public celebrations that are attended by numerous non-Italians as well. The old authentic ethnicity drew boundaries between insiders and outsiders and was reflected in a powerful Italian identity. This new ethnicity, although real, appears to be insubstantial. Its strongest expressions seem to be for contrived rather than spontaneous gatherings.

Admittedly, within generations, as within ethnic, racial, religious, political, class, and any other large groupings, there are widespread variations. No two people are alike, much less aggregates containing millions. So while we concentrate on the similarities that characterize a generation, be aware there are a good many differences. We will be concerned primarily with changes over the years in the family system, since the one indisputable fact about Italian life is the centrality of the family. The family is supreme—at least it was in Italy, when the immigrants left their towns and villages to come to America. It lost none of its strength in the passage across the Atlantic. The unacculturated immigrant simply transplanted his family lifeways in the United States.

GENERATIONAL TRANSFORMATIONS

The Immigrants: The First Generation

Italian immigrants brought with them a set of family values inseparably connected to community and religious ideals. Indeed, the beliefs, customs, and morals of the home, the state, and the church formed a seamless web around domestic relations from which there could be no escape. These three institutions joined together to forge an ironclad sense of tradition.

Part of that tradition placed the father at the head of the family. He was its indisputable ruler, be he wise or foolish, saint or scoundrel, gentle or cruel. He could, if he chose to do so, punish his children severely. No one would challenge his authority. He was to be feared, respected, and imitated; he was never to be questioned or contradicted. These rules of family conduct were sometimes violated, as are all rules of interpersonal behavior, but it was a far greater breach of propriety to challenge the father in public than in private.

Just as husbands were superior to wives, so also were boys superior to girls. A double standard of conduct was practiced, with no regard to sexual equality. There was a strong preference for the firstborn to be a male. Wives held to this view as strongly as husbands. Sons and daughters were loved alike, yet parental treatment of the two sexes was altogether different. Sons were given great latitude in exploring their interests and satisfying their needs. The older they were, the greater freedom they enjoyed. Daughters, on the other hand, were always watched very closely. The older they got, the more closely they were guarded. Once daughters were married, a sense of great relief came over the parents, especially the mother.

The protective web surrounding Italian girls extended to their mothers, who were not supposed to work outside the home. Unlike Irish, German, Polish, and other European ethnic women, immigrant Italian women were discouraged from entering the factories, which provided female jobs in very large numbers. Although some Italian wives did earn wages in factories, that circumstance was considered regrettable. A woman's place was in the home. Some employment was permissible, though. To work in a family-owned and -operated business was entirely admirable. Consequently, when Italian immigrants had family businesses, they really were family businesses. Everyone worked in them: Papa, Mamma, and all the children except infants.

Divorce was not allowed in the Old Country. In America, where it was legal, it was extremely rare among immigrants.

When it did occur, it was a disgrace for the whole family, not just for the divorced couple. The immigrant Italian family was ethnically homogamous; that is, Italians married other Italians.

The immigrant generation was imbued with a strong puritanical streak. However, Italians certainly did not avoid vulgarity. A foul mouth on a boy or man was a sign of masculinity. It was even permissible for women under certain circumstances, such as when things went wrong in the kitchen. Little children who cursed were admonished, but they were nevertheless considered cute when they did so. The discussion of sexual matters was to be strictly avoided. Husbands and wives made no public display of affection. The restraints imposed in marriage were even more rigorously required before marriage. Purity was assured during courtship through an elaborate system of chaperonage.

Dating, as we know it today, did not exist. It was not a recreational activity. From the beginning, it was a serious matter, something that was supposed to lead without interruption or delay to marriage. The Sicilian proverb has it that "long engagements turn into snakes." Children were greatly desired, especially in great numbers. They were a blessing from heaven and constituted the primary reason for marriage. Moreover, in those days, children were economic assets. They were valuable members of an agricultural economy that had not yet mechanized.

Some non-Italian whites complained about the large number of children in Tangipahoa Parish Italian households before World War II. They claimed that Italian strawberry farmers had all their unpaid children planting, cultivating, and picking berries while the non-Italians had to hire agricultural field hands to do theirs. The non-Italians also objected to the Italians working the fields on Sunday, when good Christians were supposed to refrain from worldly toil.

The Second Generation

The children of the immigrants inherited their parents' attitudes and values toward the family, but they also grew up in

America, where they were exposed to a variety of experiences that called some of the old values into question. By and large this generation subscribed to the beliefs of the old generation, but their behavior did not always conform to those beliefs. The father was supposed to be the patriarch, divorce was socially prohibited, families were expected to be large, and familistic concerns took precedence over all else. Yet, what was normally expected could not and did not always take place, making this generation somewhat marginal.

This generation had one foot firmly planted in Europe and one foot firmly planted in America. They spoke two languages. Parents spoke Italian to each other in private and to other Italian-speaking adults, and they spoke English to their children and to non-Italians. The only time they spoke Italian in front of their children was when they argued. As a consequence, many of the children of this generation spoke very little Italian, but they understood the curse words.

Immigrants who were bilingual clearly preferred Italian to English. They would speak English only when it was necessary. The immigrants' children who were bilingual, however, gradually came to prefer English over Italian. For the second generation, Italian was spoken in the bedroom, English was spoken in the parlor, and a mixture of the two became the language of the kitchen.

In this generation, divorce was unusual but not unheard of. Family size declined, and the supreme authority of the father was not always accepted. This generation typically married within the Italian community, but the rule was not followed as religiously as was the case with the immigrants. Where the Italian community was large and resentment toward it strong, marriage across ethnic lines was infrequent. Conversely, when the Italian community was spread out and attitudes were comparatively tolerant, a considerable amount of out-marriage took place. For example, in Tangipahoa Parish, where social acceptance was low, sons and daughters of immigrants overwhelmingly married other Italians.[13] In New Orleans, where acceptance was greater, the majority of the second generation married non-Italians. At this time, between 1920 and 1950, this contrasting pattern prevailed because the great majority of white non-Italians in Tangipahoa Parish were English-Scotch-Irish Protestants who treated the Italians with disdain, if not contempt, while New Orleans was predominately Catholic and decidedly more tolerant toward the Italians.

Unlike the immigrants, their children did not restrict their social contacts to other Italians. Those who went to school came in contact with non-Italian friends and acquaintances. On the job, they worked side by side with non-Italians. Eventually, this led to a lifestyle that included a variety of experiences, different from, and often at odds with, the way of life of their parents.

The second generation moved into a wider variety of occupations than did their fathers. While their fathers were day laborers in the construction industry, the second generation became carpenters, masons, plumbers, and electricians. Those who were most successful became small contractors working for themselves. As they followed their fathers into the factories, they moved up from the unskilled floor, to the semiskilled bench, to skilled occupations like machinist and tool-and-die maker. In the shipyards they became boilermakers, welders, and pipefitters. Large numbers of them moved into the ranks of foremen. However, this pattern of upward mobility was far less common in Louisiana than in Northern cities.

The most common pattern of upward mobility in rural areas was the acquisition of land. That transformation took place within the immigrant generation. Typically and in substantial numbers, they purchased land surrounding the city of New Orleans. They were the truck farmers who supplied the city with fresh produce. The overwhelming majority of the truck farmers in St. Bernard, Plaquemines, and Jefferson parishes were Italians. Prior to World War II, Kenner was a small agricultural community dominated by Italian truck farmers. Following the war, as the city expanded, property values skyrocketed, producing wealth for many of those Italians who had not previously sold out.

In Tangipahoa Parish, many of the sons and daughters of immigrants continued to farm their parents' farmsteads. More of them, however, began the long commute into New Orleans to work on the river or into Baton Rouge to work at the plants along Scenic Highway. Though most of the second-generation Italians in the parish earned their living in the cities, they did not abandon the farms. Instead, the farms, which were small to begin with, were divided among the children. Some simply sold out; others sold out to their brothers and sisters; still others built homes on the property they inherited.

Those who worked in the cities continued to plant berries, but instead of two- to five-acre fields, they planted thirty- to forty-row patches. By 1960, when the second generation was approaching the age of fifty, there was a noticeable decline in Italian involvement in the strawberry industry. In earlier days a successful immigrant would ship a hundred crates a day during the peak of the season. The second generation was more likely to sell by the pint or flat along the side of the road.

The Third and Fourth Generations

The first generation, the immigrants, were unquestionably Italian. Their children, the second generation, were reared as Italians, but they grew up with American influences. The third generation was reared as Americans with some lingering Italian attributes. The orientation of the fourth generation was even more American.

The old traditions weakened. What was required of the immigrants and expected of the children became only preferences for the grandchildren. The old obligations were breaking down and options were expanding. Among the third generation, English was not only the language of choice, it was the only language they could speak. Democratic decision making was beginning to be practiced in the family, and family size was declining. Married children were moving out of the old neighborhoods—not just across town but out of town. Friendships with non-Italians were common, and dating American style became the norm. Marriage was no longer confined to other Italians and divorce increased. Psychology became more important than tradition in rearing children. Medicine was substituted for folk remedies. Primogeniture gave way to egalitarianism. Godparenthood became peripheral to the extended family. Individualism increased as familism declined. Education emerged as a prized possession. These transformations took place between the Great Depression of the 1930s and the tumultuous decade of the 1960s.

All of America underwent major transformations during this time. The social changes in the forties were violent and visible; those of the fifties were quiet and invisible but significant. In the forties we fought the war, men died, families separated, industry expanded, jobs multiplied, and women went to work. In the fifties affluence spread to the middle class, automobiles became commonplace, those who could fled to the suburbs, television was perfected, and we invented the shopping center and drive-in movies.

Third- and fourth-generation Italian-Americans, like all other Americans, were caught up in these transformations. They could not insulate themselves from the changes sweeping across America. The combined effects of these social and economic changes presented insurmountable challenges to *la via vecchia,* the old way. The third generation was not just swept along by what was happening, they eagerly participated in it. The primary vehicle for their participation was education. Educational success for them became a conveyor belt to occupational success. College pointed the way to the professions and to management positions. As technical and skilled factory occupations opened up and expanded, Italians moved into them. This resulted in a larger Italian presence in the middle class. The barbecue pit and swimming pool in the suburb replaced furniture and a car in the old working-class neighborhood.

While it is true that Italian immigrants and their descendants became more American, it has not resulted in an equal and opposite loss of Italian identity. A few of the old ways have been consciously rejected; some have been given up reluctantly; many have been forgotten; all have been modified. Still, the heritage remains.

The fourth generation is with us now. The next two or three decades belong to them. They are pivotal because they are the first generation without direct experience with *la via vecchia*. The immigrants lived it. Their children and grandchildren were personally connected to the old way through the immigrants they knew and loved. The first generation is not here anymore. The second generation is passing on. Thus, the current generation is without a direct link to the Old Country. How this will affect the identity of the fourth generation is still emerging.

To oversimplify, one could say that the first generation, the immigrants, were Italians who lived in America. Their children are Italian-Americans with the emphasis on Italian. Their grandchildren are Americans of Italian descent. Their great-grandchildren are Americans of mixed ancestry.

VIGNETTES ON THE GENERATIONAL TRANSFORMATIONS

"Santa" and "The Old Man" represent the immigrant generation. In both stories the main characters are unacculturated Italians. "An Erstwhile Criminal" portrays the second-generation Italian-American as marginal in two worlds—one Italian, the other American. The Italian criminal, myth and fact, is its focus. The final brief literary sketch, "An American Success Story," recounts the identity problems of the third generation.

Santa

Santa looked a great deal older than her seventy years, for they had been difficult years. Her breathing was now labored as a result of asthma and other respiratory problems. Her legs were often swollen and covered with painful open sores from the complication of diabetes. She walked with the aid of an almost straight stick she called a "cane," but walking was an ordeal and stooping impossible.

In her youth she had been beautiful, small in stature but with large blue eyes. Now wrinkles covered her face and neck. But nothing—not the years, the hard work, the many illnesses—had dimmed those eyes. They were a source of other women's envy, because few Sicilian women possessed the characteristics that past invaders from northwestern Europe had contributed to the population of Sicily. But her life was hardly a thing to envy. Her husband had died and left her with five children to rear. Her two boys contributed to the family's income as day laborers. Two of the girls married early and moved some distance away outside the range of frequent visitation. The youngest daughter, Rosalie, never married and nursed the old woman until the day she died.

Grief and trouble seemed to be Santa's daily bread. Her youngest son died prematurely in his thirties, having spent the last ten years of his life in a hospital. The oldest daughter fought almost continuously with her husband and the few visits to her mother were filled with the reenactments of these conflicts.

What would have broken weaker beings, Santa took in stride. She was even able to cultivate a lively sense of humor in the face of all her troubles. Her faith in the inscrutable ways of God was unshakable. She believed that God's reasons for allowing the innocent to suffer must be part of a great plan and never questioned His goodness.

Her bedroom looked like a sacred shrine: holy-water fonts, blessed palms, and holy pictures and statues were everywhere. Next to her bed, two votive candles burned in front of an aging plaster of Paris Madonna with child. When her hands were not working, they were thumbing the large wooden beads of her rosary.

"Mamma, where are you going?" Rosalie called to her.

"Plant the beans, whata you think?"

"But, Mamma, you don't have to. You're going to fall one of these days."

The old woman paid her no mind but determinedly and slowly hobbled out into the backyard. Half-remembering a bit of Sicilian wisdom, she yelled to her daughter, "He who sows reaps."

Against the fence in the backyard, Santa rested momentarily from her long journey. When she caught her breath, she opened a very old and rumpled paper bag. She carefully extracted the dried beans from the yard-long pods. Taking several in her left hand before pinning the bag on the fence, she poked a hole next to the fence with her "cane." She dropped one bean at a time, but when a bean didn't fall into the tiny hole, she coaxed it in with her "cane." She would also drop a bean before a hole was made. When this procedure was followed, she pushed the seed into the ground with her cane, making little effort to cover it with soil. The planting was done almost as if she were repeating some sacred rite, and indeed each seed was dropped or pushed into its appointed station with a kind of prayer. "This is for you, Santa Maria," she said to one. "This is for you, San Giuseppe," she said to another. St. Francis, St. Anthony, St. Paul, and St. Rosalie were similarly memorialized. By the time she ran out of fence, she had planted a veritable litany.

In two months she would collect the long beans with as much joy as a small boy collects treasures that he secures in his pockets. With skillful eye and hand she would pick only those beans that were large enough and tender enough to make her bean omelette.

She would repeat this ritual for eleven more springs before the God she always trusted called her to His bosom. The last spring of her life, she was confined to her bed. For three days she was semiconscious, refusing food and only occasionally sipping water through a straw. Her heart grew weaker and weaker and she went into what seemed to be a coma. Rosalie kept lonely vigil at her mother's bedside. From time to time, she would reach under the covers and check to see if Santa's feet were cold. Usually the old woman would not respond to these investigations, but once, some twelve hours before her death, she raised her head and said, "This is not the hour."

*Death came to Santa slowly and reverently, and she nobly yielded to
its demands. The saints would have to find someone else next spring if
they wanted the great beans to be planted in their honor.*

The Old Man

*The old man raised his hand to tug at the crop of wiry white hair
that completely covered his head. Under that canopy of white was a
remarkable head that contained a treasury of the words and deeds of
past generations. They were not the written words of great sages or
scholars, but the many observations and experiences gathered by countless and nameless individuals woven into the fabric of Sicilian folk wisdom. This wisdom was neatly catalogued, and relevant information on
any subject could be retrieved immediately. The old man was a deposi-
tory of knowledge, a walking library.*

*Nothing in the old man's room suggested this. There were no diplo-
mas, no books, and only a few pieces of furniture, which his daughter,
in whose house he lived, thought necessary to secure his comfort. The
old chair next to his bed was used as an aid for getting in and out of
bed as much as for sitting. The bare wood of the chair, worn from age
and frequent handling, blended well with the simple iron bed. The only
other furniture was a large cabinet, the bottom of which was reserved
for his clothes and other personal possessions, such as his pearl-covered
snuff box. The top of the cabinet was used to store the wine, bread, and
cheese. These items he would "snack on" between meals. His guitar,
when not being used, was placed under his bed. Two "holy pictures,"
one of the Sacred Heart and the other of the Madonna, and a crucifix
completed the furnishings of the room. The only light was supplied by
a bulb hanging from an electrical wire, with a long pull-string switch.*

*Only the old man's reputation for knowledge could explain why so
many immigrants came to see him, and those who came were rewarded
for their efforts. They came despairing, pressed, and confused, but they
left consoled, at ease, and resolute.*

*In spite of his advanced age a steady stream of "clients" continued
to seek his counsel. "There's still some oil left in the lamp." How much,
he did not presume to know. When the subject was broached he would*

say, "When the oil is finished, the lamp goes out." The old man didn't worry about death, for he had taken his own advice and put first things first. On those occasions when he himself was tempted to follow unwise counsel, he would remind himself of the words written on the walls of the vicaria *(cemetery) in Palermo: "Run, run as fast as you can, I'll wait for you here."*

The silence of his room was broken by the ritual greeting of Angelina and his daughter, Anna, as the latter escorted Angelina to his room. Anna would always stay with the visitors in the old man's room, at least for the first part of the conversation. She could tell by looking at the old man's eyes when it was time for her to leave. Today, however, her gravy (tomato sauce) demanded her immediate attention, and because Angelina was an old friend, she didn't have to extend this courtesy of sitting and talking for a while.

As for Angelina, she was desperate because she was having trouble with her husband again. He was the type that prompted the old Sicilian advice, "Keep away from husbands and mules." To add to her difficulties, he had begun to accuse her of squandering his money. The poor creature had to beg him for money for the children's clothes. No request seemed justified to him. Antonio was tight, vindictive, and bellicose. As Angelina poured her heart out to the old man, anger swelled up in him, but his eyes revealed nothing.

As Angelina continued her litany of troubles, the old man raised his hand to interrupt. He spoke softly but his voice almost sounded stern. "Every wind is contrary to a broken ship." She knew he was asking her to stop reciting her troubles. She pondered this advice and recalled how even her pasta and gravy gave her no pleasure and seemed to turn out wrong of late.

The old man consoled her with lessons from the life of Christ. He told her how much the good suffer for the bad. He told her that God has His purpose in this and in all difficulties. "Only you could put up with such a man," he told her. "God has His reason. Marriages and bishops are made in heaven."

Adapting to the painful and unchangeable conditions of life is the most difficult task. With this last proverb, Angelina's face revealed her

continuing protest. She had not yet learned how to embellish and cap-
italize on the happy aspects of a difficult life.

"My mother-in-law thinks I'm wrong," she whined.

The old man immediately retorted, "No girl gets on well with her
mother-in-law." Weaving an intricate cloth of argument, the old man
began to match a proverb to each protest Angelina raised. Like a skill-
ful lawyer, he drew upon maxims and experiences to refute each com-
plaint. At length, she realized her case was lost. She knew the old man
was right, but what her head conceded, her heart could not accept.

The old man always left his "clients" happy, and Angelina was still
in a depressed state. On such occasions, he used the most healing of the
healing arts, humor. In an unsuccessful attempt to hide his charity, he
gave her a few dollars and told her it was an early Christmas present,
because, considering his age, he might not live to see another Christmas.

Angelina's mouth revealed her amusement at this most unartful of
lies. Because he wished her to use it for herself, he said, "St. Joseph
shaved his own beard before shaving the others." Now the smile turned
into an almost audible laugh.

"Antonio's mother is an unhappy woman. Be nice to her but don't
associate too much. Everything is bad to her and she's been complain-
ing for the last seventy-five years. 'He who consorts with wolves, growls
like one.'" Then he added, "He who associates with cripples ends by
limping." With this last pearl of wisdom, Angelina was laughing
audibly.

An Erstwhile Criminal

The November sun gently bathed the small shotgun house just off St.
Claude Avenue as Tony Ochimala emerged on the banquette followed
by his three small children. The neighbors had come to expect this rather
comical sight of "Big Tony" closely tailed by four-year-old Mike, three-
year-old Luke, and two-year-old John. It was a bit like seeing three
chicks following the rooster. Mary Doyle, the Ochimalas' next-door
neighbor, was the first to call the neighborhood's attention to the paral-
lel. Tony's wife, Lucy, felt lucky to have a husband who not only loved
children but was exceptionally tolerant of their caprices.

There was another side of "Big Tony." He could lose his temper easily and had a reputation for settling arguments with his fists. But not once in the five years that Lucy and Tony had been married did he vent this temper on his wife and children. As for others, well that was a different matter. Just as the rooster and the three chicks rounded the corner, a short, fat, baby-faced man of thirty or so rushed up to Tony. "Eh, you son of a——" Tony clapped his hand over Paul Marcudi's mouth and halted the foulest tongue in the neighborhood.

"Stupotso, there are tender ears here." Tony felt like smashing Paul's face, and indeed he had done so once before for the very same reason. But today he had more forbearance than usual and curbed his initial urge to rearrange Paul's face.

Now Paul really couldn't stop himself from uttering obscenities. His whole vocabulary, which wasn't much, consisted of half-Italian and half-English curse words. When he wasn't cursing, he was spitting. Tony swore that to stand in the same spot with Paul for more than one hour was to risk drowning. To make matters worse, his aim was terrible. Lucky victims got only their shoes wet. The not so lucky would be baptized higher up. Tony witnessed an unfortunate passer-by get it on the bridge of her nose. Fortunately for Paul, the lady thought she had been the victim of sparrows overhead.

These peccadilloes notwithstanding, Tony liked Paul. Although Paul was a rogue, a coward, and half a dozen other equally unflattering things, he could make a dead man laugh. It was precisely his worthlessness that made Paul a valuable friend.

Today, in addition to selecting winners on his scratch sheet, Paul had a serious business proposition to discuss with Tony. "You wanna make some money real quick?"

Tony's arm reached out to bring a stray chick back in the barnyard, as he digested Paul's question. "What are you talking about?"

Paul hesitated for a moment, then responded, "My cousin from Harvey knows this guy who wants someone to store some booze for a few days. I figure you can ask your uncle Angelo to keep the stuff in his shed . . . just for two or three days. All we have to do is pick the stuff up in St. Bernard and put it in Angelo's shed. Can you borrow your uncle's truck?"

"Yeah, sure. When?"

"The day after tomorrow, after dark."

Later that night, Tony walked the short distance to his uncle's house. Angelo and Sarah, his wife, freely expressed their pleasure in seeing Tony and received him with such warmth that one would have thought he had made the journey from the other side of the globe. Now ordinarily, Tony would have felt at ease with this show of affection, but because he was asking something that could cause them trouble, he was on edge. He nervously fumbled for the correct words to state the purpose of his visit. "Uncle Angelo, ca-can I borrow your truck?"

"Sure." The old man instinctively gave the affirmative response. Still patting Tony on the back, he began tugging on his arm to direct him to the nearest chair.

"I-I need to use your shed to store . . ."

"Sure. Sure!" The old man interrupted him while Sarah busied herself in the kitchen trying to find something to offer Tony. Tony really wanted to tell the old man why he wanted the truck and what he wanted to store, but he couldn't bring himself to do it. Before he had left the couple's house that night, he convinced himself he would explain things fully to the old man when he went to pick up the truck.

By the time Tony, Paul, and Paul's cousin hauled the booze to Angelo's shed it was after one o'clock. As they walked toward the street, a car emerged out of the darkness and stopped in front of the trio. A single shotgun blast broke the silence. Paul and Tony ran in opposite directions. Paul's cousin lay face down on the banquette. The police found no witnesses and had no concrete leads. They speculated that it was a typical Mafia-style slaying. "A Sicilian was killed with a sawed-off shotgun, the preferred weapon of the Mafia" was the following morning's headline.

As for Paul and Tony, they were never to work on the wrong side of the law again. Tony, for his part, never breathed a word of it. Years later Paul would tell his grown children. His children would tell their children how their grandfather stood up to the Mafia and narrowly escaped death.

An American Success Story

Anthony. An-tho-ny. Was the name really Italian? He remembered how his friends in high school and college and even a few of his teachers *called him "Antonio." Their faces were full of expectation when they sounded it out. Sometimes he was actually embarrassed by it. At times he was a bit annoyed, particularly when they acted as if he should play the Italian buffoon. He would think, "Should I get a monkey and organ grinder and sing 'Ridi Pagliaccio'?"* But in truth, there were times when he was a young man that he played their game and feigned being Italian, as if exaggerated hand gestures and talk of Italian food could make someone Italian. Antonio! Antonio! His friends would sound out the name as if to conjure up some ghost from the past. At times, he resented references to his ancestry and interpreted them as prejudice and stupidity.*

Anthony was the grandchild of Sicilian immigrants. He wasn't an Italian. He didn't consider himself to be an Italian-American. He thought of himself as an American businessman who happened to have Italian grandparents. He was as far from being Italian as Louisiana is from Sicily. No, he was farther! One could always cross the ocean, but how does one make the journey into another self? Yet gradually, almost unconsciously, he was being drawn into reflection.

As a successful businessman he had become part of mainstream America, but he no longer savored his success as he once did. At times, he felt a strange disquiet. He was, like many of his American friends, an engine driven at breathtaking speed, coming from nowhere and going no place. He wasn't driving the engine. He was merely along for the ride. And for what purpose? Is success enough for a man to be content? He had "made it." In making it, he had distanced himself from his past. In severing himself from his roots, he had lost himself.

Now from time to time he would read works written by and on Italians in America. At first his desire was prompted by a half-awakened curiosity, but what had started as curiosity turned into a compelling search. Somehow he knew he could salvage something of his identity by searching the past. And thus he began his quest . . . his journey back in time to his childhood and to life in the old house he knew as a child with his parents and grandparents.

When he wasn't gleaning old family records, he was picking the brains of his parents, who patiently endured his persistent questions.

The biographies of his grandparents came to have new meaning for him. He relished what his parents remembered of the "old ones." He delighted in the Sicilian proverbs his parents managed to recall. He collected old family photographs, letters, and anything that could link him with his ancestors. He would spend hours scrutinizing these, devouring their meaning with the rapacity of a wolf, and still he was hungry for memory.

Antonio? No! Anthony. He couldn't lie. Those memories were too dear. American success is not bought cheaply. But by sheer will or luck, he had managed to find the lines of continuity that connected him with his past; and in doing so, he fancied he had found himself.

Anthony is struggling to find himself. Despite his material success, the world has lost meaning for him. He uses the knowledge of his ancestry to anchor himself. However, he resists the temptation to trivialize it. He refuses to delude himself by accepting the fact that he is American and no amount of celebrating ancestry can change that. However, his dilemma points unequivocally to the overriding importance of memory in the formation of our self-definitions. Juan Sanchez, a Brooklyn-born painter of Puerto Rican descent, speaks for all of us in declaring, "I had to find my way back to my culture, not for the sake of leisure education or memory but for survival—to understand the cultural complexity of my heritage."[14] Self is held together in an important sense by our memories. Our identities are threatened when memory is fragmented. For too many of us, our identities have become as fragmented as reflections in a broken mirror. Perhaps we should look upon all the inspirations that summon memories of our Italian ancestors the way Noah was told to look upon rainbows. Just as the bow in the clouds is the perpetual sign that God will not forget his people, our rainbows will remind us of who we are and of those who have come before us.

Notes

Chapter One
1. Mario Puzo, "Choosing a Dream: Italians in Hell's Kitchen," in *Generations,* ed. Jim Watts and Allen F. Davis (New York: Knopf, 1974), 32-41.
2. Bruno Roselli, *Let the Dead Speak!* (New York: Poughkeeper Artcraft Press, 1929).
3. Ruth Benedict, *Patterns of Culture* (Boston: Houghton Mifflin, 1934); Margaret Mead, *Coming of Age in Samoa* (New York: Modern Library, 1940). See also Margaret Mead, *Four Families* (New York: McGraw-Hill, 1959), filmstrip.
4. Ralph Linton, *The Cultural Background of Personality* (New York: Appleton-Century, 1945).
5. The purely cognitive components of culture are not divorced from emotional elements. Words have meanings, which more or less can be translated from one language to another, but they also evoke feelings that are best appreciated by the community of speakers who use them. Culture in general, or any single aspect of culture, must, therefore, be felt in order to be understood. Speaking of honor (respect), Peristiany and Pitt-Rivers argue that "honor is too intimate a sentiment to submit to definition . . . it must be felt." See J. G. Peristiany and Julian Pitt-Rivers, ed., *Honor and Grace in Anthropology* (Cambridge: Cambridge University Press, 1992), 4.

Chapter Two
1. Jerre Mangione and Ben Morreale, *La Storia: Five Centuries of the Italian American Experience* (New York: Harper Perennial, 1992), xix-xx.
2. Ibid., 69.
3. Robert F. Foerster, *The Italian Immigration of Our Times* (New

York: Anro Press and *New York Times*, 1969), 3-22. Italians emigrated to other European countries, North Africa, Canada, and Australia.

4. D. S. Walker, *A Geography of Italy*, 2nd ed. (London: Methuen, 1967), 183-88. See also Phyllis H. Williams, *South Italian Folkways in Europe and America* (1938; reprint, New York: Simon & Schuster, Scribner, Russell & Russell, 1969), 1-7.

5. Dennis Mack-Smith, *A History of Sicily* (New York: Viking Press, 1968), 181-87.

6. A. L. Maraspina, *The Study of an Italian Village* (Paris: Morton, 1968), 79-98.

7. Mack-Smith, 469-79.

8. Ibid., 279.

9. Cecil Woodham-Smith, *The Great Hunger* (New York: Harper & Row, 1962), 33-37.

10. Foerster, 3-22.

11. This was not only true for Italian immigrants but for all immigrants who arrived in the late nineteenth and early twentieth centuries.

12. Foerster, 32. Over 72 percent returned from the United States in the period 1907-11. The return rates were smaller for subsequent and earlier periods but were substantial and reflect among other things the goal of the immigrant only to sojourn abroad.

13. *New Orleans Daily Picayune*, December 17, 1880, 2.

14. Bennett H. Wall, ed., *Louisiana: A History*, 2nd ed. (Arlington Heights, Ill.: Forum Press, 1984), 36.

15. John Kemp, *New Orleans: An Illustrated History* (Woodland Hills, Calif.: Windsor Publications, 1981), 37.

16. Fulton's steam engine found application aboard ships long before it was widely used in locomotives. Fulton's first steamboat began to ply the Mississippi River in 1812, nearly fifty years before interstate locomotion came to the city. Even after the railroad steam engine came into existence, right of ways had to be secured, rail beds prepared, and rails laid before people and materials could move along them. These developments took time.

17. Jean Ann Scarpaci, "Italian Immigration in Louisiana's Sugar Parishes: Recruitment, Labor Conditions, and Community Relations, 1880-1910" (Ph.D. diss., Rutgers University, 1972), 10.

18. Ibid., 109, 111.

19. Eliot Lord, John J. D. Trenor, and Samuel J. Barrows, *The Italians in America* (New York: B. F. Buck, 1905). This work contains Americans' reactions to Italian immigrants and generally extols the

immigrants while deprecating the black workers. John V. Baiamonte, Jr., speaks of the high praise given by planters to their Italian field hands in his "Immigrants in Rural America: A Study of the Italians of Tangipahoa Parish, Louisiana" (Ph.D. diss., Mississippi State University, 1972), 1-30. Scarpaci discusses the same point, 97-190.

20. *New Orleans Daily Picayune,* January 11, 1881. Not all were field hands. There were two masons, two carpenters, one blacksmith, and two wives.

21. Based on mortality during the period of 1880-1930, we estimate that 11,000 Italian immigrants could have died before being counted by the census. If we add 11,000 to the actual census count of the immigrants in 1910 (approximately 20,000), we arrive at an estimate of 31,000.

22. Bureau of the Census, *Fifteenth Census,* vol. 3, part 1 (1932), 993.

23. Herbert J. Gans, *The Urban Villagers: Group and Class in the Life of Italian Americans* (New York: Free Press, 1962).

24. Baiamonte, "Immigrants in Rural America," passim.

25. Scarpaci, 50-52.

26. Betty Boyd Caroli, *Italians From the United States, 1900-1914* (Staten Island, N.Y.: Center for Migration Studies, 1973), 34-40.

27. National Archives, Passenger Lists for Port of New Orleans, November 1-December 30, 1898; January 2-June 28, 1899; July 5-December 20, 1899; January 2-February 28, 1900; passim.

28. The major newspapers carried accounts of immigrants arriving from other U.S. cities. See Scarpaci, 109, and Baiamonte, "Immigrants in Rural America," 10.

29. *New Orleans Daily Picayune,* December 17, 1880.

30. Ibid., October 17, 1890, 2.

31. Ibid.

32. Ibid.

33. Ibid., December 17, 1900, part 2, 4.

34. Ibid., October 21, 1900, part 2, 4.

Chapter Three

1. Ignasio Silone, *Fontamara* (New York: Atheneum Press, 1960), 30-31.

2. Bruno Arcudi, "Italian Americans and *Il Saper Vinere*" (paper presented in the Italian-Americans in South Louisiana series funded by the American Italian Renaissance Foundation and the Louisiana Committee for the Humanities, Baton Rouge, La., 1982).

3. *New Orleans Daily Picayune,* October 22, 1900, 3.

4. Peter Berger, Brigitte Berger, and Hansfred Kellner, *The Homeless Mind* (New York: Vintage Books, 1976), 83-96.

5. Maria Pia Di Bella, "Name, Blood and Miracles: The Claims to Renown in Traditional Sicily," in Peristiany and Pitt-Rivers, 151-65. The concept of honor is worldwide, but scholars have found the Mediterranean basin a fruitful area to study. See J. G. Peristiany, ed., *Honour and Shame: The Values of Mediterranean Society* (Chicago: University of Chicago Press, 1966). In that region, the oral pact or covenant is the basis for all exchanges. Thus, it is necessary to be known as a person of honor. Individual and collective honor guarantees oral agreements, according to Di Bella. However, there are competing notions of honor among societies and between groups in the same society, and these represent the struggle for power (Peristiany, 4). It is also true that inasmuch as concepts of honor validate the legitimacy of groups and society, stability is assured (Di Bella, 164).

6. Di Bella, 152-53.

7. Thomas Merton convincingly argues the case for the spiritual virtues of all useful work in his beautiful and insightful analysis of Christian monasticism. See *The Silent Life* (New York: Farrar, Straus & Giroux, 1957).

8. See Foerster.

9. Gans, *The Urban Villagers*, 4.

10. Ibid.

11. Irving Howe, *World of Our Fathers* (New York: Simon & Schuster, 1976), 151.

12. Ibid., 148.

13. There is an endless argument in Louisiana over the definition of Creole. When we use the term we are referring to the American descendants of the early French settlers of New Orleans and Louisiana who came directly from France in the early eighteenth century. If the descendants are racially mixed, they are referred to as *créoles de couleur*. The French Canadians who found their way to Louisiana after being forcibly expelled from Nova Scotia in the 1750s and 1760s are known as Acadians or Cajuns, not Creoles. Some writers also consider the American descendants of Spanish settlers to be Creoles. We are not considering them in our definition.

14. Thomas Kessner, *The Golden Door: Italian and Jewish Mobility in New York City 1880-1915* (New York: Oxford University Press, 1977), 30-31.

15. Russell M. Magnaghi, "Louisiana's Italian Immigrants Prior to 1870," in *The Louisiana Purchase Bicentennial Series in Louisiana History*, vol. 10, *A Refuge for All Ages: Immigration in Louisiana History*

(Lafayette, La.: Center for Louisiana Studies, 1996), 580-602. Unless otherwise noted the remainder of this section draws heavily from Magnaghi's excellent article.

16. Edwin Adams Davis, *Louisiana: The Pelican State* (Baton Rouge: Louisiana State University Press, 1959), 12-13.

17. Mangione and Morreale, 9-10.

18. Magnaghi, 582.

19. Ibid., 583.

20. Anna Lundberg, "The Italian Community in New Orleans," in *New Orleans Ethnic Cultures,* ed. John Cooke (New Orleans: Committee on Ethnicity in New Orleans, 1978), 38.

21. Ibid.

22. Magnaghi, 590.

23. Giuseppe Garibaldi was one of the founding fathers of the modern nation of Italy. In his country, Garibaldi is thought of as the equivalent of George Washington because he led the military expeditions that resulted in the unification of Italy in 1860.

24. Lundberg, 38-39.

25. Alcée Fortier, *Louisiana, Comprising Sketches of Parishes, Towns, Events, Institutions and Persons Arranged in Cyclopedic Form,* vol. 3 (Madison, Wis.: Century Historical Association, 1914), 742-43.

26. Peirce F. Lewis, *New Orleans: The Making of an Urban Landscape* (Cambridge, Mass.: Ballinger, 1976), 11-16.

27. Ibid. See also H. W. Gilmore, "The Old New Orleans and the New: A Case for Ecology," *American Sociological Review* (1944): 385-94.

28. Bureau of the Census, *Twelfth Census: 1900, Louisiana Census Rolls* (handwritten microfilm).

29. Bureau of the Census, *Sixteenth Census of the United States: 1940. Population and Housing: Statistics for Census Tracts: New Orleans, La.,* prepared by the U.S. Government Printing Office (Washington, D.C., 1941).

30. Ibid.

31. Scarpaci, 118-23.

32. Humbert S. Nelli, "The Italian Padrone System in the United States," *Labor History* 5 (spring 1964): 155.

33. For a complete discussion of the *padrone* system, see Nelli, "Italian Padrone System," 153-67.

34. Scarpaci, 77-78.

35. Bayou Teche originates in St. Landry Parish in the south-central part of Louisiana and meanders south and southwesterly until it empties into the Atchafalaya River near Morgan City, Louisiana.

36. Scarpaci, 117.
37. Ibid., 124-25.
38. The grinding operations separated soil, cane juice, and bagasse, the material (cellulose) left after extracting the juice. In subsequent steps, sugar and molasses were separated.
39. Scarpaci, 125.
40. Ibid., 117.
41. Florence Dymond, "Sketches of a Plantation" (New Orleans: Tulane University, 1968), manuscript.
42. Ibid.
43. Geographical Positions of Stone Lime Benchmarks from Donaldsonville to Head of Passes, Louisiana (New Orleans: Army Corps of Engineers, 1892-93), 28.
44. Ibid., 24.
45. Bureau of the Census, *Twelfth Census, Census Rolls,* Plaquemines, vol. 32 (1900), roll 1577.
46. Ibid., St. James, vol. 37 (1900), roll 580.
47. Salvatore Panzeca, "Family Reflects on a Beautiful Life," *Italian-American Digest* 26, no. 3 (1999): 7, 19.
48. *Census Roll in St. Mary Parish,* vol. 41, roll 582.
49. *Census Rolls in Jefferson Parish,* vol. 17, roll 566.
50. Baiamonte's study of the Italians in Tangipahoa Parish ("Immigrants in Rural America") is complete and imaginative. In this section, and elsewhere in our discussion of the Italians in Tangipahoa Parish, we draw heavily from his original research.
51. *Census Rolls in Tangipahoa Parish,* vol. 42, roll 583.
52. Baiamonte, "Immigrants in Rural America," 56.
53. Ibid., 36-37.
54. Ibid., 44-46.
55. Ibid.
56. Ibid.

Chapter Four
1. As we began to work on this chapter, fate did not treat two of our friends very well. Joe Costa died unexpectedly in his sleep, and Steve Costanza was in Kentucky at his father's deathbed. It is was if Fortune herself was sending a signal that she should not be treated too harshly in this analysis.
2. Boethius, *The Consolation of Philosophy,* trans. Richard Green (Indianapolis: Bobbs-Merrill, 1962), ix.
3. Ibid., 121.

4. Niccolo Machiavelli, "The Prince," in *The Portable Machiavelli*, trans. Peter Bondanella and Mark Musa (New York: Penguin Books, 1979). See especially chapter XXV, "On Fortune's Role in Human Affairs and How She Can Be Dealt With," 159-62.

5. We are alluding, here, to the Protestant ethic, a body of religious thought that morally justifies the acquisition of material wealth and by extension success in life. This is, of course, Max Weber's famous thesis expressed in *The Protestant Ethic and the Spirit of Capitalism*.

6. Widespread is perhaps too weak a term. Maybe ubiquitous would be more appropriate. Richard Epstein, in the preface to the first edition of *The Theory of Gambling and Statistical Logic*, called gambling "a near universal pastime." Soon thereafter, in the preface to the second edition, he claimed that gambling is one of the few *constants* in the human condition (italics ours). Apparently, between editions he had come to agree with Balzac that "the gambling passion lurks in the bottom of every heart." See *The Theory of Gambling and Statistical Logic* (New York: Academic Press, 1977), xiii.

7. For a recent, comprehensive, worldwide treatment of the topic, consult *Parabola*, a journal emphasizing the study of myth, tradition, and the search for meaning. See the special issue devoted entirely to a consideration of fate and fortune among the Greeks, Romans, Christians, Hindu, and Chinese: *Parabola* 25, no. 4 (winter 2000).

8. Robert D. Herman, ed., *Gambling* (New York: Harper & Row, 1967).

9. Robert K. Merton, *Social Theory and Social Structure*, rev. and enlarged ed. (Glencoe, Ill.: Free Press, 1957).

10. Mary E. Murrell, "Why People Gamble," in *Gambling Today*, ed. D. Lester (Springfield, Ill.: Charles C. Thomas, 1979), 84-105.

11. Andrew Greeley, *Ethnicity, Denomination, and Inequality* (Beverly Hills: Sage Publications, 1976).

12. The Florida Parishes consist of nine parishes east of the Mississippi River and north of Lake Pontchartrain. They get their designation from the fact that the inhabitants of this region in 1779 came under Spanish rule as the Florida Territory, which, at that time, extended westward to the east bank of the Mississippi River. A successful rebellion in 1810 against the Spanish resulted in the creation of the Free State of West Florida (sometimes referred to as the Republic of West Florida), which lasted a brief two years before it was officially joined to the state of Louisiana by Congressional act on April 14, 1812.

13. Joseph DeMarco, Jr., interview by authors, Hammond, La., July 11, 2001.

14. Joseph DeMarco, Ledger of Grocery Accounts, 1933.

15. Bureau of the Census, *Population Schedules of the Twelfth Census of the United States: 1900,* prepared by the U.S. Government Printing Office (Washington, D.C., 1978), microfilm.

16. The communities of Harvey and Kenner are in Jefferson Parish, which borders Orleans Parish. Today Harvey is an unincorporated suburban development with a well-defined industrial economy of its own, and Kenner is one of the fastest growing cities in Louisiana. It is an incorporated place with a population of more than sixty thousand. In 1900 both places were small, isolated settlements devoted exclusively to agriculture, much of which was vegetable farming in support of the urban population in New Orleans. St. James and St. Mary parishes are in the sugarcane belt in Louisiana. St. Mary Parish is about eighty miles southwest of New Orleans. St. James Parish is upriver, about forty miles northwest of New Orleans. Today, both parishes are substantially different from what they were in 1900. Now, their economies are mixed, but in 1900 they were nearly exclusively dependent on "King Cane."

17. The most populated wards in 1900 were adjacent to the French Quarter. These were wards 4, 5, 6, and 7.

18. While we are convinced of the validity of these conclusions, as the following discussion illustrates, there is no easy (or absolutely certain) way to interpret the data in table 5. To be engaged in a white-collar occupation in 1900 overwhelmingly meant to own your job. Your job was your property. It belonged to you. You could do what you wanted with it because you were more than likely a merchant or a free professional who owned your own business. Together with farmers and merchants, free professionals comprised the Old Middle Class. In modern times, the white-collar world is referred to as the New Middle Class and is predominately a collection of managers, salaried professionals, salespeople, and office workers who share one thing: they do not retain their jobs as their own personal property. Rather, they are employees whose children cannot inherit their parents' jobs. Fifty-two percent of the New Orleans sample held white-collar jobs. This is an exceptionally high figure, but it is undoubtedly a conservative assessment because in table 5, craftsmen are considered skilled laborers. If craftsmen who owned their own businesses were removed from the skilled-and-semiskilled category and placed in the white-collar category, as many of them should, then the white-collar percentage would be higher, and the percentage of laborers would be correspondingly

lower. How much higher and lower we cannot say for sure, because there is no way from the original data to distinguish between craftsmen who work for themselves and craftsmen who work for others. On the other hand, merchants are treated as white-collar workers although many of them were street peddlers who went around the neighborhoods in horse-drawn wagons selling produce, while others were grocers and fishermen. Most of them were functionally illiterate, hardly the image of the white-collar world. Assuming half the craftsmen were owners and the other half were non-owners of the establishments for which they worked would inflate the percentage of white-collar workers, while removing merchants whose work was more manual than mental would deflate the white-collar category. We estimate the gains and the losses would balance each other out, and conclude that about 50 percent of the New Orleans sample was, indeed, white collar.

For a detailed analysis of the Old and New Middle Class, see C. Wright Mills, *White Collar* (New York: Oxford University Press, 1956), 63-76.

19. John J. D'Alesandre, "Occupational Trends of Italians in New York City," in *The Italians,* ed. Francesco Cordasco and Eugene Bucchinoni (1935; reprint, Clifton, N.J.: Augustus M. Kelley, 1974), 417-31. A more recent analysis of the data reported that 42 percent of the Italians in New York were laborers and about 25 percent were merchants and peddlers. Kessner, 30-31. Samuel L. Baily has reported that at the turn of the century, approximately three-quarters of the Italians in New York were blue-collar workers and most of these were in unskilled and semiskilled jobs. By contrast, he reported a higher percent of skilled workers for Buenos Aires and a substantially higher percentage of owners of small businesses. See Baily, "The Adjustment of Italian Immigrants in Buenos Aires and New York, 1870-1914," *American Historical Review* 88, no. 2 (1983): 281-305.

20. Judith E. Smith, *Family Connections* (Albany: State University of New York Press, 1985).

21. Lewis, 12.

22. West Bank means on the western side of the Mississippi River in the New Orleans metropolitan area.

23. *New Orleans Times-Picayune,* May 7, 1978, sec. 2, 2.

24. William Francis Lawrence and Debra Nance Lawrence, *Biographical Sketches of the European Immigrants of Northeast Louisiana, 1880-1900* (Baton Rouge: Claitor's, 1982).

25. The expression "The City" is used without any other identifying appellation by New Orleanians to refer to the city of New Orleans. To the chagrin of other Louisianians, it implies that everyone should

know there is only one city in Louisiana and that is New Orleans, the Crescent City.

26. Edna Bonacich and John Modell, *The Economic Basis of Ethnic Solidarity* (Berkeley, Calif.: University of California Press, 1980).

27. Evans Casso, *History of the Casso Family in Louisiana* (New Orleans: Jackson Square Press, 1972).

28. Evans Casso in collaboration with Mrs. Gregorio Noto, *A Brief History of the Noto Family* (n.p., n.d.).

29. Scarpaci, 127.

30. Linda Serio, "Ships of Our Ancestors," *Italian-American Digest* 22, no. 3 (1995): 13.

31. Scarpaci, 130.

32. Ibid., 131.

33. Ibid., 193.

34. Baiamonte, "Immigrants in Rural America," passim.

35. Ibid., 83. See also Hodding Carter, *Southern Legacy* (Baton Rouge: Louisiana State University Press, 1950), 105-18.

36. American Italian Renaissance Foundation, oral-history tapes, New Orleans, n.d.

37. Dymond.

38. Scarpaci, 202.

39. Christine L. Bordelon, "Family Makes Great Impact on Kenner," *New Orleans Times-Picayune,* January 21, 2001, sec. E, 1, 8.

40. Joan Kent, "New Orleans, Italian Style," *New Orleans States Item,* March 17, 1979, Lagniappe sec., 6.

41. Rudolph Vecoli, "*Contadini* in Chicago: A Critique of the Uprooted," in *The Aliens,* ed. Leonard Dinnerstein and Frederie Cople Jaher (New York: Appleton-Century-Crofts, 1970).

42. A. V. Margavio and J. Lambert Molyneaux, "Residential Segregation of Italians in New Orleans and Selected American Cities," *Louisiana Studies* 12 (1973): 639-45.

Chapter Five

1. Luigi Barzini, *The Italians* (New York: Atheneum, 1965), 190.

2. We are not denying the prominence of the universal functions of the family as described by social scientists. But over and above the universal functions, the Italian family served as a refuge from the insecurities faced in that region. Any family can serve this function, and most do. Our contention is that this became a primary function for the Italian family.

3. Modernization theory links resistance to change to authoritarian

personality traits. See E. E. Hagen, *On the Theory of Social Change* (Homewood, Ill.: Dorsey Press, 1962). See also Alex Inkeles, "The Modernization of Man in Socialist and Nonsocialist Countries," in *Social Consequences of Modernization in Communist Societies,* ed. M. G. Fields (Baltimore: Johns Hopkins Press, 1976), 50-59; Alex Inkeles, *Exploring Individual Modernity* (New York: Columbia University Press, 1986); and W. W. Rostow, *The Stages of Economic Growth* (Cambridge: Cambridge University Press, 1960).

4. Modernization theorists link the traditional backwardness of peasants with familism. Some theorists argue that the cause of backwardness is amoral familism. This is the position taken by Banfield in his study of a southern Italian village. See Edward C. Banfield, *The Moral Basis of a Backward Society* (New York: Free Press, 1958). However, he fails to see that the absolute lack of opportunities for the peasants in the Old Country did not permit progress. In Louisiana, with its relatively abundant land, the immigrants moved quickly to improve their situation. There is a connection between values and opportunities. A belief in the efficacy of hard work in the face of persistent failure is hard to sustain. We believe that Banfield fails to appreciate how quickly the human spirit turns to hope and a commitment to hard work when opportunities really improve.

5. Humbert S. Nelli, *From Immigrants to Ethnics: The Italian Americans* (Oxford: Oxford University Press, 1983), 22-26.

6. Francis Ianni with Elizabeth Reuss-Ianni, *A Family Business* (New York: Russell Sage Foundation, 1972), 16.

7. Richard Gambino, *Blood of My Blood: The Dilemma of the Italian-Americans* (Garden City, N.Y.: Doubleday, 1974), 4-5.

8. Materials for this section were drawn from Williams, 73-107.

9. Ibid.

10. Andrew Montalbano, *Sicilian Sun* (Metairie, La.: New Writer's, 1997).

11. At current exchange rates, 252 lire is equivalent to .12 cents.

12. A. V. Margavio and Jerome Salomone, "The Passage, Settlement and Occupational Characteristics of Louisiana's Italian Immigrants," *Sociological Spectrum* 1 (1981): 345-59.

13. We will call the immigrant generation the first generation, then call their children, the first generation born in America, the second generation. Often, the second generation is referred to as the first-generation Italian-American, which, of course, they are technically. The grandchildren of the immigrants will be called the third generation, and so forth.

14. A. V. Margavio and Jerome Salomone, "The Economic Advantages of Familism: The Case of the Sicilians of New Orleans," *Sociological Spectrum* 7 (1987): 101-19.

15. Pitirim A. Sorokin, *Society, Culture, Personality* (New York: Harper, 1947). See his discussion of multibonded groups.

16. Jerry Wilcox and A. V. Margavio, "Fertility, Economy, and Household Structure in Nineteenth-Century America: A Comparative Study of French Canadian, Irish, Italian, and Native Born Patterns" (paper presented at Mid-South Sociological Association Meetings, Baton Rouge, La., October 1989). For a discussion of Italian family life in "strawberry country," see Carter, 105-18.

17. Massimo Levi-Bacci, *A History of Italian Fertility* (Princeton, N.J.: Princeton University Press, 1977).

18. Paul J. Campisi, "Ethnic Family Patterns: The Italian Family in the United States," *American Journal of Sociology* 53 (1948): 443-49.

Chapter Six

1. For the classic discussion of basic human needs in the sociological literature, see the works of W. I. Thomas. His previously famous Four Wishes for security, status, adventure, and response, though largely now forgotten, continue to be the theoretical foundation for all modern conceptions of social needs. The Four Wishes first appear in "The Persistence of Primary Group Norms," in *Source Book for Social Origins,* 4th ed. (Boston: Richard Badger, 1909), 13-16. They reappear in (with Florian Znaniecki) *The Polish Peasant in Europe and America,* 5 vols. (Chicago: University of Chicago Press, 1918-20) and they receive their fullest treatment in *The Unadjusted Girl* (Boston: Little, Brown, 1923).

2. Charles Speroni, *Wit and Wisdom of the Italian Renaissance* (Berkeley: University of California Press, 1964), 208.

3. The reader can understand what is meant by bread from the context in which it is used. Earlier we used the word to mean making a living. Here it is used to designate food.

4. Vecoli.

5. J. W. Purseglove, *Tropical Crops: Dicotyledons I and II* (New York: John Wiley & Sons, 1968), 318.

6. Ethelyn Orso and Peggy Kaveski, "Undisclosed Aspects of Saint Joseph Altars," *Louisiana Folklore Miscellany* 3 (1975): 15-16. A hereditary disease has been linked with the consumption of fava beans. Favism is an acute form of hemolytic anemia caused by eating the bean or breathing its pollen.

7. Purseglove, 321-26.

8. Ibid., 124-25.

9. Howard Lafay, "Sicily, Where All the Songs Are Sad," *National Geographic* 149 (1976): 419.

10. *New Orleans Times-Picayune,* November 26, 1978, Dixie sec., 48.

11. Barbara Monteleone, "Tony Monteleone: Childhood Memories." Unpublished manuscript in the possession of Howard Nichols, Hammond, La., November 5, 1990.

12. A. V. Margavio, "Folklore of New Orleans Sicilians," *Louisiana Folklore Miscellany* 3 (1975): 9-13.

13. "WO" is used to signify sayings that are found in a written and oral tradition and an "O" to signify sayings we believe to be part of an oral tradition only. Most proverbs reported here can be found in Giovanni Verga's *House by the Meddlar Tree,* which was published in 1881. The English translation used here was by Eric Mosbacher (New York: Grove Press, 1953). This work is unique in that it extensively employs proverbs used by nineteenth-century Sicilians.

14. Ibid.

15. John Cabibi, interview by authors, Metairie, La., November 18, 1995. Cabibi was editor of the New Orleans weekly Italian newspaper, *La Voce Coloniale,* which ceased publication in the 1950s.

16. Joy J. Jackson, "Foreign Images and Influences in Nineteenth Century New Orleans Drama and Music," *Southeast Louisiana Historical Papers* 15 (1991-92): 18-19.

17. Jack Stewart, "The Original Dixieland Jazz Band's Place in History," *The Jazz Archivist* 6, no. 1 (1999): 7.

18. Linda Serio, "Nick LaRocca, Creator of Jazz," *Italian-American Digest* (spring 1989): 3-4.

19. Magnaghi, 592-94.

20. Ibid., 592-93.

21. Ibid.

22. Joseph Maselli and Bette Cadwell, "Italian Hall Remembered," *Italian-American Digest* 24, no. 3 (1999): 1, 15.

23. Ibid.

24. Montana Josephine Mudge, "The Italian Union Hall—As I Remember It," *Italian-American Digest* 26, no. 1 (1999): 7.

25. "Progressive Men's Club Celebrates 50 Years," *Italian-American Digest* 20, no. 2 (1993): 15.

26. Raphaella Maggiore, "Societa di Principessa Jolanda-Margarita," *Italian-American Digest* 6, no. 1 (1979): 5.

27. *New Orleans Times-Picayune,* June 28, 1901, sec. 2, 1.

28. Ibid., March 24, 1920, 14. An Italian Americanization organization was formed and called the Italian Democratic Club, which launched a massive campaign to Americanize 30,000 Italians in the New Orleans area. Its purpose was to teach the principles of Americanism and point out the advantages of learning English and attending night school. Ibid., June 16, 1920, 24.

29. "Who Really Killed the Chief?" *Italian-American Digest* 7 (1981): 3.

30. Social historians claim that the black Civil Rights movement of the 1960s and early 1970s had aftereffects on other racial and ethnic groups, serving as a catalyst for their explosion of consciousness. Roman Heleniak, professor of history at Southeastern Louisiana University, says, "There seems little doubt that racial and ethnic multiculturalism was enhanced at this time among native American Indians, hillbillies, rednecks, and white ethnics like the Irish, Germans, Poles, Greeks, French Cajuns, and Italians, among others." Heleniak, interview by authors, New Orleans, September 15, 1997.

31. "Joseph Maselli: The Man of Honor," *Italian-American Digest* 26, no. 3 (1999): 10-11.

32. Rocco C. Blasi, "Italianism Chicago Style," *La Parola del Popolo* 29 (1979): 68.

Chapter Seven

1. The discerning reader will recognize this allusion to Karl Marx and Friedrich Engels' *Communist Manifesto.*

2. Based on their examination of the historical record, the authors of *La Storia,* Jerre Mangione and Ben Morreale, conclude that the gangster stereotype is undeserved. Others who agree with this assessment include Mario Cuomo, Geraldine Ferraro, and Tommy Lasorda, as reported in the television documentary entitled "Italians in America," aired on WYES, Channel 12 (New Orleans: March 18, 2001).

3. B. Schrieke, *Alien Americans: A Study of Race Relations* (New York: Viking Press, 1936), 70-104. See also Mangione and Morreale, chapter 15.

4. Mangione and Morreale, 241.

5. Everett V. Stonequist, *The Marginal Man: A Study in Personality and Culture Conflict* (New York: Russell & Russell, 1961), 2-3.

6. Oscar Handlin, *The Uprooted: The Epic Story of the Great Migrations that Made the American People* (Boston: Little, Brown, 1952), 263.

7. Vecoli, 216-28.

8. Ibid., 220.

9. Vern Baxter and A. V. Margavio, "Honor, Status, and Aggression in Economic Exchange," *Sociological Theory* 18, no. 3 (2000): 399-416.

10. Ibid.

11. Thomas and Znaniecki.

12. *New Orleans Daily Picayune,* December 1, 1892, 2.

13. Anthony V. Margavio, "The Reaction of the Press to the Italian American in New Orleans, 1880 to 1920," *Italian Americana* 4, no. 1 (1978): 72-83.

14. *New Orleans Daily Picayune,* August 9, 1896, 2, and August 10, 1896, 1.

15. Scarpaci, 248. Reported also in John V. Baiamonte, Jr., *Spirit of Vengeance: Nativism and Louisiana Justice, 1921-1924* (Baton Rouge: Louisiana State University Press, 1986), 9, and Edward F. Haas, "Guns, Goats, and Italians: The Tallulah Lynchings of 1899," *Journal of North Louisiana History* (spring-summer 1982): 45.

16. *New York Times,* July 22, 1899, sec. 7, 3.

17. Ibid., July 23, 1899, sec. 1, 5.

18. Ibid., July 28, 1899, sec. 4, 6.

19. Ibid., August 9, 1899, sec. 2, 4.

20. Haas, 45.

21. Richard Gambino, *Vendetta* (Garden City, N.Y.: Doubleday, 1977).

22. Ibid., 130.

23. Ibid.

24. Ibid., 4.

25. Samuel J. Hyde, *Pistols and Politics* (Baton Rouge: Louisiana State University Press, 1997). See also the chapter entitled "Bloody Tangipahoa" in Baiamonte, *Spirit of Vengeance..*

26. Joy J. Jackson, *New Orleans in the Gilded Age: Politics and Urban Progress, 1880-1896* (Baton Rouge: Louisiana State University Press, 1969), 232-33. Reprinted by permission of Louisiana State University Press. Copyright © 1969 by Louisiana State University Press for the Louisiana Historical Association.

27. Don Gennaro, "The Gennaro Family," *Italian-American Digest* 23, no. 1 (1996): 11.

28. John S. Kendall, "Who Killa da Chief?" *Louisiana Historical Quarterly* 22 (1939): 492-530.

29. Ibid., 495.

30. Ibid., 501.

31. The monument has since been moved to Lafayette Square, a park in New Orleans located at the intersection of Julia and Camp streets.

32. Kendall, 524.

33. Baiamonte, *Spirit of Vengeance,* passim.

34. Michael L. Kurtz, "Organized Crime in Louisiana History: Myth and Reality," *Louisiana History* 24, no. 4 (fall 1983): 357-74.

35. Ibid., 364.

36. House Committee on Assassinations, *Staff and Consultant Reports on Organized Crime,* vol. 9, 95th Cong., 2nd sess., 1979.

37. Ibid., 62.

38. Sen. Estes Kefauver chaired the U.S. Senate Committee on Organized Crime in the United States, which held hearings in New Orleans in 1950.

39. House Committee on Assassinations, 62.

40. Kurtz, 374-75.

41. Jerome Salomone attended this funeral and observed this incident firsthand.

Chapter Eight

1. Williams, 138. Williams goes on to say that the original statue still standing in the crypt of the Church of the *Vescuvato* has two fingers pointing toward the heavens. Another statue erected later where the miracle is said to have taken place has four fingers outstretched skyward.

2. The same point has been made about French anticlericalism in France and Louisiana. See Laurence Wylie and Armand Begue, *Village in the Vaucluse* (Cambridge: Harvard University Press, 1958); Roger Baudier, *The Catholic Church in Louisiana* (New Orleans: Archdiocese of New Orleans, 1939), 473-93; and James G. Dauphine, *A Question of Inheritance: Religion, Education, and Louisiana's Cultural Boundary, 1880-1940* (Lafayette: Center for Louisiana Studies, 1993), 81-99.

3. Gambino, *Blood of My Blood,* 195.

4. Holy days are specially designated consecrated times other than Sundays set aside by the Catholic Church for religious ceremonies in honor of a member of the Holy Family or one of the saints.

5. Williams, 142.

6. E. J. Hobsbawn, *Primitive Rebels,* 2nd ed. (New York: Praeger, 1963), 97.

7. Ibid., 98.

8. Ibid., 100.

9. Ibid.

10. Ibid.

11. Ibid., 103.

12. Baiamonte, "Immigrants in Rural America," 57. Recently,

Father De Priest, rector of New Orleans' Notre Dame Seminary, began organizing worship services for Byzantine-rite Catholics. According to his stated plan, a Mass in the Byzantine rite will be celebrated the first Sunday of each month at 10:00 A.M. in the chapel of Notre Dame Seminary.

13. George Gurtner, *Historic Churches of Old New Orleans* (New Orleans: Friends of St. Alphonsus, 1997), 48-50.

14. Silvano M. Tomasi, "The Ethnic Church and the Integration of Italian Immigrants in the United States," in *The Italian Experience in the United States,* ed. Silvano M. Tomasi and Madeline H. Engel (Staten Island, N.Y.: Center for Migration Studies, 1970), 163-93.

15. Nicholas John Russo, "Three Generations of Italians in New York City: Their Religious Acculturation," in Tomasi and Engel, 195-209.

16. Ibid.

17. *Catholic Directory Almanac* (Milwaukee: Hoffman Brothers, 1920), 230-38.

18. Ibid.

19. Ibid., 83-93.

20. *New Orleans Times-Picayune,* August 16, 1914, sec. 1, 10.

21. Ibid., August 17, 1900, 6. Professor Paoletti regularly played at the Spanish Fort, a popular place for Sunday entertainment.

22. Ibid.

23. The brief life of Mother Cabrini described here was taken primarily from *Mother Cabrini* (Boston: Daughters of St. Paul Publications, 1977). The author's name is not given.

24. Lundberg, 39.

25. *New Orleans Daily Picayune,* May 22, 1896, 2. Some New Orleans residents may be surprised to learn how far back the May Festival goes. It is not exclusively a Catholic schools event either. In most places in Protestant America, it would not have been possible to use gambling and alcohol sales to raise money for charity, but in New Orleans, the most European of American cities, such occasions were almost weekly fare.

26. It should be noted that members of these Catholic religious communities served everyone who sought their aid, not just Catholics. This was especially true of institutions like hospitals, soup kitchens, hostels for the homeless, and orphanages. It was true also of the Catholic schools, which were open to non-Catholics should they choose to attend them, and some did do so.

27. Baudier, index under "Schools," 637-38.

28. There was a tension between the immigrants and education, as

a general rule. Since they were peasants, the immigrants could see little value in book learning. They wanted their children to learn how to work, which could be taught by parents. Besides, as an Americanizing influence, the school had a tendency to challenge the supreme authority of the family. Such a challenge was anathema to Italians.

29. Patron saints are specially chosen or designated protectors of persons, places, things, conditions, and causes. Indeed, anything of importance may be assigned a patron saint. The patrons are heroic figures in the history of the church who exemplified in their lives the attributes or virtues that they will oversee. St. Jerome, for example, who was a scholar, is the patron saint of scholars; and St. Frances Xavier Cabrini, an alien herself who ministered to émigrés to the United States, is the patron of immigrants. The list of patron saints is virtually inexhaustible because they can be adopted locally without ecclesiastical approval. Often, the church fathers are more or less forced to officially designate a patron that has become a local institution. Mary, the Mother of Christ, is the most popular patron by far, followed by St. Joseph.

30. Herbert Thurston, S.J., and Donald Attwater, ed., *Butler's Lives of the Saints,* vol. 1 (New York: P. J. Kenedy & Sons, 1956), 631-33.

31. Stephen Duplantier, "The Cult of St. Joseph in Kenner," *Louisiana Folklore Miscellany* (1983): 42-43. Originally reported in Italo Colvino, *Italian Folktales,* trans. George Martin (New York: Pantheon Books, 1980).

32. The phrases St. Joseph altar and St. Joseph table are used interchangeably. The altar or table is an elevated structure upon which is placed the offerings of fresh and cooked vegetables, fruits, fish, baked goods, nuts, and other foodstuff, except meat. Immediately forward of the altar is a table used to feed the saints in a special ceremony.

33. Karen Wright Warren, "The Sicilian Saint Joseph Altar Celebration in Southeastern Louisiana" (master's thesis, Southeastern Louisiana University, 1983); and Ethelyn Orso, *The St. Joseph Altar Traditions of South Louisiana* (Lafayette: Center for Louisiana Studies, 1990).

34. *Italian-American Digest* 28, no. 1 (spring 2001): 1, 5. Similar notices of many other altars could be found in newspapers like the *New Orleans Times-Picayune, Baton Rouge Morning Advocate,* and *Hammond Daily Star.*

35. Mary Ann Tusa McColloster, "New Light on the New Orleans St. Joseph Altar," *Louisiana Folklore Miscellany* 3, no. 1 (April 1970): 38-45.

36. Roslynn Plemer, "Feast of St. Joseph," *Louisiana Folklore Miscellany* 2, no. 4 (August 1968): 85-90.

37. McColloster.

38. Ibid.

39. Lyle Saxon, Edward Dreyer, and Robert Tallant, *Gumbo Ya-Ya* (1945; reprint, Gretna, La.: Pelican, 1998).

40. *New Orleans Daily Picayune*, March 19, 1858, 6.

41. Saxon, Dreyer, and Tallant, 99.

42. Ibid., 105.

43. Ibid., 97.

44. Ibid., 107. Saxon's source is Thurston and Attwater, vol. 3, 486-87, which contains the most complete discussion of her life and importance in Catholic martyrology as exists in the literature.

45. Saxon, Dreyer, and Tallant, 109.

46. Ibid., 118-19.

47. Ibid., 120.

48. *New Orleans Times-Picayune*, June 14, 1919.

49. B. B. Swank, "Chapels Are Testimonials of Love," *Clarion Herald* (Archdiocese of New Orleans) 17, no. 18 (June 14, 1979): 8.

50. The chapel is under the care of Our Lady of Grace Society, whose members maintain the building and grounds and supervise the annual procession.

51. *Hammond (La.) Sunday Star*, December 10, 2000, 5A.

52. The Italian verb *spedire* means to expedite. The adjective *spedito(a)* means rapid.

53. Tevye, a Jew, is the main character in the musical "Fiddler on the Roof." Anatevka is the early-twentieth-century Russian village where the musical is set.

54. Baudier, 473-93.

Chapter Nine

1. Richard Rodriguez, *Hunger of Memory: The Education of Richard Rodriguez, an Autobiography* (Boston: Bantam Doubleday Dell, 1982).

2. Herbert J. Gans, "Symbolic Ethnicity: The Future of Ethnic Groups and Culture in America," *Ethnic and Racial Studies* 2, no. 1 (January 1979): 1-20.

3. Richard D. Alba, *Italian Americans: Into the Twilight of Ethnicity* (Englewood Cliffs, N.J.: Prentice-Hall, 1985).

4. Marcus Lee Hansen, *The Problem of the Third Generation Immigrant* (Rock Island, Ill.: Augustana Historical Society, 1938), 9-10.

5. Alba, 125-26.

6. James A. Crispino, *The Assimilation of Ethnic Groups: The Italian Case* (Staten Island, N.Y.: Center for Migration Studies, 1980), 43-78.

7. Alba, 139.

8. Mrs. Joseph Iverstine, now a widow in her seventies, said her father-in-law, Joseph Di Agistino, changed his name to Iverstine because Di Agistino was too hard for people to understand. When she was asked, "Why Iverstine and not some other name?" she did not know.

9. Vasilios Kapenekas, owner and son of Demetrois Kapenekas, interview by authors, October 28, 2000.

10. Alba, 111, 147.

11. Arthur E. McEnany, ed., *The Membership Roster in the Louisiana Senate from 1880-2004* (2001). Carlisle's ancestry is probably Italian, but that fact could not be conclusively established.

12. Alba, 86.

13. Baiamonte, "Immigrants in Rural America."

14. Miguel Luciano, "The Amnesia of History: A Discussion with Juan Sanchez," *National Forum* 81, no. 3 (summer 2001): 29-31.

Bibliography

Alba, Richard D. *Italian Americans: Into the Twilight of Ethnicity.* Englewood Cliffs, N.J.: Prentice-Hall, 1985.

American Italian Renaissance Foundation. Oral-history tapes. New Orleans, n.d.

Arcudi, Bruno. "Italian Americans and *Il Saper Vinere.*" Paper presented in the Italian-Americans in South Louisiana series funded by the American Italian Renaissance Foundation and the Louisiana Committee for the Humanities. Baton Rouge, La., 1982.

Baiamonte, John V., Jr. "Immigrants in Rural America: A Study of the Italians of Tangipahoa Parish, Louisiana." Ph.D. diss., Mississippi State University, 1972.

———. *Spirit of Vengeance: Nativism and Louisiana Justice, 1921-1924.* Baton Rouge: Louisiana State University Press, 1986.

Baily, Samuel L. "The Adjustment of Italian Immigrants in Buenos Aires and New York, 1870-1914." *American Historical Review* 88, no. 2 (1983): 281-305.

Banfield, Edward C. *The Moral Basis of a Backward Society.* New York: Free Press, 1958.

Barzini, Luigi. *The Italians.* New York: Atheneum, 1965.

Baudier, Roger. *The Catholic Church in Louisiana.* New Orleans: Archdiocese of New Orleans, 1939.

Baxter, Vern, and A. V. Margavio. "Honor, Status, and Aggression in Economic Exchange." *Sociological Theory* 18, no. 3 (2000): 399-416.

Benedict, Ruth. *Patterns of Culture.* Boston: Houghton Mifflin, 1934.

Berger, Peter, Brigitte Berger, and Hansfred Kellner. *The Homeless Mind.* New York: Vintage Books, 1976.

Blasi, Rocco C. "Italianism Chicago Style." *La Parola del Popolo* 29 (1979): 68.

Boethius. *The Consolation of Philosophy.* Translated by Richard Green. Indianapolis: Bobbs-Merrill, 1962.

Bonacich, Edna, and John Modell. *The Economic Basis of Ethnic Solidarity.* Berkeley: University of California Press, 1980.

Bordelon, Christine L. "Family Makes Great Impact on Kenner." *New Orleans Times-Picayune,* January 21, 2001, sec. E, 1, 8.

Cabibi, John. Interview by authors. Metairie, La., November 18, 1995.

Campisi, Paul J. "Ethnic Family Patterns: The Italian Family in the United States." *American Journal of Sociology* 53 (1948): 443-49.

Caroli, Betty Boyd. *Italians From the United States, 1900-1914.* Staten Island, N.Y.: Center for Migration Studies, 1973.

Carter, Hodding. *Southern Legacy.* Baton Rouge: Louisiana State University Press, 1950.

Casso, Evans. *History of the Casso Family in Louisiana.* New Orleans: Jackson Square Press, 1972.

Casso, Evans, with Mrs. Gregorio Noto. *A Brief History of the Noto Family.* N.p., n.d.

Catholic Directory Almanac. Milwaukee: Hoffman Brothers, 1920.

Census Roll in St. Mary Parish. Vol. 41. Roll 582.

Census Rolls in Jefferson Parish. Vol. 17. Roll 566.

Census Rolls in Tangipahoa Parish. Vol. 42. Roll 583.

Colvino, Italo. *Italian Folktales.* Translated by George Martin. New York: Pantheon Books, 1980.

Crispino, James A. *The Assimilation of Ethnic Groups: The Italian Case.* Staten Island, N.Y.: Center for Migration Studies, 1980.

D'Alesandre, John J. "Occupational Trends of Italians in New York City." In *The Italians,* edited by Francesco Cordasco and Eugene Bucchinoni, 417-31. 1935. Reprint, Clifton, N.J.: Augustus M. Kelley, 1974.

Dauphine, James G. *A Question of Inheritance: Religion, Education, and Louisiana's Cultural Boundary, 1880-1940.* Lafayette: Center for Louisiana Studies, 1993.

Davis, Edwin Adams. *Louisiana: The Pelican State.* Baton Rouge: Louisiana State University Press, 1959.

DeMarco, Joseph. Ledger of Grocery Accounts. 1929, 1933.

DeMarco, Joseph, Jr. Interview by authors. Hammond, La., July 11, 2001.

Di Bella, Maria Pia. "Name, Blood and Miracles: The Claims to Renown in Traditional Sicily." In *Honor and Grace in Anthropology,* edited by J. G. Peristiany and Julian Pitt-Rivers, 151-65. Cambridge: Cambridge University Press, 1992.

Duplantier, Stephen. "The Cult of St. Joseph in Kenner." *Louisiana Folklore Miscellany* (1983): 42-43.

Dymond, Florence. *Sketches of a Plantation.* New Orleans: Tulane University, 1968.

Epstein, Richard. *The Theory of Gambling and Statistical Logic.* New York: Academic Press, 1977.

Foerster, Robert F. *The Italian Immigration of Our Times.* New York: Anro Press and *New York Times,* 1969.

Fortier, Alcée. *Louisiana, Comprising Sketches of Parishes, Towns, Events, Institutions and Persons Arranged in Cyclopedic Form.* 4 vols. Madison, Wis.: Century Historical Association, 1914.

Gambino, Richard. *Blood of My Blood: The Dilemma of the Italian-Americans.* Garden City, N.Y.: Doubleday, 1974.

———. *Vendetta.* Garden City, N.Y.: Doubleday, 1977.

Gans, Herbert J. "Symbolic Ethnicity: The Future of Ethnic Groups and Culture in America." *Ethnic and Racial Studies* 2, no. 1 (January 1979): 1-20.

———. *The Urban Villagers: Group and Class in the Life of Italian Americans.* New York: Free Press, 1962.

Gennaro, Don. "The Gennaro Family." *Italian-American Digest* 23, no. 1 (1996): 11.

Geographical Positions of Stone Lime Benchmarks from Donaldsonville to Head of Passes, Louisiana. New Orleans: Army Corps of Engineers, 1892-93.

Gilmore, H. W. "The Old New Orleans and the New: A Case for Ecology." *American Sociological Review* (1944): 385-94.

Greeley, Andrew. *Ethnicity, Denomination, and Inequality.* Beverly Hills: Sage Publications, 1976.

Gurtner, George. *Historic Churches of Old New Orleans.* New Orleans: Friends of St. Alphonsus, 1997.

Haas, Edward F. "Guns, Goats, and Italians: The Tallulah Lynchings of 1899." *Journal of North Louisiana History* (spring-summer 1982): 45.

Hagen, E. E. *On the Theory of Social Change.* Homewood, Ill.: Dorsey Press, 1962.

Hammond (La.) Sunday Star. December 10, 2000.

Handlin, Oscar. *The Uprooted: The Epic Story of the Great Migrations that Made the American People.* Boston: Little, Brown, 1952.

Hansen, Marcus Lee. *The Problem of the Third Generation Immigrant.* Rock Island, Ill.: Augustana Historical Society, 1938.

Heleniak, Roman. Interview by authors. New Orleans, September 15, 1997.

Herman, Robert D., ed. *Gambling*. New York: Harper & Row, 1967.

Hobsbawn, E. J. *Primitive Rebels*. 2nd ed. New York: Praeger, 1963.

Howe, Irving. *World of Our Fathers*. New York: Simon & Schuster, 1976.

Hyde, Samuel J. *Pistols and Politics*. Baton Rouge: Louisiana State University Press, 1997.

Ianni, Francis, with Elizabeth Reuss-Ianni. *A Family Business*. New York: Russell Sage Foundation, 1972.

Inkeles, Alex. *Exploring Individual Modernity*. New York: Columbia University Press, 1986.

———. "The Modernization of Man in Socialist and Nonsocialist Countries." In *Social Consequences of Modernization in Communist Societies*, edited by M. G. Fields, 50-59. Baltimore: Johns Hopkins Press, 1976.

Italian-American Digest (1979-2001).

"Italians in America." Television documentary aired on WYES, Channel 12. New Orleans, La.: March 18, 2001.

Jackson, Joy J. "Foreign Images and Influences in Nineteenth Century New Orleans Drama and Music." *Southeast Louisiana Historical Papers* 15 (1991-92): 18-19.

———. *New Orleans in the Gilded Age: Politics and Urban Progress, 1880-1896*. Baton Rouge: Louisiana State University Press, 1969.

"Joseph Maselli: The Man of Honor." *Italian-American Digest* 26, no. 3 (1999): 10-11.

Kapenekas, Vasilios. Interview by authors. October 28, 2000.

Kemp, John. *New Orleans: An Illustrated History*. Woodland Hills, Calif.: Windsor Publications, 1981.

Kendall, John S. "Who Killa da Chief?" *Louisiana Historical Quarterly* 22 (1939): 492-530.

Kent, Joan. "New Orleans, Italian Style." *New Orleans States Item*, March 17, 1979, Lagniappe sec., 6.

Kessner, Thomas. *The Golden Door: Italian and Jewish Mobility in New York City 1880-1915*. New York: Oxford University Press, 1977.

Kurtz, Michael L. "Organized Crime in Louisiana History: Myth and Reality." *Louisiana History* 24, no. 4 (fall 1983): 357-74.

Lafay, Howard. "Sicily, Where All the Songs Are Sad." *National Geographic* 149 (1976): 419.

Lawrence, William Francis, and Debra Nance Lawrence. *Biographical Sketches of the European Immigrants of Northeast Louisiana, 1880-1900*. Baton Rouge: Claitor's, 1982.

Levi-Bacci, Massimo. *A History of Italian Fertility*. Princeton, N.J.: Princeton University Press, 1977.

Lewis, Peirce F. *New Orleans: The Making of an Urban Landscape.* Cambridge, Mass.: Ballinger, 1976.

Linton, Ralph. *The Cultural Background of Personality.* New York: Appleton-Century, 1945.

Lord, Eliot, John J. D. Trenor, and Samuel J. Barrows. *The Italians in America.* New York: B. F. Buck, 1905.

Luciano, Miguel. "The Amnesia of History: A Discussion with Juan Sanchez." *National Forum* 81, no. 3 (summer 2001): 29-31.

Lundberg, Anna. "The Italian Community in New Orleans." In *New Orleans Ethnic Cultures,* edited by John Cooke. New Orleans: Committee on Ethnicity in New Orleans, 1978, 38-46.

McCollister, Mary Ann Tusa. "New Light on the New Orleans St. Joseph Altar." *Louisiana Folklore Miscellany* 3, no. 1 (April 1970): 38-45.

McEnany, Arthur E., ed. *The Membership Roster in the Louisiana Senate from 1880-2004.* 2001.

Machiavelli, Niccolo. "The Prince." In *The Portable Machiavelli,* translated by Peter Bondanella and Mark Musa. New York: Penguin Books, 1979.

Mack-Smith, Dennis. *A History of Sicily.* New York: Viking Press, 1968.

Maggiore, Raphaella. "Societa di Principessa Jolanda-Margarita." *Italian-American Digest* 6, no. 1 (1979): 5.

Magnaghi, Russell M. "Louisiana's Italian Immigrants Prior to 1870." *The Louisiana Purchase Bicentennial Series in Louisiana History.* Vol. 10, *A Refuge for All Ages: Immigration in Louisiana History.* Lafayette, La.: Center for Louisiana Studies, 1996. First published in *Louisiana History* 27 (1986): 60-62.

Mangione, Jerre, and Ben Morreale. *La Storia: Five Centuries of the Italian American Experience.* New York: Harper Perennial, 1992.

Maraspina, A. L. *The Study of an Italian Village.* Paris: Morton, 1968.

Margavio, A. V. "Folklore of New Orleans Sicilians." *Louisiana Folklore Miscellany* 3 (1975): 9-13.

———. "The Reaction of the Press to the Italian American in New Orleans, 1880 to 1920." *Italian Americana* 4, no. 1 (1978): 72-83.

Margavio, A. V., and Jerome Salomone. "The Economic Advantages of Familism: The Case of the Sicilians of New Orleans." *Sociological Spectrum* 7 (1987): 101-19.

———. "The Passage, Settlement and Occupational Characteristics of Louisiana's Italian Immigrants." *Sociological Spectrum* 1 (1981): 345-59.

Margavio, A. V., and J. Lambert Molyneaux. "Residential Segregation of Italians in New Orleans and Selected American Cities." *Louisiana Studies* 12 (1973): 639-45.

Maselli, Joseph, and Bette Cadwell. "Italian Hall Remembered." *Italian-American Digest* 24, no. 3 (1999): 1-15.

Mead, Margaret. *Coming of Age in Samoa.* New York: Modern Library, 1940.

———. *Four Families.* New York: McGraw-Hill, 1959. Filmstrip.

Merton, Robert K. *Social Theory and Social Structure.* Rev. and enlarged ed. Glencoe, Ill.: Free Press, 1957.

Merton, Thomas. *The Silent Life.* New York: Farrar, Straus & Giroux, 1957.

Mills, C. Wright. *White Collar.* New York: Oxford University Press, 1956.

Montalbano, Andrew. *Sicilian Sun.* Metairie, La.: New Writer's, 1997.

Monteleone, Barbara. "Tony Monteleone: Childhood Memories." Unpublished manuscript in the possession of Howard Nichols. Hammond, La., November 5, 1990.

Mother Cabrini. Boston: Daughters of St. Paul Publications, 1977.

Mudge, Montana Josephine. "The Italian Union Hall—As I Remember It." *Italian-American Digest* 26, no. 1 (1999): 7.

Murrell, Mary E. "Why People Gamble." In *Gambling Today,* edited by D. Lester, 84-105. Springfield, Ill.: Charles C. Thomas, 1979.

National Archives. Passenger Lists for Port of New Orleans. Lists for November 1-December 30, 1898; January 2-June 28, 1899; July 5-December 20, 1899; January 2-February 28, 1900.

Nelli, Humbert S. *From Immigrants to Ethnics: The Italian Americans.* Oxford: Oxford University Press, 1983.

———. "The Italian Padrone System in the United States." *Labor History* 5 (spring 1964): 153-67.

New Orleans Daily Picayune, March 19, 1858-October 22, 1900.

New Orleans Times-Picayune, August 17, 1900-November 26, 1978.

New York Times, July 22-August 9, 1899.

Orso, Ethelyn. *The St. Joseph Altar Traditions of South Louisiana.* Lafayette: Center for Louisiana Studies, 1990.

Orso, Ethelyn, and Peggy Kaveski. "Undisclosed Aspects of Saint Joseph Altars." *Louisiana Folklore Miscellany* 3 (1975): 15-16.

Panzeca, Salvatore. "Family Reflects on a Beautiful Life." *Italian-American Digest* 26, no. 3 (1999): 7-19.

Peristiany, J. G., ed. *Honour and Shame: The Values of Mediterranean Society.* Chicago: University of Chicago Press, 1966.

Peristiany, J. G., and Julian Pitt-Rivers, ed. *Honor and Grace in Anthropology.* Cambridge: Cambridge University Press, 1992.

Plemer, Roslynn. "Feast of St. Joseph." *Louisiana Folklore Miscellany* 2, no. 4 (August 1968): 85-90.

"Progressive Men's Club Celebrates 50 Years." *Italian-American Digest* 20, no. 2 (1993): 15.

Purseglove, J. W. *Tropical Crops: Dicotyledons I and II.* New York: John Wiley & Sons, 1968.

Puzo, Mario. "Choosing a Dream: Italians in Hell's Kitchen." In *Generations,* edited by Jim Watts and Allen F. Davis, 32-41. New York: Knopf, 1974.

Rodriguez, Richard. *Hunger of Memory: The Education of Richard Rodriguez, an Autobiography.* Boston: Bantam Doubleday Dell, 1982.

Roselli, Bruno. *Let the Dead Speak!* New York: Poughkeeper Artcraft Press, 1929.

Rostow, W. W. *The Stages of Economic Growth.* Cambridge: Cambridge University Press, 1960.

Russo, Nicholas John. "Three Generations of Italians in New York City: Their Religious Acculturation." In *The Italian Experience in the United States,* edited by Silvano M. Tomasi and Madeline H. Engel, 195-209. Staten Island, N.Y.: Center for Migration Studies, 1970.

Saxon, Lyle, Edward Dreyer, and Robert Tallant. *Gumbo Ya-Ya.* 1945. Reprint, Gretna, La.: Pelican, 1998.

Scarpaci, Jean Ann. "Italian Immigration in Louisiana's Sugar Parishes: Recruitment, Labor Conditions, and Community Relations, 1880-1910." Ph.D. diss., Rutgers University, 1972.

Schrieke, B. *Alien Americans: A Study of Race Relations.* New York: Viking Press, 1936.

Serio, Linda. "Nick LaRocca, Creator of Jazz." *Italian-American Digest* (spring 1989): 3-4.

———. "Ships of Our Ancestors." *Italian-American Digest* 22, no. 3 (1995): 13.

Silone, Ignasio. *Fontamara.* New York: Atheneum Press, 1960.

Smith, Judith E. *Family Connections.* Albany: State University of New York Press, 1985.

Sorokin, Pitirim A. *Society, Culture, Personality.* New York: Harper, 1947.

Speroni, Charles. *Wit and Wisdom of the Italian Renaissance.* Berkeley: University of California Press, 1964.

Stewart, Jack. "The Original Dixieland Jazz Band's Place in History." *The Jazz Archivist* 6, no. 1 (1999): 7.

Stonequist, Everett V. *The Marginal Man: A Study in Personality and Culture Conflict.* New York: Russell & Russell, 1961.

Swank, B. B. "Chapels Are Testimonials of Love." *Clarion Herald* (Archdiocese of New Orleans) 17, no. 18 (June 14, 1979): 8.

Thomas, W. I. *The Unadjusted Girl.* Boston: Little, Brown, 1923.

Thomas, W. I., ed. *Source Book for Social Origins.* 4th ed. Boston: Richard Badger, 1909.

Thomas, W. I., and Florian Znaniecki. *The Polish Peasant in Europe and America.* 5 vols. Chicago: University of Chicago Press, 1918-20.

Thurston, Herbert, S.J., and Donald Attwater, ed. *Butler's Lives of the Saints.* New York: P. J. Kenedy & Sons, 1956.

Tomasi, Silvano M. "The Ethnic Church and the Integration of Italian Immigrants in the United States." In *The Italian Experience in the United States,* edited by Silvano M. Tomasi and Madeline H. Engel, 163-93. Staten Island, New York: Center for Migration Studies, 1970.

U.S. Bureau of the Census. *Population Schedules of the Twelfth Census of the United States: 1900.* Prepared by the U.S. Government Printing Office. Washington, D.C., 1978. Microfilm.

———. *Sixteenth Census of the United States: 1940. Population and Housing: Statistics for Census Tracts: New Orleans, La.* Prepared by the U.S. Government Printing Office. Washington, D.C., 1941.

———. *Twelfth Census, Census Rolls.* Plaquemines. Vol 32. Roll 577. 1900.

———. *Twelfth Census, Census Rolls.* St. James. Vol. 37. Roll 580. 1900.

U.S. House Committee on Assassinations. *Staff and Consultant Reports on Organized Crime.* Vol. 9. 95th Cong., 2nd sess., 1979.

Vecoli, Rudolph. "*Contadini* in Chicago: A Critique of the Uprooted." In *The Aliens,* edited by Leonard Dinnerstein and Frederie Cople Jaher. New York: Appleton-Century-Crofts, 1970. First published in *Journal of American History* 54 (1964): 404-17.

Verga, Giovanni. *The House by the Meddlar Tree.* 1881. Translated by Eric Mosbacher. New York: Grove Press, 1953.

Walker, D. S. *A Geography of Italy.* 2nd ed. London: Methuen, 1967.

Wall, Bennett H., ed. *Louisiana: A History.* 2nd ed. Arlington Heights, Ill.: Forum Press, 1984.

Warren, Karen Wright. "The Sicilian Saint Joseph Altar Celebration in Southeastern Louisiana." Master's thesis, Southeastern Louisiana University, 1983.

Weber, Max. *The Protestant Ethic and the Spirit of Capitalism.* 3rd Roxbury ed. Los Angeles: Roxbury, 2002.

"Who Really Killed the Chief?" *Italian-American Digest* 7 (1981): 3.

Wilcox, Jerry, and A. V. Margavio. "Fertility, Economy, and Household Structure in Nineteenth-Century America: A Comparative Study of

French Canadian, Irish, Italian, and Native Born Patterns." Paper presented at Mid-South Sociological Association Meetings. Baton Rouge, La., October 1989.

Williams, Phyllis H. *South Italian Folkways in Europe and America.* 1938. Reprint, New York: Simon & Schuster, Scribner, Russell & Russell, 1969.

Woodham-Smith, Cecil. *The Great Hunger.* New York: Harper & Row, 1962.

Wylie, Laurence, and Armand Begue. *Village in the Vaucluse.* Cambridge: Harvard University Press, 1958.

Index

ability to negotiate, 115
Accardo, Nick, 110
advice of elders, 174
Airoldi, Giuseppe, 59
Algiers, Louisiana, 68
Almerico, Tony, 179
American Civil War, 31, 34
American Italian Federation of
    the Southeast, 184; Museum
    and Library, 184
anglicized names, 262
Anthony of Padua, 18
anticlericalism, 225
Arcudi, Bruno, 49
Arnone, Nick, 169
Ascension Catholic Church,
    Donaldsonville, 251
Audicio, Giovanni, 59

Barzini, Luigi, 17
beauty, 16
Benedict, Ruth, 15
Bertrandville, Plaquemines
    Parish, 78
black Creoles, 108; blacks, 106;
    blacks and Italian immi-
    grants, 108
Black Hand, 88

blasphemy, 223
blessed beans, 245
"Bloody Tangipahoa," 206
boarding, 84, 132
Bocchio, Joseph, 212
Boethius, 91
Bonana, Sharkey, 179
Borgia, Caesare and Lucrezia, 18
bragging, 158
bread, 16, 162, 169
business community, 104
Byzantine Catholics, 229

Cabrini, Mother, 235-36
Cabrini Day Care Center, New
    Orleans, 235
campanilismo, 30, 124, 189
Captain Tony, 77
card games, 180
Casamento, Joe, 105
Casso, Lorenzo, 109
Catherine of Siena, 18
Catholic Church, 120, 225, 232-
    33; in America, 229; in South
    Louisiana, 126, 231; piety, 225
Cefalutana Benevolent Society,
    182
celebrations, 128